D0916832

A Woman of the *Times*

JOURNALISM,

FEMINISM,

AND THE

CAREER OF

CHARLOTTE

CURTIS

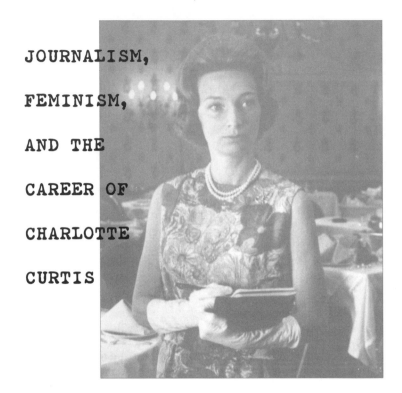

A Woman of the *Times*

Marilyn S. Greenwald

Foreword by Liz Smith

OHIO UNIVERSITY PRESS
ATHENS

Ohio University Press, Athens, Ohio 45701
© 1999 by Marilyn S. Greenwald
Printed in the United States of America
All rights reserved

Ohio University Press books are printed on acid-free paper ⊗™

03 02 01 00 99   5 4 3 2 1

Book design by Chiquita Babb

Library of Congress Cataloging-in-Publication Data
Greenwald, Marilyn S.
    A woman of the Times : journalism, feminism, and the career
of Charlotte Curtis / Marilyn S. Greenwald.
        p.   cm.
    Includes bibliographical references and index.
    ISBN 0-8214-1265-5 (alk. paper)
        1. Curtis, Charlotte, 1928–1987. 2. New York Times.
3. Feminism—United States. 4. Women journalists—United
States—Biography. 5. Journalists—United States—Biography.
I. Title.
PN4874.G698A3 1999
070'.92—dc21
    [b]   98-50091

For Tim

Contents

Illustrations

Foreword

BY LIZ SMITH

WHAT CAN YOU SAY about a woman who was brilliant, unique, and never let her own success go to her head—a woman who died all too young at the tender age of fifty-eight and at the top of her game?

Well, I can say, like a cat looking at a queen (or like a lowly gossip columnist looking at an acclaimed society observer who had reached the journalistic peak) that Charlotte was in a class by herself. She was at least the Marcel Proust of her era—the sixties and seventies—and she brought her own kind of "New Journalism" to the coverage of the high and mighty in government, politics, society, and the arts.

Charlotte's friend David Schneiderman, who worked with her on the op-ed page, described her as "the tiny lady who went to all those chic, elegant dinner parties with a firecracker in her beaded purse. . . . A trouble-maker in the best sense." Her mentor Sydney Gruson, who was a vice president at the *Times*, said she was "a conspirator of world-wide order. She was always trying to figure out ways of bending things to her will. I never thought she'd try to break things, just bend things." Her boss Arthur Sulzberger of the *Times* said of the people about whom Charlotte wrote that she "skinned them without Novocaine, yet they never felt a thing. Focusing a bright light on the foibles of society, yet they never blinked."

Charlotte began her twenty-five-year career with the *Times* in 1965. She had grown up in Ohio and in spite of her rise to the top of the *crème de la crème* of the Fourth Estate, she never left Ohio in her heart and head. She remained the ultimate inside outsider and urged other journalists to follow her lead.

When I was only a lowly and unknown ghost writer for the Hearst newspapers' long-lived Cholly Knickerbocker society column, Charlotte was already the brightest feature writer of the *Times* style pages. We met at the pool of the Colony Hotel in Palm Beach and she was appropriately attired in a little pink dress. I had on blue jeans because I'd never been to Palm Beach before and thought this was appropriate "informal" attire. It was appropriate in Texas, after all. Charlotte laughed: "Liz, you are very brave not to care what Palm Beach thinks. Be sure you keep that quality. Don't ever become a part of them."

Of course I did care what Palm Beach thought. I was young, callow, ambitious. But I cared more what Charlotte thought. She was the most generous journalist I ever met. Not for her the petty one-upmanship of mean competition. She wanted to see newspapering improve on every front. Anything written well or honestly or with perception was in her interest.

Charlotte helped me at every turn. When she'd see me standing in the cold with the rest of the gang outside the Metropolitan Opera on opening nights, she'd sidle up to me and whisper, "That's Mrs. So-and-So, who is going with So-and-So and believe me, you can mention her and write that and you'll be ahead of the others." She gave me tip after tip. I could not exhaust her good will. She would call me with ideas she knew the *Times* could never develop. She enjoyed having a secret protégé. But in this world, she kept a dispassionate, fair-minded, disinterested "cool." She treated duchesses and charladies exactly the same and had a mordant wit, a fine talent for expression, and a deep sense of ethics. She was always for the underdog.

I perceived that working for the *Times* was a bit like wearing a straitjacket. You were constantly exposed to stories you couldn't do — they were too trivial, too tasteless, or perhaps too unprovable by *Times* standards. This frustrated Charlotte, who had piercing instincts about getting it all out if it was worth telling. I was the perfect receptacle for her overflow of a fund of information perhaps unfit for the *Times* to print.

Charlotte loved helping me, pointing out where the bodies might be buried, hinting that this or that would be a great story if only I'd look into it. And over and over she cautioned me, "Don't become one of them—the people you write about." She would whisper to me at parties where she felt I was having too much fun and not really working, "Don't forget Texas. Don't forget Ohio—that's where America really is. Not here." And she kept her own independence although she was, in a way, "one of them," invited everywhere. She was adored, feared, and appreciated by the very subjects she covered, but she always kept her notepad handy and let everyone know she was "on the job."

When Charlotte fell ill and returned to Ohio, she kept in touch with me on the phone. She continued to be the most generous idea person in the world. She took great delight in knowing that the old world was going along without her. She was incredibly brave and never complained or talked about her fatal illness.

When Charlotte graduated from writing her society column to becoming the op-ed editor of the *Times*, she relished being a part of the old cabal of *Times* people who didn't always get along with Executive Editor Abe Rosenthal's new regime. She took a secret delight in the fact that no one at the *Times* had any power over her work except the publisher-owners and she made a brilliant job of being at the top where the power really lay.

I recall going to talk to her for *Interview* magazine. That was the day she tried to make me feel good about a personal career writing gossip. She said that of course gossip was history and it only depended on how one handled it. She reminded me of the marvelous old Adolph Ochs story that other newspapers publish gossip, but when the *Times* prints it, it's sociology! (Ochs was one of the *Times*'s first publishers.)

It was there in her elegant office that I urged her to do something daring with her high position. I wanted her to pose for our photographer like Charlie Chaplin in *The Great Dictator* where he is seen with the globe of the world balanced on his foot. I said, "Charlotte, you are now handling editorial advice to the entire world. It's a perfect picture!" Charlotte thought it over. "Liz, I think I shouldn't. It's too much fun for a *Times* editor to have!" She was later pleased with the more formal portrait of herself created by Cris Alexander. It had been retouched into a super glamorous youthfulness and she found that simply hilarious.

I recall saying to her during our interview: "You have reached the top as one of the most influential women in journalism. Are you like Alexander with no more worlds to conquer?" She said no. "I could leave the *Times* and do other things, write books, edit a magazine, but what I'd like would be to work in a garden — on a rich person's estate. I don't see the *Times* as the end of the line at all, because there are all those horizons out there."

Soon after, she left the *Times* because she was so ill. And the garden she entered was a Gethsemane. But now, still acutely missing Charlotte's wit and advice and perspicacity, I like to think of her improving some rich person's garden in the great hereafter, improving it as she improved me and so many others. This is as good a hope for life after death as any other.

Acknowledgments

OVER THE YEARS, many friends and colleagues made it possible for me to complete this book, and I could never adequately express my gratitude.

My friends Nancy Lewis, Doug Daniel, and Fred and Sarah Heintz were unwavering in their support, as were Mark Tatge, Julie Truck, and Sally Walters.

I am also very grateful for the generosity of Dr. William Hunt, whose kindness, cooperation and openness made it possible for me to closely examine the life and career of his wife; and to Mary Curtis Davey, who was also very generous with her time and information.

I would also like to thank many of Charlotte's co-workers and friends at the *Times* and in Columbus who took the time to meet with me and who were candid in their observations and insights. These include, among others, Clifton Daniel, David Schneiderman, Leslie Wexner, Robert Shamansky, A. O. Sulzberger and C. J. Satterwhite. My gratitude also goes to Liz Smith.

This project would never have been started had it not been for several people and organizations. The enthusiasm of Goodwin Berquist fueled my own initial interest in the project and made me believe in its worth. Patrick Washburn and Joseph Bernt discussed the project with me many times and edited initial drafts; and many of my colleagues at Ohio University continually offered me encouragement and moral support. I am grateful, also, for support provided by the Department of Women's Studies at Ohio State University, the College of Communication at Ohio University, and the Freedom Forum.

Thank you, also, to the people at the Ohio University Press, who had faith in me and who helped me revise and improve the manuscript. I am particularly indebted to Gillian Berchowitz for her insight and sensitivity, and to Nancy Basmajian, Richard Gilbert, and Trudie Calvert for their months of hard work.

And special thanks to my husband, Tim, whose patience, sense of humor and faith in me made this book possible.

Introduction

WHEN CHARLOTTE CURTIS was thirty-four and a fledgling women's news reporter on the *New York Times* in 1963, she won an award for reporting from the Newspaper Women's Club of New York. A reporter covering the awards for the trade publication *Editor and Publisher* asked Charlotte and the five other recipients how they managed to succeed in the male-dominated world of newspaper journalism. Charlotte was asked specifically if she ever used her "feminine charms" to get a story. "Honey," she replied, "I don't have any, damn it."

Of course, Charlotte was joking. She grew up in a genteel environment that stressed the importance of civility and manners, particularly for women, and was educated at an exclusive private girls school and Vassar College. Her flip response was no doubt meant to indicate that she did not take the question seriously.

Thirty-five years after Charlotte rose through the ranks of the *Times* to become associate editor of the paper, the question *is* a serious one. How did Charlotte Curtis, who described herself as a "little girl from Ohio," maneuver through the Byzantine internal political structure of the *New York Times* to become its first top female editor and the first woman whose name appeared on the paper's masthead? How did she thrive in a culture dominated by men, many of whom grew up in the East and were educated at Ivy League and prep schools? And how did she impose change at one of the most static institutions in the country? Did she indeed have to employ "feminine charms" to succeed?

The staff of the *New York Times* had its own personality and culture. When Charlotte joined the paper in 1961, it was a boy's club, and its "culture" reflected white male attitudes and points of view. Most of the reporters, and all but one of the section editors, were men.

As the most prestigious newspaper in the world, the *Times* was able to hire the "best and the brightest" journalists from around the world. Charlotte was highly intelligent, talented, motivated, and an extremely hard worker, but, then, so were many men and women at the paper. These usually rare qualities did not set her apart at the great *New York Times*.

In this book I examine how Charlotte Curtis broke into the journalistic boy's club of the *Times* and describe the personal qualities that enabled her to make the climb from home-furnishings writer to associate editor. I also address the question of whether she had to act like a man to succeed among men, whether she had to flirt or use sex to get their attention, or whether she used or betrayed other women at the paper. Finally, I ask what sacrifices she had to make to succeed.

～

I first heard about Charlotte Curtis in 1979, when I began working as a news reporter on the *Columbus Citizen-Journal*. The *C-J*, as it was known, was the smaller of the two daily newspapers in Columbus, but it had a reputation for being "feisty." Its editors were not afraid to take on the power structure of the town, and what the *C-J* lacked in size, it made up for in ambition and competitiveness.

Because the staff was small, most of us were overworked and underpaid, and we frequently grumbled about our underdog status. Shortly after I began working there, one of the older photographers told me, sarcastically, that my hard work would pay off one day. After all, he said, a former *C-J* reporter was now an editor at the *New York Times*. The photographer chortled, "We're all headed for the *New York Times!*"

That reporter was Charlotte Curtis, and I was to hear her name many times during my seven years at the *C-J*. The half dozen staff members who worked with her years earlier often described her derisively. They said she was a classic "Type A" personality: driven, competitive, and zealous about her work. One photographer said she was "weird."

It is easy to see why he thought of her as odd: she was a self-sufficient Vassar-educated woman who worked in a newsroom full of working-class men, few of whom had college educations; unlike most women of the 1950s, her ambition was not to marry and have a family but to rise to the top of her field. Strangest of all, she did not believe the world began and ended in Columbus, Ohio.

At the time, I wondered how Charlotte could work among a group of people who considered her weird. She was a reporter-editor during most of her eleven years at the paper, and she worked closely with other staff members. I knew firsthand that your job at the paper was much easier if you blended in with your colleagues and they found you "normal." I got the impression she was anything but conventional.

I had little interest in Charlotte then, other than the fact that she was a former CJ'er who now worked at the lofty *Times*. Nearly ten years later, however, I had changed careers and was studying the role of women in journalism. I learned of her death at the relatively young age of fifty-eight. She had risen to a top editorial spot on the *Times* and was a weekly columnist when she died. I knew a woman needed more than brains and talent to prevail at the *Times*. So I wondered what special qualities Charlotte possessed and what she did to distinguish herself on the paper.

Charlotte joined the *Times* during an era of great social change in the United States. The civil rights and feminist movements burgeoned during the mid-1960s and for nearly two decades influenced most aspects of life, from the family to the workplace. The highly structured office environment was particularly affected. Women were entering the work force at increasing rates, changing the social dynamics there, and relations between the sexes were in flux. Hence Charlotte's rise at the *Times* must be viewed in the context of the relations between men and women.

If Charlotte's *C-J* co-workers considered her weird, she was thought of as perfectly normal by some of those who ran the *New York Times*.

Charlotte's rise there can be directly attributable to the close friendships she established with some of the powers at the paper, most notably, its managing editor, Clifton Daniel; publisher A. O. "Punch"
Sulzberger; and Pulitzer Prize–winning foreign correspondent and
author Harrison Salisbury. Charlotte became friends with one member of this power structure, who introduced her to others. Next thing
she knew, she was a part of that structure.

Her close friendships with these powerful men came naturally.
All three were worldly, well-educated, and well-traveled—as was
Charlotte. She could mingle seamlessly at their social gatherings,
she knew how to dress appropriately, and she knew the difference between a salad and a dessert fork. But to assume she succeeded merely
because she blended in with them is overly simple; although Charlotte was too refined to mimic the way men spoke and acted and too
proud to flirt with them to get ahead, she was the perfect mix of "male"
and "female." Her ambition, cosmopolitan outlook, cynicism, loyalty,
and quick sense of humor were "male" attributes that made the men
respect and like her; her meticulous and classic grooming and discreet
demeanor made her attractive to them in a "feminine" but nonthreatening way. These personal qualities drew them to her and indirectly
led to her professional success. And she enjoyed being with and conversing with men. When she was a young child, few women were as
well-traveled, well-educated, and well-read as she. At that time men
were the ones who had the opportunity to leave home and see the
world.

Former *Times* reporter Molly Ivins said Charlotte succeeded at the
male-dominated *Times* because she was smarter than any of the men
there. That may be true—but it is also an oversimplification. If she
was smarter than the men, she was also clever enough not to let it
show.

But Charlotte's success did not stem simply from her relations with
men like Daniel, Sulzberger, and Salisbury. She understood her environment and knew how to work with her colleagues and employees. Although she was not highly confrontational, and, indeed, hated

personal arguments, she picked her battles carefully, rarely backed down or compromised if she thought she was right, and had a strong sense of loyalty to her job and to her friends. This loyalty sometimes got her in trouble when her journalistic obligations conflicted with her personal views.

Equally important, Charlotte had a will of steel that made her immune to personal feelings. For instance, her news judgment and professional outlook were often in direct opposition to those of *Times* news executive A. M. Rosenthal, and the two battled for nearly two decades. Charlotte, however, never took their professional differences personally and remained cordial toward Rosenthal, although some of her close friends believe he severely damaged her career. She claimed she had no time for personal animosity and wasted no time worrying about those who disagreed with her or mocked her. She was far too goal-oriented to be deterred.

This phenomenal detachment and mental toughness allowed her to overcome illness and prove doctors wrong in a terrifying prognosis, which would have been enough to prevent many from doing their best work. Charlotte, instead, did not speak about it, received a promotion, and traveled around the world before cancer reentered her life in 1986. When she lay weak and dying in her Columbus home, she gathered the energy for one last activity that meant the world to her: the planning—down to the last detail—of her memorial service. God forbid, Charlotte thought, that the wrong florist provide the decorations or that inappropriate music be played.

In this book I examine how Charlotte Curtis rose through the ranks of the *Times* to become op-ed editor and a member of the editorial board, positions that gave her a key voice in deciding whose opinion was published each day in one of the most influential newspapers in the world. It is impossible to chronicle her career without understanding the *New York Times* of the era. How did the paper and other media outlets respond to the dramatic social and cultural upheavals of the 1960s, 1970s, and early 1980s? How did the women's movement, in particular, impose change in story content, news judgment, and language in the media? What changes did the *Times* allow so it could survive during the years of the phenomenal growth of television?

This biography of Charlotte Curtis starts before her birth—with the life and career of her mother, Lucile Atcherson, a pioneer in her own right. Charlotte was clearly her mother's daughter, and their lives paralleled each other in many ways. Lucile was a women's suffrage leader in Ohio who later became the first American female diplomat to serve overseas. After she gave up her career to marry and raise a family, Lucile Atcherson Curtis was a tireless social activist, community leader, and volunteer in Columbus and the recipient of many local and national service awards. She served as a role model to her two daughters throughout their lives and instilled in them a social consciousness and respect for hard work. Lucile was a daunting figure to Charlotte, and she spent her life trying to please her mother and live up to her lofty expectations.

Also chronicled here are Charlotte's years at Vassar and their influence on her political and social outlook; her early years at the *Columbus Citizen* (later the *Citizen-Journal*), where she was given the license to experiment with her unique and unorthodox writing style and news judgment; and her twenty-five-year career at the *New York Times*. During her years as a society writer and editor, she initiated a previously unheard-of and brutally frank style of society reporting that acknowledged that, in reality, "not all brides are beautiful." She spent eight years as editor of the newly formed op-ed page, a revolutionary commentary section that first appeared in the *Times*; and finally she became a weekly columnist.

Overall, this biography portrays a woman with a deeply contradictory nature, who observed strict decorum in her manners, mode of dress, and personal tastes but broke many rules of conventional journalism in her writing; a woman who longed to be a part of the rough, working-class world of newspapering despite a genteel and conservative upbringing; a woman who sought out the company of men socially, despite the fact that she attended an all-female high school and college and worked much of her life surrounded by women in the "women's" section of newspapers.

I also attempt to assess the legacy of Charlotte Curtis and her long-term influence. I examine whether she paved the way for the success of other women at the *Times*, or if the price of her own success was losing the respect and friendship of other women at the paper. I ask whether she was naïve in her view that women managers need not be vocal or showy but that they can "burrow from within" and subtly use their influence to make the workplace fairer to women. Most important, I try to determine whether the men at the paper who nurtured and promoted her eventually betrayed her. Comments she made late in her life indicate that Charlotte may indeed have admitted her own naïveté about how women can achieve equality in the workplace.

Charlotte did not live in an age of cable television when print journalists regularly appear on television talk shows and comment on current events, so her face may not have been familiar to national audiences. But she, fashion editor Eugenia Sheppard of the *New York Herald-Tribune*, and John Fairchild, publisher of *Women's Wear Daily*, wielded enormous power and influence through their frank and sometimes caustic coverage of fashion and society. Their names were household words in Manhattan in the mid-twentieth century, and they were key players in its culture. Their legacy endures—particularly in New York.

To say that the story of Charlotte Curtis is relevant more than ten years after her death is to acknowledge that women still have a long way to go to achieve equality in the work force; unfortunately, women still face the same struggles and roadblocks she did. Her career provides a fascinating glimpse into the workings of an American institution and how it responded to major social upheavals. And her life is a study of how one woman overcame the handicap of her gender and was clever and hardworking enough to use her "feminine charms" to succeed.

~

Charlotte Curtis's personal papers are now stored at the Schlesinger Women's Studies Library at Radcliffe College. The papers of her mother, Lucile Curtis, are also stored there.

Memos and letters from Lucile Curtis's years in the U.S. Foreign Service are stored at the U.S. Department of State, although some duplicates are stored among her papers at the Schlesinger Library. The author received access to most of these under the Freedom of Information Act.

A Woman of the *Times*

1

A Life in Public Service

BY THE TIME Charlotte Murray Curtis and her sister Mary Darling Curtis were born in 1928 and 1930, respectively, their parents had lived full lives and received national recognition. Their mother, Lucile Atcherson Curtis, who graduated from high school at the age of fourteen, had been a pioneering U.S. diplomat who was the subject of stories in numerous major newspapers, including the *Christian Science Monitor*, and the *Philadelphia Public Ledger*.[1] Their father, George Morris Curtis, a physician, earned medical, master's, and Ph.D. degrees and had done groundbreaking research into the effect of iodine on the thyroid, all before he was forty.

Charlotte and Mary could have resigned themselves to mundane lives, assuming they would never repeat the accomplishments of their parents; they could have tried to compete with their parents; or they could have assumed that being unusual and brilliant was the norm. The Curtis girls unconsciously selected the last option. As Charlotte noted decades later, they *had* to succeed—it never occurred to them to do otherwise.[2] Their parents excelled in widely diverse areas. Lucile devoted most of her ninety-one years to social causes and international diplomacy, while George was a dedicated scientist and teacher.

1

It was not unusual for two such accomplished people to meet and fall in love. Both had traveled around the world, and both had made their careers their top priority in an era when family came first—especially for women. But in 1926, when Lucile Atcherson, a thirty-two-year-old diplomat for the U.S. State Department, met thirty-six-year-old George Curtis in Bern, Switzerland, they moved quickly. It was unusual then for people their age to be unattached, no matter how important their lifework. Within two years, they had married and moved to Chicago, where Curtis was appointed associate professor of surgery at the newly established University of Chicago Medical School. A year later, Charlotte was born, and sixteen months later, Mary came along. Lucile gave up her career to take care of their infant daughters.

As a child, Lucile was the apple of her father's eye. Fred Wayland Atcherson was a widower when he married Charlotte Ray, who was fifteen years his junior, and he showered affection on his only child, who was born on October 11, 1894, when he was thirty-nine. He had both the inclination and the means to spoil her. A prominent citizen in Columbus, Ohio, he was a county commissioner and the owner of much commercial and residential real estate, including the landmark Normandie Hotel on Long Street in downtown Columbus, which he built in 1906, and a downtown livery stable on Gay Street. The elegant ten-story Normandie had an Old World grace, with terra-cotta and marble floors and walls and a caged exterior elevator. Fred, a Massachusetts native who spent his adult life in Columbus, devoted much of his time to his business and politics. What time was left he spent doting on Lucile. He gave her everything she wanted from the moment she was born.

His wife, Charlotte Ray Atcherson, was born in 1871 into a family with roots in Wartrace, Tennessee. Charlotte's father was a doctor in the Civil War, and the family moved north after the war ended. Charlotte was a tiny and energetic woman who loved elegance and the finer things in life. But she also was a natural storyteller and a nurturer, whose top priority was Lucile, her only child.[3]

Fred Atcherson was a shrewd businessman. He and his father, both of whom held managerial positions in the horse-drawn railway system, came to Columbus in the late 1800s. They opened a small livery stable downtown in 1878 — a venture that became so profitable that they were soon forced to move it to bigger quarters a few blocks away.

Atcherson was one of the first in town to realize the potential of automobiles, and in 1914 he opened one of the nation's first taxi services at a time when "taxi" was not a part of the American lexicon. The progressive-thinking Atcherson could provide his customers with either a horse-drawn taxi or an automobile. His businesses grew more lucrative, and he soon learned that autos required much better roads than horses. The best way to get better roads, he knew, was to take action himself. A Republican, he ran for the Franklin County Commission, on which he served from 1918 to 1933, including four years as chairman. He also helped found the Ohio Club (later the Columbus Athletic Club), an exclusive organization that was a meeting place for businessmen like himself. By the time he retired in 1933, thanks to him, Franklin County had a network of blacktop streets that was acclaimed throughout the country.[4]

Lucile wanted for nothing as she grew up on the outskirts of Columbus on 4690 Sunbury Road, a sprawling country home the Atchersons called Brookwood. She loved riding horses, so her father bought her one. She attended the prestigious private Columbus School for Girls (CSG), where she excelled as a student. Being an outstanding student at CSG was no easy feat. Many of the wealthy people of Columbus sent their daughters there for intellectual stimulation while they learned the finer points of etiquette. Lucile graduated at age fourteen and, with her horse, was sent to Smith College. To Lucile, Smith was an extension of CSG. It was a school for reserved, well-to-do young women who seriously wanted an education but who knew that their main purpose in life was to marry well and raise a family. One did not get a fine education there to prepare for a career but rather to become a well-rounded individual who would be a capable and gracious wife, mother, and hostess.

Lucile was on the fast track at Smith, and she graduated at age eighteen. Graduating early from high school and college was both a blessing and a curse. Although she was challenged academically and did not have to stay in lockstep with her slower peers, she often missed out socially and faced a dilemma when she graduated: what should she do with the rest of her life?

Despite the Atchersons' affluence, both parents were driven and intense, and they taught their daughter to scorn idleness. During her summers home from Smith in 1910 through 1912, she volunteered as an aide to Columbus's only visiting nurse, an activity that gave her a lifelong interest in public health. In 1913, she returned to Columbus with a college degree in finance and economics and no plans. She worked for her father at the Normandie and, briefly, as a secretary for William Oxley Thompson, the president of Ohio State University. She took a few business courses at the University of Chicago and also worked for a short time as a secretary for the president of that university. Lucile grew bored with these jobs, however, and she quickly learned that her greatest fulfillment came from activities that gave her no money or academic credit. She began doing volunteer work for several health and cultural organizations in Columbus and in 1914 embarked on a mission that would change her outlook on life: for $30 a week, she worked as executive secretary of the Franklin County Suffrage Society.

In 1912, five thousand women marched through staid, conservative Columbus, the state capital, advocating a constitutional amendment that would give women the right to vote. They were unsuccessful in the short run, but they helped establish the momentum that would lead to future victories. By the end of World War I, women were allowed to vote in Columbus school board elections, and their efforts gave them visibility and drew thousands of supporters.[5] Lucile was one of the marchers, and she initially joined the women's suffrage movement because, she said sixty-five years later, "it was better than sitting on the front porch swing."[6]

The headstrong Lucile worked tirelessly for women's suffrage and later became the first Columbus woman to join the National Women's Party. She also helped organize the Ohio Suffrage Association. Lucile's biggest success as a suffrage leader was her effort to persuade black women's groups to join the movement, which resulted in black women in Columbus distributing thousands of leaflets urging male voters to support suffrage.[7]

Her activities as a suffrage leader in Ohio encouraged Lucile to realize that her gender did not have to limit her career goals. She knew by then that she could not work day after day at a monotonous white-collar job, so in 1917, at age twenty-three, she volunteered overseas with the staff of the American Fund for the French Wounded (AFFW), a joint effort of the French and American governments; she was transferred a year later to the newly organized civilian division of the AFFW called the American Committee for Devastated France, whose purpose was to aid the physical restoration of eleven villages and provide social and medical services. Lucile worked for the administrator of the program, Anne Morgan, sister of industrialist J. P. Morgan. Lucile's efforts were rewarded when she was transferred to Paris to become director of personnel there for the organization. In December 1919, she was honored by the French government for her efforts and given a medal—the Medaille de la Reconnaissance Francaise.

Her activities in France whetted her appetite for foreign service, but in 1919, women did not yet have the vote and were not considered U.S. citizens and therefore were ineligible for foreign diplomatic service. In 1920, however, women won the right to vote, and Lucile applied to take an exhaustive series of tests that would make her eligible for the Foreign Service. She was the first woman to apply for the test.

That a woman had the audacity to apply for the exam drew national attention. The three-day Foreign Service exam asked detailed questions about international law, history, and foreign governments, and it required proficiency in a minimum of one foreign language. In addition, students' diplomatic skills, manners, and character were tested.[8] Like most others who took the test, Lucile received extensive tutoring beforehand. At first, Charles Hill, head of the political science department at George Washington University, feared that a woman in his all-male class might distract the men who were preparing for the exam. But Lucile caused him to change his mind: "It was an inspiration to come in contact with a mentality like Miss Atcherson's," he said. "She is far above the average man or woman."[9] She and twelve men passed the test.

A newspaper story at the time described Lucile as a tall brunette with brown eyes who was no "frump": "She is beautifully groomed from belt to buckle. All of her clothes have that indefinable thing called style, following fashion in a dignified—not extreme—way. . . . There is no place for frumps in the Diplomatic Corps," the story said.[10]

As Lucile quickly learned, qualifying for the Foreign Service and serving overseas were two different things. In 1922, she made history when President Warren G. Harding nominated her as the first woman in the U.S. Foreign Service, but the male-dominated U.S. Senate did not think it appropriate for a young single woman to travel overseas as a diplomat, and it refused to approve the appointment. Instead, Lucile was appointed to the State Department's division of Latin American Affairs in Washington, D.C., where she worked actively to maintain relations between the United States and ten Latin American countries.

Lucile worked hard to pass the Foreign Service exam, but if she was angry at not being allowed to serve overseas, she did not show it. When a reporter asked her reaction, she was coy: "As for Miss Atcherson, you couldn't get any reaction out of her as she considers herself a soldier ready to obey orders without question," the reporter wrote. "In fact, she insisted smilingly that she loved Washington, that it was a lovely city and that it would give her still better training for the foreign service."[11]

Lucile's participation in the suffrage movement taught her about the power of numbers, and she sought support for the cause. After being by swamped by letters and telegrams of support from the Women's Suffrage Society, the League of Women Voters, and other women's and political groups, the Senate Committee on Foreign Relations recommended her appointment overseas and the full Senate approved it in 1923. She became a U.S. diplomat based in Bern, Switzerland, or, officially, "third secretary of the legation" in Bern. The appointment made history, and it was heralded on the front page of the *Christian Science Monitor* as "an expansion of women's political aspirations."[12]

Lucile's appointment, combined with her family's affluence, gave her the opportunity and means to travel throughout Europe by car. "She had her own Buick," said William Hunt, Lucile's future son-in-law, who, seventy years later, was amused at the image of the thirty-year-old Lucile roaming around prewar Europe in her car. Hunt's favorite anecdote about the bold Lucile—an anecdote passed on by her daughter Charlotte—involves Lucile's attempt to cross the Swiss border. Traveling from one country to another was routine for Lucile, who would flash her diplomatic pass at the border and go on her way. "It was unusual for a woman to have a diplomatic pass, and the Swiss border guard didn't believe it was valid," Hunt said. The guard refused to grant her passage, but Lucile would not be deterred. Although it was a Saturday, she managed to locate the American ambassador, who happened to be out on the golf course, and she eventually was permitted passage. This stubbornness and resourcefulness "was very Lucile," Hunt said.[13]

It was a carefree and interesting life for the unconventional and independent Lucile, who had a natural interest in history and in the way people lived. But her younger daughter, Mary, remembers her mother telling her that this unusual life was not always what it seemed: "She was a free spirit—as free as you could be in that era," Mary Curtis Davey said seven decades later. "Yet as she told me one time, it was lonely going home at night and not having anyone to share it with."[14]

While Lucile was traveling through Europe as a diplomat, Dr. George Morris Curtis was in Bern conducting research on the effect of iodine on the thyroid. Curtis was born in 1890 in Big Rapids,

Michigan, and grew up in nearby Greenfield, the home of Gibson refrigerators. The son of a Unitarian minister, he graduated from the University of Michigan in 1910 with master's and bachelor's degrees and received a doctorate in anatomy four years later. In 1914, at age twenty-four, he became an assistant professor of anatomy at Vanderbilt University and became head of the department a year later.

Holding three degrees and running a department was not enough for Curtis, who loved learning. After serving in the U.S. Army Medical Corps during World War I, he entered Rush Medical College in Chicago and received a medical degree in 1920. In 1924, he was awarded a fellowship by the National Research Council to study iodine metabolism at the University of Chicago and the University of Bern. It was important that Curtis study in Switzerland because populations of such landlocked areas frequently lacked adequate supplies of iodine, and he tried to determine if this lack was responsible for unusually high levels of cretinism in Switzerland. He eventually became one of several researchers who helped ensure that table salt contained adequate levels of iodine.[15]

George Curtis and Lucile Atcherson met in Bern in 1926, and their courtship was unusual by any standards. Lucile was stationed in Bern, but she traveled throughout Europe, so they had to conduct a romance through the mail. By the summer of 1927, Lucile had been transferred to Panama, limiting their time together even more. As their relationship grew, so did their written correspondence. From the time they met in mid-1926 until the time they married in on January 16, 1928, Lucile and George Morris Curtis wrote each other nearly every day they were separated and sometimes two or three times a day.

At first, the two were unfailingly polite to each other. In a letter from Oslo, Curtis described the sights in detail and flirtatiously asked Lucile if, despite her lofty position, he could call her by her first name: "Do you mind if I commence this letter so? It seems so formal to use Miss, in spite of the fact that you are the trusted Secretary of American Legation in Bern."[16]

Within a year, Curtis and Lucile were engaged, and Curtis wrote to her happily about marriage plans and his announcement of their engagement to friends: "It is such happiness to think that you are coming to live with me and be my comrade, my sweetheart and my wife. I shall try hard to make you happy dearest one . . . I have told my dear friends of our engagement and they all are warm in their congratulations and warm in their admiration of you."[17]

By mid-1927, however, Lucile was transferred out of Bern and to Panama, a move that did not please her. She rarely complained, but some of her letters to her fiancé lacked their characteristic interesting commentary and upbeat tone. Shortly after she was transferred, she remarked that the bugs and the heat made life difficult. In one letter, she said she was grateful she had not contracted malaria.

Although Lucile had accomplished her goal of becoming a pioneering diplomat, she found it nearly impossible to gain acceptance in the male-dominated world of diplomacy. The Swiss with whom she worked in Bern—and her own colleagues—had trouble accepting a woman in their line of work, and Lucile was not promoted, even though the men who entered the Foreign Service with her had gained promotions in the five years they had served.

In the summer of 1927, Lucile wrote a courteous letter to the legation's personnel chief, asking when she could expect a promotion and why others had been promoted ahead of her. She painstakingly documented the dates of the promotions of seven of the eight men who joined the Foreign Service when she did (one had dropped out) and noted that she had not been told why she was not promoted.[18]

Lucile's letter triggered a flurry of correspondence among high-ranking members of the Foreign Service. Since she began her job working overseas in 1925, she had received two job evaluations—the first, in late 1925, was positive. Her ratings in various categories of "personality" and "quality of work" were good to excellent. In written comments, her superior, Hugh Gibson, noted that the appointment of a female diplomat amused the Swiss, "and they have not always been kindly in their comments . . . [but] Miss Atcherson has conducted herself with dignity and good sense by showing a desire to be inconspicuous and has done a good deal to disarm criticism."[19]

Lucile's situation had changed dramatically by October 1926. In a detailed "annual efficiency report," Gibson stated Lucile's inability to mingle with her male colleagues was devastating to her career. Her status as a woman officer was a novelty and made her conspicuous: "She is by nature reserved and formal with little facility in personal relationships. . . . She does not possess the *savoir vivre* necessary to meet a difficult situation." Further, Lucile received substantial help from her colleagues—much more than any man in her position would receive, he wrote.

Gibson acknowledged repeatedly in his evaluation that a woman diplomat can never be successful simply because she does not have the access to and personality of the men with whom she works: "[A male secretary] cultivates the society of colleagues and officials of the Government. He frequents their company in spare time, encourages them to come to his home and otherwise seeks to cultivate their . . . confidences. . . . A woman secretary is at a disadvantage."[20]

Shortly after Lucile wrote the letter asking why she had not been promoted, the personnel board provided its members with a more exhaustive and damning summary of her work, noting that her overall numerical ranking had declined in each of the three years she had served overseas. By 1927, her ranking of seventy-six made her eighty-fifth in her class of ninety-two officers. Further, the report said, she lacked character ("Lacks initiative and has little sense of responsibility"), ability ("Lacking in resource, tact, judgment and sense of what is fitting"), and a positive personality ("Egotistical; has harmed prestige of Legation with her actions. . . . Her sex a handicap to useful official friendships").[21] The last comment is the most telling—up to this point in her life, she had been nearly perfect in every way. These universally negative rankings were uncharacteristic of her, and they may be seen as evaluations not just of Lucile but of those with whom she worked. The challenges facing her as a woman made the job more difficult for those around her, and her colleagues were not willing to change to accommodate her.

Lucile evidently was never shown these evaluations and simply was told that her performance record did not merit promotion.[22] But it was the transfer to Panama combined with her deepening relationship with George Curtis that prompted her resignation from the Foreign Service. Yet her resignation worried the State Department's personnel office. Officials erroneously believed that it was prompted by Lucile's failure to be promoted and that it might become a public relations nightmare.[23]

Their fears were unfounded, however, and in the fall of 1927, Lucile resigned from the Foreign Service to make final preparations for her January wedding. Shortly thereafter Curtis returned to his post at the University of Chicago. Letters between the two at that time show the eagerness — and amazement — Lucile felt about the upcoming wedding. Twelve days before their wedding, she wrote how pleased she was to have received three letters from him in one day, and she happily described three wedding presents they had received by mail. At the end, she was giddy: "Thank you for the New Year's wishes — this year does bid fair to bring my heart's chief desire — the best husband in the world. LA. The idea of my having a husband!"[24] Lucile and George were married in a small ceremony in Trinity Episcopal Church in downtown Columbus; the reception was held at the bride's home, Brookwood. George's sister was the matron of honor and only attendant and his brother the best man.

By the following year, they were living in Chicago, where he began work as associate professor of surgery at the University of Chicago Medical School. Lucile's life undoubtedly became more mundane when she moved back to the United States, but once she was married, she had no choice about continuing in the Foreign Service. Diplomatic service was restricted to unmarried women. By the end of 1928, Lucile's life changed dramatically again — on December 19, 1928, her daughter Charlotte was born; another, Mary, came less than two years later.

~

When Mary Curtis was born in 1930, the Curtises had become a typical Midwest family. George spent most of his time as a professor and researcher, and he earned a reputation as a driven teacher—one who was tough but who took a deep interest in his students. Lucile stayed at home to care for their two baby daughters. The new arrangement put a damper on their traveling; until this time, both George and Lucile had spent much of their adult lives living in various cities around the world.

But their travel schedule resumed in a limited way as soon their children were old enough to travel with them. After Charlotte and Mary grew up, George and Lucile Curtis traveled more extensively. Even a series of strokes George suffered while he was in his fifties did not prevent numerous trips, although in 1952, at sixty-two, he became permanently disabled and needed a wheelchair. Curtis's family had a history of fatal cerebral hemorrhages. His three siblings all died of them: his younger sister, Martha, a nurse, died at age thirty-eight; an older sister, Lucille, at age fifty; and a younger brother, Arthur, a dermatologist, at age fifty-six. When George Curtis died of pneumonia in 1965 at age seventy-five, he had lived to an older age than any of them.

After the Curtises had lived in Chicago for about two years, Lucile moved back to Columbus to help manage her father's hotel. Fred Atcherson was in his seventies. Managing the Normandie was a full-time job for him and his daughter, and the pair usually worked six or seven days a week. George Curtis visited on most weekends after Lucile, Charlotte, and Mary moved to the house in Sunbury Road with Lucile's mother, Charlotte. Fred Atcherson maintained a residence at the Normandie, although he spent much time at Brookwood.

This unconventional family arrangement—with George living away from his family—lasted only about a year or two. By 1932, George Curtis was promoted to full professor at the University of Chicago, but that year he was offered a position as professor of surgery at Ohio State University (OSU) in Columbus. The OSU medical school was expanding at this time, and its administrators believed that Curtis, as a brilliant researcher and teacher, would help establish the national recognition they sought. And the match endured: George Morris Curtis was named chairman of OSU's department of research surgery in 1936, a job he would hold until the end of his career. His two daughters would grow up in their mother's hometown in a closely knit extended family that included their maternal grandparents.

~

Lucile Curtis lived twenty years after her husband, filling her life with extensive travel and public service. Although she was physically healthy for most of her adult life, Lucile battled depression, and long after her husband had died and her children were grown, she attempted suicide. The energetic and upbeat Lucile was the last person anyone would have suspected of suffering depression. With her exhausting travel schedule and volunteer efforts, she was rarely idle, and she took pride in blending in with the natives during her travels and handling adversity with a sense of humor. Her daughter Charlotte once described two exotic excursions taken by her septuagenarian mother: "Last summer . . . she ate bits of goat for breakfast in Outer Mongolia and lived in a yurt, one of those funny little tent things. She was also in Siberia, which she later said reminded her of Columbus in early days."[25] In a 1980 résumé, Lucile wrote, "I have crossed the Atlantic and returned more times than I have fingers and the Pacific more times than toes. Three trips completely around the world, one by air, two by ship (one of these by Chinese freighter). Jamaica visited first in 1924—returned 4 times. Barbados 4 winters. Cuba, Colombia, Hong Kong, Taiwan, So. Korea, Cambodia, S. Vietnam."[26]

Lucile made some trips to accept national public service awards. Ironically, despite her poor performance evaluations as a member of the Foreign Service, she and Clifton Wharton, the first black person in the Foreign Service, were honored for their pioneering efforts as part of the U.S. State Department's Foreign Service Day on May 19, 1978. Secretary of State Cyrus Vance presented Lucile, then eighty-four, with a twelve-by-sixteen-inch copper plate mounted on a rosewood plaque, on which a map of the world was etched with dots to mark the places she served as a diplomatic officer. An inscription noted her pioneering role: "[She] broke the barriers for equality among the sexes in the Foreign Service."

As an indirect result of the State Department honor and for five decades of volunteer work in Ohio, the mayor of Columbus declared May 19, 1976, Lucile A. Curtis Day, calling her a "Franklin County treasure." The *Columbus Citizen-Journal* editorialized that she was deserving of the title, listing nearly two dozen organizations of which she was an officer or board member.[27]

At age seventy-seven, she was named a delegate to the White House Conference on Aging and received outstanding alumni awards from Smith College and the Columbus School for Girls, as well as honors from Temple Israel in Columbus, Citizens' Research, a community organization, and the service club Sertoma.

Lucile Curtis demonstrated to her daughters the importance of public service and hard work, cultivated their curious minds and tenacious spirits, and taught them to respect unconventional lifestyles. If it is possible for a woman to inherit the ability to navigate successfully in a man's world, Charlotte surely acquired that trait from her mother. There is little doubt, however, that Charlotte also inherited from her an oddly paradoxical personality—one that allowed Lucile, a world traveler and pioneering diplomat, to settle calmly into a life of domesticity. But Lucile, for most of her life, fooled everyone by masking periodic attacks of severe depression with a serene facade.

2

A Progressive Upbringing

MARY DAVEY BELIEVES that their early upbringing had a dramatic effect on the personalities of her and her sister. After George Curtis moved to Columbus to join his family, the four Curtises lived in Brookwood, the rambling country house that Lucile's father, Fred Atcherson, had built on Sunbury Road. Because Columbus was relatively undeveloped in the early 1930s, the fifteen or so miles they lived outside of the center city could well have been one hundred, and the girls learned to appreciate and respect nature. Because they had few playmates, they enjoyed each other's company almost exclusively.[1]

As close as the girls would become to their parents, another adult became a major influence in their lives: their maternal grandmother, Charlotte Ray Atcherson, who lived with them and cared for them each day while their mother worked at the Normandie Hotel. Charlotte Atcherson, after whom Charlotte Curtis was named, was known as "Gargie" to her granddaughters because of their inability as toddlers to pronounce "Grandmother." It was Gargie who played with the girls, fed them, braided their hair, and instilled in them an early love of books and facts. The diminutive Charlotte Atcherson also introduced the little Curtis girls to a civilized way of life. Mary and

Charlotte ate plenty of elaborate salads and other unconventional foods for the era, and each day they dropped what they were doing for a midday teatime. "We had cottage cheese and chives and exotic things like that before it became chic," Davey said. Teatime was particularly important because it provided an opportunity to read, chat, and tell stories. During teatime, the Curtis girls would hear for the first time a lesson that would be repeated throughout their childhood and adolescence: that, with persistence, they could achieve in life whatever they wanted. "Gargie was a special influence on us because of this can-do attitude," Davey said. "She'd tell us, 'You can do anything.'"[2]

When they were little girls, their grandparents and parents instilled in them the power of the written word, and whenever they went to camp or out of town with their parents, Charlotte and Mary wrote numerous letters and postcards homes, recounting their activities. George and Lucile Curtis relied heavily on letters when the two lived apart during their courtship, and they kept these letters their entire lives. They considered this written link with friends and loved ones important, and Charlotte, too, would heavily rely on written communication to maintain friendships and family relationships.

The Curtis girls and their grandmother were close because the three usually spent their days together. Their grandfather, Fred Atcherson, lived at the Normandie Hotel, although he frequently came to the Sunbury Road home to visit and to do odd jobs there. A poor economic climate resulting from the Depression was hard on businessmen and property owners like Atcherson because many of his tenants could not pay their rent. Consequently, Lucile was kept busy as manager of the Normandie, taking care of many of the day-to-day activities there and making sure her father's property was in order.

Mary Davey remembered her early upbringing as pastoral and peaceful, and this rustic existence gave Charlotte and Mary an abiding respect for nature and the environment. But Mary was much more the "outdoors" type: tall and large-framed with blond hair and brown eyes, she was, like her mother, and, in her own words, a "little horse" who loved to play hard outdoors. Charlotte, in contrast, took after her grandmother: she was short, thin, and pale with red hair and blue eyes. Charlotte, unlike her sister, was prone to a variety of illnesses as a child, including whooping cough and encephalitis. Consequently, she spent far more time indoors and was, in her sister's words, "very much self-contained."[3]

The girls' schooling was carefree and unorthodox for the times. They attended the freewheeling experimental University School, which stressed creativity over academics, an environment Davey described as "individuality plus." Most of the students there were children of Ohio State University faculty members who believed in what Davey called a "free-flowing" education. Instead of studying history, reading, writing, and the like in conventional fashion, the students would focus on one topic — Egypt, for example — and study those subjects in relationship to Egypt. They would learn all there was to know about the assigned topic and would put on plays, readings, and other such activities to stimulate interest in it.[4]

Teachers at the University School did not like to put undue pressure on their students: "I have to confess, we didn't do well in mathematics and I didn't read, literally, until I was shamed into it," said Davey, who later became an activist, social worker, city council member, mayor, and pilot. "We laughed about it later because we're both weak at multiplication tables and some basic things. I'm a creative speller." Or, as Charlotte's husband said decades later, "It was apparent [they] could make little crystal radios but they didn't know their multiplication tables."[5] The creative education of Mary and Charlotte ended when they were in the fifth and seventh grades, respectively. The family moved out of the Sunbury Road home and into Bexley, a Columbus suburb only a few miles east of the city's downtown. The move was a turning point for them for several reasons: their beloved Gargie moved back into the Normandie Hotel with her husband; living in the city, the girls were much less reliant on nature and each other for amusement; and the proximity of their new home to town meant their parents could spend more time with them.

Fred Atcherson owned much residential property in Bexley, an upper-middle-class, conservative suburb that was home to many of the professional men of Columbus and their families, and the family moved into a house on 311 North Drexel Avenue, several blocks from the private Capital University. Bexley was a conventional white Anglo-Saxon Protestant community, but it had an unusually large percentage of Jewish residents, although few Jews lived in Columbus at the time. The Columbus School for Girls, the private and exclusive school that Lucile had attended, later moved to the city. Many of the well-to-do families in Columbus sent their daughters to CSG to prepare for a college education at an Ivy League college or one of the Seven Sisters.

The girls' CSG schooling was the opposite of their education at the University School: they went from an unstructured style of learning with no homework to a highly structured, rigid curriculum heavy on homework. Education at CSG also included religion. Charlotte and Mary attended chapel each day at school, and it was a long time before they realized that not everyone was Episcopalian as they were. "I remember several of our best friends were Jewish, but it never occurred to anyone that Jews would not want to sing the Christian prayer or hymns," Davey said.[6] When the Curtis girls attended CSG in the early 1940s, a handful of Jewish girls attended but only two or three black students. Davey does not remember this as discriminatory but as a function of economics: the school welcomed anyone who could afford its tuition. But CSG catered to the majority of its students, who were white Anglo-Saxon Protestants. In Bexley, marriage between couples of different religions was frowned on and gossiped about, but Jews and non-Jews did date. Decades later, when she was a *Times* society editor, Charlotte noted with a biting irony in dispatches from Florida that many country clubs prohibited Jewish members, and she noted that other organizations, including the Junior League, were also discriminatory.

It took the Curtis girls a year or so to become accustomed to the grueling academic pace of CSG and the competition from their intelligent and driven classmates. The girls excelled at French, and an inspiring teacher gave Charlotte a particular interest in chemistry.[7]

Charlotte's report cards during her years at CSG indicate that she may have had some trouble with her studies shortly after she transferred to the school, but her grades improved steadily over time. In March 1941, when she was thirteen, she earned a B in English, a B+ in spelling, a B+ in Math, a C+ in Science, a C+ in History, and a B in French. In February 1944, she earned a B in English, a B+ in French, and a B- in biology but a C in Latin and C+ in French. Her grades improved the next year. In March 1945, they were all As and Bs: an A- in English, a B in algebra, a B+ in French, and a B- in Latin.[8]

The competition for good grades at CSG was subtle but tough. "It was lady-like, civilized competition, but it was there," Davey said. A well-rounded education there included more than academic subjects. The girls participated in a wide variety of extracurricular activities and after-school lessons—the riding club, the choir, the dance club, the Cercle Français.[9]

Charlotte's extracurricular activities at CSG did not center on writing but instead took on a cultural dimension. According to the 1946 CSG yearbook *The Top Knot*, Charlotte belonged to the Dramatic Club, the French Club, choir, and the hockey team all four of her high school years. At various times she belonged to the swim team, was a member of the yearbook board, served on the student council, and was class treasurer.[10]

In the group photo of the class of 1946, Charlotte blends in perfectly with her twenty-seven classmates, all of whom wore demure pageboy haircuts and school uniforms of dark blazer, beige skirt, white anklets, and saddle shoes. But other references in the yearbook indicate that she might have been more of a free thinker than her classmates, and she was hardly demure. The inscription next to her senior picture described her as "a flash of red hair and a shriek of laughter. . . . Charlotte is always ready to argue about anything from the right shade of lipstick to the latest bills in Congress and she refuses to be budged when she has formed an opinion."[11]

Fifty years later, Tibi Sterner Johnson remembered Charlotte, one of her partners in the Debate Club, as a firebrand whose favorite pastime was discussing politics. But Charlotte was no shrinking violet: "She was gutsy—not afraid to say what she believed," Johnson said. Even at age sixteen, "she could have an acid tongue."[12] Charlotte's rebellious side was noticeable at home, too. As a teenager, she once hung a flag with a communist symbol outside the Curtis home—presumably to annoy her politically conservative father.

The Columbus School for Girls in the 1940s instilled a schizophrenic mind-set in its students. On one hand, it gave them a solid education and insisted that they take their studies very seriously. On the other hand, according to Davey, it reflected society's unspoken philosophy that women should be seen and not heard. "You didn't say tiddley boom as a woman," she said. "You observed the conventions, your skirt was always below your knees, and your knees were glued together. You didn't speak until spoken to, you didn't make waves. There were individuals who flourished there, though. Individualism was there—it was *sotto voce*—but it was there."[13]

This contradictory lifestyle was reinforced in the Curtis home. George and Lucile Curtis insisted that their daughters get the high-quality education offered at CSG, but they hardly wanted the girls to be silent. They insisted that they state opinions based on logical arguments and wanted them to set high goals. After she became a successful editor at the *New York Times*, Charlotte told a reporter about this gender-neutral upbringing: "In a way, I was raised as much like a boy as a girl. I was never told not to get dirty or to keep my clothes clean. I was encouraged to take part in any kind of sport and to excel academically. It was never considered that I would not excel. And because there was no son on whom expectations could be placed, they were placed on me."[14]

Charlotte maintained that it was at home that she learned the art of debating and the importance of stating her opinions in concise, reasoned arguments. At the dinner table, the four Curtises often debated current events, and the girls were expected to back up their points logically with evidence. "From the time I was four, I was trained in self-assertion," Charlotte once said. "If you could win against my father, you could win against anyone."[15]

Charlotte also said that she learned from these early dinner table debates to select her fights carefully—a philosophy that would help her negotiate the internal politics at the *New York Times*. She discussed it decades later: "Some areas are worth fighting about 24 hours a day, like civil rights. I don't have the strength to fight in areas that don't matter . . . I'm not going to fight with taxi drivers, grocers, etc. . . . You should speak up in areas that matter to you personally. But the area should be of some consequence."[16]

Because their father was an educator and a scientist, the Curtis girls' day-to-day lives were a learning experience. To teach them anatomy, George Curtis required his daughters to arrange the food on their dinner plates as the internal organs of the body, with the meat as the heart, the vegetables as the lungs, and so on. "By the time we were ten, we could recognize and draw pictures of every part of the body," Charlotte said. "To this day, I could draw you a pituitary."[17] On warm summer nights, the girls would lie on their backs in the grass and identify the constellations and planets, and they could name and identify a great number of birds, flowers, and trees.

George Curtis adored his daughters, but the top priority in his life was his job as a research surgeon and teacher, and it was there that he invested most of his time and energy. George Curtis was known internationally for his research in thoracic surgery, was a founder and active member of several international surgical associations, and was a pioneer researcher after World War II on the treatment of blast injuries to the lungs. He was devoted to his medical students, whom he called "his boys," and over the years he became a close friend and mentor to many of them.

He depended on his hands for his livelihood, so he could not participate in sports or other activities that might injure them, and they were insured by Lloyds of London. Although his top priority was his work, the Curtis family benefited indirectly from George Curtis's job. He delivered research papers at medical conferences all over the world, and frequently the family accompanied him. Before they graduated from high school, the Curtis girls had visited Oslo, Norway, Yellowstone National Park, and the Canadian Rockies, among other places; they frequently traveled cross-country on trains. They always wrote postcards or letters to their parents or grandparents as they traveled. The thirteen-year-old Charlotte, in a letter to Fred Atcherson, once chronicled in detail her days at camp in Portland, Maine, describing in meticulous detail her swimming classes and evening activities.[18]

The Curtis girls also delighted in the parties and gatherings their parents gave at their home, usually for George Curtis's medical students and colleagues. Curtis's students frequently visited the family home, where the girls observed them from the top of the stairs.

Charlotte, of course, did not know that her future husband was among the scores of medical students who visited the Curtis home: William Hunt, who would become chief of neurological surgery at Ohio State, was one of George Curtis's students. He was seven years older than Charlotte and in the mid-1940s paid little attention to his professor's adolescent daughter. They would become better acquainted more than twenty years later.

George and Lucile were careful to emphasize to their daughters that their gender should not restrict their success professionally, yet George, an avid fisherman and bird-watcher, may have wished for a son to share these traditionally male avocations. Mary, however, also loved the outdoors, and the two became close by going fishing together and participating in other outdoor activities. Charlotte, who was sickly through much of her adolescence, grew closer to Lucile. When Mary was little, she and her father would practice fly fishing in the backyard of their big Sunbury Road home. George Curtis would put a white handkerchief on the road and shoot the fly, and it was Mary's job to unscramble the hook from the handkerchief. Later, when Mary was older, the two took fishing trips to Lake Michigan. George Curtis attacked fishing with the same dedication and zeal he devoted to everything else.[19]

Lucile Curtis—the daughter of a Republican county commissioner —was devoted to social causes, and, as she grew older, her politics became increasingly liberal. She was active in many social, political, and medical groups, including the League of Women Voters, the YWCA, and the Columbus Urban League. She had a deep influence on Charlotte, who at a young age began to understand the value of such organizations.

The Curtis girls learned as children about the rewards of hard work—and that idleness was a sin. Charlotte explained this way of life to a reporter: "I . . . came from a family that believed in doing worthwhile things even on vacation time. I got my first newspaper job because it was assumed we would have jobs in the summer—not for financial reasons but because we had to do something."[20]

This attitude was so ingrained in Charlotte that even after she became a successful *New York Times* editor and spent far more than forty hours a week at her job, she abhorred being labeled a workaholic. Instead, she believed, one's work and personal life should mesh smoothly. As one reporter wrote, "Since 1961, Charlotte has worked at the *Times*, perhaps harder than anyone else on the staff. . . . Charlotte finds 'no conflict . . . between work and play. . . . The two are perfectly blended.'"[21]

After Charlotte and Mary moved to Bexley, their lives gradually took divergent paths. By the time they moved, they were surrounded by girls their own age, and each developed her own circle of friends. They remained close to many of these school and neighborhood friends for decades. Like Charlotte and Mary, many of these girls were expected to continue their education at prestigious colleges, and a few of Charlotte's good friends in Bexley attended Vassar with her.

When it became time for Charlotte to select a college before her high school graduation in 1946, there was little question that she would leave Columbus. Well-educated, upper-middle-class young women from Bexley did not attend Ohio State, the nearby land-grant public institution. They were expected to attend private schools, preferably one that would give them a high-quality academic education as well as lessons in the finer points of being a lady.

Lucile enjoyed her years at Smith College, and Charlotte considered applying to Smith, but she applied to and was accepted by Vassar. Mary believes the decision not to attend Smith might have been indicative of a small rebellion on the part of Charlotte: "I think she was making a statement, although she may not have known it at the time. I think that she, while deeply influenced by Mother, early on knew that if she were to flourish she had to be different."[22] For her entire life, Charlotte had sharply contradictory feelings toward her mother. She respected and loved her, but, even when she was a top editor at the *New York Times*, feared her disapproval. Charlotte felt she must be a high achiever to live up to her mother's exacting standards. And she continually worried about her mother's bouts of depression and where they might ultimately lead.

But, Davey said, the two Curtis girls were torn when it came to Columbus and their family life—they both enjoyed their lives in Columbus, but by the time they were adolescents, they felt they had to get away. Charlotte's ambivalence about living in Columbus would remain throughout her life, and she would always maintain strong ties to the city. Mary, however, left Columbus in 1952 to attend Smith College and she would never live there again.

3

Leaving Home

WHEN SHE ENTERED Vassar, Charlotte continued the same type of rigorous education she was introduced to at CSG. And most of her classmates were well-bred, upper-middle-class women such as those who attended CSG. But her life was to change dramatically that September of 1946 when she moved out of Bexley and to Poughkeepsie, New York. For the first time, she viewed life outside the confines of Columbus and away from the watchful eye of her parents. She now lived less than two hours from New York City, one of the most exciting cities in the world, and she was exposed daily to a variety of people and philosophies. Her four years at Vassar would change her and make her realize that she must live in Manhattan if she was serious about a career.

While she was a college student, Charlotte continued her habit of corresponding by letter with her family—particularly her mother. The hundreds of letters she sent her mother throughout her life reflected Charlotte's personal thoughts and political views and the general status of her life. They became a vital form of communication between the two, a way for Charlotte to sort out her own thoughts and a historical record of their lives. The countless letters Charlotte wrote her mother over three decades also show how she craved and valued Lucile's opinions on everything from the latest fashions to politics to career choices. And they were a way for Charlotte to monitor Lucile's occasional bouts with depression.

During her college years and shortly thereafter, Charlotte for the first time exhibited deep contradictions in her character. She felt a strong need to conform to her parents' ideas of an acceptable lifestyle and behavior, yet she had an independent and iconoclastic spirit that opposed convention. Her paradoxical nature was an enigma to many who knew her, and it caused her self-doubt until she learned to be true to herself.

~

Selwa Showker Roosevelt recalled her sophomore year at Vassar and the two best friends with whom she shared adjoining single rooms in Main North dormitory. The two women, Charlotte Curtis and Harriette Moeller, came from an affluent suburb of Columbus, Ohio, and roomed together as freshmen. Selwa joined them during their sophomore year, and they formed an unlikely and nearly inseparable trio, complete with new nicknames. The tiny, outspoken, and vigorous redhead, Charlotte, became known as "Rusty"; Harriette, tall, blond, and willowy, adopted the nickname "Ronnie"; and Selwa Showker, a Lebanese American with a dark complexion and jet black hair, became "Lucky."

"The three of us were quite something," Roosevelt said fifty years later. "Harriette was this absolutely gorgeous blond—ravishingly beautiful and tall. I'm middle-sized and dark, and Charlotte was tiny and had this bright red hair. So we were a funny trio."[1] Charlotte and Harriette were friends from Bexley, and they met Selwa during their freshman year. The three became best friends despite some glaring differences in temperament and goals. Moeller, Roosevelt recalled, was "glamorous, attracted to the bright lights"; Roosevelt herself was very studious and ultra-serious about her grades and classwork, and

Curtis was single-minded in deciding on a lifelong career and gearing her studies in that direction. The personalities they displayed in college evidently shaped their later lives: the glamorous Ronnie became the Vicomtesse de Rosiere and moved to Palm Beach; Lucky married Archibald Roosevelt Jr.—a Central Intelligence Agency agent and the grandson of Theodore Roosevelt—and she became White House chief of protocol during the Reagan administration; and the politically aware Rusty became associate editor of the *New York Times.*

Another future celebrity in their dormitory was Jacqueline Bouvier, who was one year behind Lucky, Rusty, and Ronnie. Roosevelt remembered Jacqueline Bouvier Kennedy Onassis as sophisticated and glamorous but also dignified and poised.[2] Charlotte much later wrote a book about her former classmate's first year in the White House.[3]

Lucky Roosevelt believes her two roommates had a dramatic influence on her life. A scholarship student from Kingsport, Tennessee, she had little in common with many of her classmates because of her modest economic and social background. Ronnie became her social mentor and taught her how to be stylish.[4] Rusty engaged her mind, challenging her to debates about politics and culture. Lucky's education was nearly complete, thanks to her teachers at Vassar and her two best friends there.

But like most students at elite private colleges in the 1940s and 1950s, the schooling of the three women went far beyond Vassar's lush green campus. They spent weekends in New York City, hitting Broadway plays, nightclubs, and stores. It was a charmed life, Roosevelt remembers: "In those days you went to places like El Morocco, the Stork Club, places like that, and the Biltmore [Hotel] under the clock. That was the era. It was a WASP world. I wasn't a WASP, but they took me in, so to speak." If Vassar was a snooty place, Lucky Showker did not notice: "It didn't matter how much money you had. That was one of the great things about it. There were so many people like me who didn't have a lot of money, but I never felt any different from anyone else."[5]

"Romanticism" exemplified this carefree Vassar class of 1950, the yearbook *Vassarian* proclaimed on its pages: "Romanticism: On weekends you ventured forth to see how the other half lives. You discovered the aberrations of New York Central and the idiosyncrasies of the New Haven Bus. You also found that college ranged into spheres beyond the academic."[6] The girls liked to think of themselves as multifaceted: "Our lives at Vassar are composed of many elements which, though in constant motion and juxtaposition, maintain a certain balance and harmony."[7]

Weekends at Ivy League colleges also became an integral part of the social scene, and Ronnie Moeller excelled during such weekends, according to Bexley native Robert Shamansky, a lifelong friend of Charlotte's and Moeller's. Shamansky recalled Charlotte telling him that her roommate Ronnie drew men like a magnet—she would come back to Vassar from the "weekends," as they were known, her purse filled with the fraternity pins and rings infatuated men had given her. Charlotte's job was to return the jewelry to its proper owners.[8]

Politics was a key part of Roosevelt's and Curtis's education at Vassar. According to Roosevelt, she and Rusty changed their ideological opinions while at Vassar and adopted political views there that they maintained the rest of their lives. Ironically, these views took opposite paths. Charlotte came to college as a political moderate and, for the first time in her life, wrote for a newspaper—the *Chronicle*, the more conservative of Vassar's two school papers.[9] Roosevelt worked on the *Miscellany News*, the voice of the left. Their experiences at Vassar changed the political views of both women. Charlotte's took a turn to the left, and scholarship student Selwa Showker's headed rightward.

Roosevelt said her thinking was shaped by an outstanding teacher who instilled in her students the ability to separate propaganda from fact. Evalyn Clark, who taught European history, was an exacting instructor who insisted that her students read an exhaustive collection of Soviet tracts, accounts of wars, and Comintern periodicals. As a result, Showker became disillusioned with the left and what she labeled its authoritarianism. But current events at the time and the influence of classmates prompted Charlotte to turn leftward into what Roosevelt termed "a bleeding heart."[10] The two women attended Vassar during the days of debates about the guilt or innocence of Alger Hiss and the Rosenbergs, and it was natural for college students of that era to adopt views that were far more liberal than their parents'. Lucile Curtis had always been a liberal politically, but many people in conservative Columbus did not share her ideology. At Vassar, Charlotte met a variety of people, and her liberal views intensified. But her favorite part of politics and of Vassar was that they prompted open debate and arguments. Decades later, she remembered that it was exciting to be on campus during a pivotal time in politics: "There was such a lot of intellectual and political ferment on campus what with it being 1948 and an election year," she said. "[Vassar] was an extremely open college and one that tolerated all kinds of ideas."[11]

Although Charlotte had already been all over the United States and overseas by the time she entered Vassar, living away from home with other women was an eye-opening experience. As soon as she moved to Poughkeepsie in September 1946, she wrote a steady stream of letters home, describing her new surroundings and offering commentary about the people she met and the environment. Her excitement and amazement are reflected in one of her first letters home, before classes started: "I've been initiated to faculty, halls, seniors, veterans, physical exams, meals—which are, by the way, a race to see who can eat the most in the least time." "Vassar clothes are a panic," she wrote. "Breakfast in pajamas or evening clothes. There's absolutely no telling."[12]

Three days later, Charlotte again wrote to her family and once again mentioned eating, which evidently was a favorite pastime of Vassar students. "Your little Vassar cherub reports again," she wrote. "I've gained 3 pounds already. Somehow the 'great college atmosphere' brings out the hunger in everyone and we really gobble."[13] It was unusual for Charlotte to mention food so frequently. Even as a child, she was a picky eater with unusual tastes, and food was never important to her. Throughout her life, her weight rarely rose above 100 or 105 pounds.[14]

Once she began classes in earnest, Charlotte was faced with the task of selecting a major. Vassar allowed an interdepartmental course of study that did not restrict its students to rigid, conventional majors such as history, political science, and the like. Students could mix and mingle subjects to form majors such as, in Roosevelt's case, International Studies. Charlotte's interest in sociology, history, and political science resulted in her becoming an American Culture major. Charlotte and her sister, Mary, experienced culture shock when they transferred from the unstructured University School to CSG, and Charlotte may have felt the same way at Vassar. Her first term grades were hardly Dean's List material: Cs in Chemistry, English, French, and Religion. The second term was even worse. She maintained her Cs, but her chemistry grade dropped to a D.[15] Mary Davey attributes the low grades to an overactive social life that brought Charlotte and her friends too frequently into New York City. Roosevelt attributes her former roommate's average and low grades to her vision of a "bigger picture"—she became so interested in deciding on a career that grades became a minor distraction at times.[16] And her course of study bears out that observation. Absent from her transcript are any courses in subjects such as drama, art, or comparative literature. Instead, she focused almost exclusively on political science, history, and English, with a sprinkling of French and Italian.

Charlotte's grades improved, however, as her academic career progressed. Although As were rare for her—she earned only two during her years at Vassar—she began by late in her sophomore year to raise the Cs to Bs and B-pluses. But her grades at Vassar did not always indicate her diligence; letters to her parents and class notes show that Charlotte worked hard at her studies and did not take them lightly. She filled countless brown-covered spiral notebooks with detailed, meticulous notes written in blue fountain pen in her left-leaning handwriting. In her philosophy notebook, for instance, she noted in painstaking detail the elements of theories by Darwin, Hegel, Huxley, and others.

In letters to her parents during her junior and senior years, Charlotte claimed to be spending much of her time on her studies: "Dear Family—Again small red headed daughter reports on recent activities. Actually, I haven't done anything but study for so long that I'm in rut—just two weeks and everything will be better."[17] Or, in a neatly typed letter, "Dear Family, Nothing much happens to me— I seem to sit at this machine day in and day out. And thesis takes so much time and as a result I'm weeks behind on other work—oh grades, they will definitely have a low blow this term."[18]

Charlotte's study habits during college set the tone for her work habits throughout her life. Later, as a society writer, she would spend much time with her head in books, researching the people, cities, and traditions about which she wrote. Then, if she were not on deadline, she would painstakingly write her stories, sometimes perfecting draft after draft. Most of Charlotte's letters home were neatly typed, double-spaced, fact-filled accounts of either her social or academic activities or her views of current events and politics. For instance, a critique she offers of a Broadway show, *Inside the USA*, contains the minute detail and detached opinion of a theater critic: "As a parody of the book by John Gunther, there were scenes from various areas of the United States. The inimitable Beatrice Lillie and Jack Haley were good, but as stars they seemed to have passed their heyday."[19]

Charlotte's letters home, with their detailed commentary on plays, government programs, and history, may seem uncharacteristic of an eighteen-year-old girl away from home for the first time. But she also addressed more conventional topics for someone of her age and situation such as the decor of her dormitory room and her plants. She described her room with delight: "The room looks just wonderful. The blue green ties the pale blue walls and the pale green rugs and bedspread together. Then, also, the Yale blue pennants go with the dark green table. Oh yes, I bought a maroon day bed cover with green, blue and red flowers on the pillows. You will never know the tremendous improvement! Just to top it off, I bought a lovely African violet."[20] The detail, whether she was describing the decor of her room, a play, or a discussion about current events, is the common thread among all the letters Charlotte wrote home. It was this recollection of and attention to the smallest facts that a decade later would earn her fame at the *New York Times*.

~

Charlotte's hectic life as a Vassar student, with its intense studying, forays out of town, and spirited political and social debates, was fairly typical of young women who attended private eastern colleges in the late 1940s and early 1950s. In her remembrances of her life in Manhattan in the early 1950s, journalist Mary Cantwell noted that even the hairstyle and "uniform" of the era's young women varied little. Most wore their hair in pageboys, often decorating them with gold barrettes or headbands. The ensemble of choice was Shetland sweater and Bermuda shorts, a mode of dressing many favored for decades: "Some women, of course, never give up the wardrobe," Cantwell wrote. "I see it wherever WASPS gather, in the headbands and gold bobby pins that hold back still pageboyed hair, and in little belgian shoes on little bony feet."[21]

Amid this whirlwind life and demure bearing was, frequently, the ubiquitous boyfriend—often men these women met early in college and dated throughout their four years as students. Many of these women led sheltered lives at home so their knowledge of men was minimal, and these college sweethearts were often their first serious boyfriends. That was the case with Cantwell and with Charlotte. Throughout her years at Vassar, Charlotte dated Dwight "Butch" Fullerton Jr., a Yale student who was raised in Circleville, Ohio, about twenty miles outside of Columbus. Charlotte and Butch met during their sophomore year and became constant companions. It is not hard to understand their alliance—both came from well-to-do families in Ohio (Fullerton's father was a judge), both attended prestigious eastern colleges, and both knew that each was a "suitable" choice in the eyes of their parents. Butch was a prelaw student who had served in the air force and graduated from a prestigious prep school. And their relationship was convenient. Neither had to worry about getting dates for events, and each had a built-in traveling companion for college weekends and evenings in Manhattan. But as was the case in many of the romantic alliances of the era, theirs was a mismatch, which Charlotte and Butch realized much later.

Like Charlotte, Butch spent much of his youth in a rambling farmhouse in the country. Mary Davey said the two were inseparable during college and had a "comfortable" relationship.[22] This low-key aspect of their relationship may have been its most appealing quality to Charlotte. As Cantwell noted, many of the young women in the late 1940s and early 1950s had little knowledge of sex, nor did they think it an acceptable topic to discuss even with their closest friends: "Doing so would have implied that the speakers knew something about it, and if we did, we . . . kept it a secret."[23]

Charlotte and Dwight's liaison also enabled them to enjoy the social whirlwind that was a vital part of their college years. So when they became engaged during their senior year, it was a natural progression, and Charlotte and her mother busied themselves for nearly a year with plans for the wedding. During her senior year, Charlotte's letters home rarely described the details of plays, ski trips, and her studies. Now they dealt with honeymoon itineraries, bridesmaids' gowns, availability of a church, and travel plans for the wedding party.

Charlotte's friends during this era remembered her tremendous energy, her eclectic interests, and her wry and often caustic sense of humor. She would maintain the latter two traits for the rest of her life. But limited energy levels caused by illness would limit her as she grew older, although she eventually learned to compensate with economy of movement and physical efficiency.[24] A longtime friend of hers, Larry Leeds, remembers first meeting her one weekend when he visited Vassar from Yale when both were freshmen. Leeds recalls that his friend Rusty stood out from her classmates because of her confident nature and tirelessness—unlike some of her insecure classmates: "Rusty Curtis was feisty, self-reliant, and self-confident," he said. "But mostly she was active. She was interested in everything and bouncy. She was wired."[25] The first signs of a diminishing energy level that would recur sporadically for the rest of her life came during her senior year in college, when she developed a strange body rash, high fever, and joint pain. It puzzled her so much that she visited the college infirmary, and, within a week, consulted two specialists. Ever the physician's daughter, she described the symptoms in great detail to her mother, even questioning the treatment and the diagnosis:

> I am now confined to bed. . . . Dr. Bean informed me that I had rhumatic [sic] fever which is tommy rot—they can't prove it. I have .6 degrees of fever. My pulse is 88 which is not rapid enough for rhumatic [sic] fever. My sediment rate is 24 having jumped from 15—but as Dr. Wright has pointed out, any human being with anything wrong would have this jump. It is also just 5 points above normal which is not high enough for rhumatic fever. . . . And Dr. Wright is almost dead positive that I don't have rhumatic fever, and I honestly believe that she is the only one around this place who knows anything. . . . They have just bungled everything all the way along the line.[26]

Charlotte's rash and fever eventually disappeared. But this illness occasionally recurred, robbing her of energy. Decades later, her husband determined that it was the first sign of an underactive thyroid, a condition that went undiagnosed for most of her life. And this was first of many times Charlotte would do her own research into treatment of her illness and offer commentary about the talents of her doctors.[27]

~

As an adult, Charlotte would proudly relate that her parents did not believe in idle time and that vacations could be learning experiences.

Thus it was unlikely that Charlotte would spend her first summer vacation from Vassar lounging around a swimming pool. What she did was a surprise to everyone, including herself. She applied and was hired for a job at the afternoon *Columbus Citizen*, one of three daily newspapers in the city.

It seems odd that Charlotte applied for a newspaper job. She expressed no interest at the time in working in journalism. Although she helped produce the CSG yearbook and worked on the *Vassar Chronicle*, her interest was mainly in expressing her opinions, and she had strong opinions on many subjects, from current events to fashion to gardening. Larry Leeds believes this initial interest in newspaper work was a by-product of her opinionated nature. Newspapering, he said, "allowed her an outlet to express all her other interests. It was a way for her to put them on paper as commentary."[28] The general education Vassar provided certainly prepared her to collect bits and pieces of eclectic information and general knowledge as a reporter. Vassar, like most other small colleges, did not teach journalism then, nor did most universities have journalism schools. Throughout her life, Charlotte disdained the idea of journalism schools to prepare journalists, believing that a varied college education was the best training for any reporter or editor.[29]

Some of her co-workers at the *Citizen* thought the tiny freshman from Vassar was overeducated. Few if any of the hard-bitten men who worked for the *Citizen* had college degrees. Their worldliness did not please George Curtis, who believed his daughter's selection of a summer job was odd, as Charlotte related years later.

> There wasn't anyone like me when I went to the Citizen to work. . . .
> I was teased constantly. I was never called Charlotte or Miss Curtis.
> I was called "Vassar." . . . It was used in a pejorative way because
> somehow there was something snobbish, there was something not
> nice about being a rich girl from a rich suburb . . . and going to
> what was considered a rich women's college. . . . Certainly in the
> Middle West, nice people . . . didn't go into newspapering. Newspa-
> pering was a job for itinerants, for cab drivers, for railroad engineers

—I'm literally talking about people I worked with, people who had only eighth-grade educations. If you couldn't get a job doing anything else, if you weren't quite respectable, you went into this crazy business.[30]

But it was precisely this illicit aspect of the business that made it glamorous to Charlotte—and it made her work hard: "I'm grateful for [the teasing by co-workers] because if I hadn't had that extra challenge, I probably would have been much more mediocre than I probably am."[31] Charlotte evidently was immune to the teasing, even though she had never been exposed to a working-class environment. Her ability to withstand it, and even to acknowledge that it improved her, was an integral part of her character. She never let the opinions of others bother her or alter her actions, and, unless she could learn from criticism, ridicule, or teasing, she simply ignored it. Further, Shamansky said he marveled at his friend's ability to blend in wherever she went, a quality she acquired because she was a good listener. This chameleonlike quality later helped her immensely as a society reporter at the *Citizen* and the *Times*—it allowed her to mingle unobtrusively with those she covered, even though what appeared in the next day's paper was not necessarily flattering.[32]

Charlotte was hired for $40 a week to work primarily on the society and women's pages because few women worked as news reporters then. The job was considered too dangerous. She wanted to work on the news section but was told at the *Citizen* that the newspaper "already had a woman" news reporter.[33] Charlotte's stories, however, were not restricted to the society pages, and she wrote many general feature stories, including her first story about where people in Columbus took vacations. She found her next story more exciting —it focused on a circus that came to town and described traveling with the circus.

After that first summer at the *Citizen*, Charlotte was hooked on the newspaper business. She loved its illicit mystique and its variety, and being a reporter enabled her to satisfy an insatiable curiosity about the world. As she said nearly forty years later, she could not see how anyone would want to do anything else: "I adored [reporting]. I thought newspapering was the most glamorous thing in the world and I still think it is. Why anybody would do anything else, I mean, clearly they need their heads examined!"[34]

As a writer, Charlotte was able to exercise her fey sense of humor and love of words, and she often used puns, alliteration, and other literary techniques in her stories. One story about an "autumn prelude" fashion show and fund-raiser for the city orchestra, for instance, employs several of these techniques: "Autumn Prelude, that much talked about symphony of frocks, femininity and fun, will be held on Sept. 6 at the Neil House," the story begins. "And the whole job of planning this rests in the hands of a devoted group of young women who have the 90 degrees of heat to work for the Columbus Philharmonic benefit."[35]

Charlotte was given much creative license at the *Citizen* and could cultivate a freewheeling writing style, and the paper, in turn, had a real-life college student to write about campus styles and to explain how college girls *really* dressed. Charlotte's conversational style and directness made the stories easy to read and even a little shocking to some readers, who were used to formulaic fashion stories that read like press releases. In one story, she revealed how college women scoffed at such accepted and traditional fashion staples as hats and taffeta: "They are amused when told that hats are the things this year," Charlotte wrote. "They reject taffeta when told to wear it because it ruffles—they are not interested in ruffling."[36] Charlotte's enthusiasm for her summer job did not waver after four summers, even though she was a newsroom nomad who wandered from desk to desk filling in for vacationing employees.

Shortly before her college graduation and her wedding to Butch Fullerton, she was offered a full-time job at the paper—an offer that thrilled her because she loved the work, and she and Fullerton had planned to move to Columbus when he entered law school at Ohio State. Charlotte wrote her family with unabashed enthusiasm about the $40-a-week job offer: "Well, I just got the most exciting letter from [*Citizen* editor] Mr. [Don] Weaver concerning a job starting next September at the Citizen. He said something to the effect that the society department needs reorganization and we need to revamp the whole page and that I'm just the girl to do it!! I'm just so excited. . . . He seemed very enthusiastic and really wants me to come back to the Citizen and make society first rate."[37]

As her years at Vassar wound down, Charlotte busily made plans for her wedding and honeymoon while writing her senior thesis. The thesis was a pivotal part of the education of students at elite private schools; Charlotte, an avid student of history and political science, selected an interdepartmental topic: Theodore Roosevelt and his concept of the new nationalism.

Charlotte and Butch planned to spend the summer in Europe for their honeymoon, after which he would begin law school and Charlotte would start work on the *Citizen*. The couple would move to an apartment in Bexley that was owned by Lucile Curtis, who had just inherited much of her father's property and was helping to settle his estate. Fred Atcherson died in March 1950 at his home in the Normandie Hotel at age ninety-four. He was survived by his wife, Charlotte, who was well into her eighties. The burden of settling the estate fell largely to their only child. Lucile's life had always been filled with travel and her volunteer work, and now, with her children in college, her participation in these activities intensified. But these years were also worrisome to her; in addition to the aging of her parents and, later, the death of her father, George Curtis, too, had severe health problems. He had the first of what would be several cerebral hemorrhages in 1946 at the age of fifty-six.[38] Although this first one was not severely debilitating, it marked the beginning of health problems that continued through the rest of his life.

As one of the 250 graduates of the Vassar class of 1950, Charlotte was no different from many of her classmates: they had just received an elite education and were exposed to a vibrant and exciting social scene but now were expected to marry the "right" man, settle down, and have a family. These tacit expectations had been reinforced since their childhood, and, despite an education that encouraged them to question authority and speak their minds, most of them felt a need to conform to these long-accepted standards.

A childhood need to please her mother persisted during Charlotte's years at Vassar; Lucile had always believed in the importance of home and family. This need to please her mother, and, consequently, to conform to society's norms, was a factor in Charlotte's decision to go through with the marriage to Butch Fullerton. Her summer jobs at the *Citizen* may have bothered her father, who did not think newspaper work was the proper job for a well-to-do young lady,[39] but Lucile may have seen it as a way for Charlotte to contribute to society. Lucile was also pleased that her older daughter was returning to Bexley to live because it appeared that Mary Curtis would not return home after her graduation from Smith in 1952. In 1951, while still a junior in college, Mary married John Davey, an air force man. She became pregnant during her senior year, and although she was married by then, her condition was shocking to many. She remembered: "I was six months pregnant when I graduated in 1952 and I scandalized the Smith women. I was made to live separately in the dormitory because I might contaminate the unmarried ladies."[40] Mary and her new husband lived in Dayton, Ohio, and Baltimore before they moved to northern California in 1960, where they raised their three children and have lived for nearly forty years.

Lucile was delighted that Charlotte planned to return to Bexley, and the two busily completed wedding plans shortly before Charlotte's graduation from college in June 1950. The evening wedding would be a small but traditional one, they decided, and would take place at Trinity Episcopal Church near their home, with a reception following at the Curtis house. Mary Curtis was her sister's maid of honor, and the four bridesmaids were all longtime Bexley friends of Charlotte's: Babs Sayre and her twin sister, Jean, Doran Ritter, and Patricia LeVeque. Three Yale classmates of Butch's were also members of the wedding party.[41]

On July 7, 1950, Charlotte became one of countless young women of her generation to marry within a year or so after graduating from college. Like many of the others, she felt pressure from many quarters to marry quickly and get on with a secure, neat life designed to last forever. After all, these women believed, if they waited too long, the suitable men might be taken. Furthermore, they felt that once they slept with their boyfriends the unspoken understanding was that they would marry them. In her book about young well-educated women in the early 1950s, Mary Cantwell described these thoughts: "Marrying young, a classmate used to say, was like getting to a sale on the first day. God knows what, if anything, would be left if you waited till you were twenty-five or -six. Besides, I had slept with him [her fiancé], and the flesh, I believed, was an unbreakable link."[42]

But the proper wedding between Butch Fullerton and Charlotte Curtis was not all that it seemed. A handwritten undated letter to Butch found among her personal papers shows that Rusty Curtis had reservations about their relationship. In this note, Charlotte told Butch that their relationship was not strong enough to last, and she implied that he, too, had mentioned that he had reservations.[43] It is not known whether Butch received this letter. The two evidently ironed out their differences before their wedding, although Charlotte's doubts remained. Mary Curtis Davey remembers a brief but frantic bedtime conversation she had with her sister the night before Charlotte's wedding. Charlotte confided that the marriage would be a mistake: "Charlotte came into my room and said, 'Mary, I've made a big mistake.' I'll never forget it. She said, 'Mary, what should I do?' Here I was, on the pickle boat. I didn't know anything about relationships or marriage."[44] After the honeymoon, Charlotte again voiced concerns to Mary about the marriage. But in the fall of 1950, Charlotte and Butch Fullerton began their new lives together in Bexley, and, much like her mother did two decades earlier, the free-spirited Charlotte traded her life of independence for one of domesticity.

4

Charlotte's Ruse

WHEN CHARLOTTE AND Butch Fullerton returned from their European honeymoon and moved into their apartment on Sherwood Avenue in Bexley, they appeared to be the typical upwardly mobile young couple of their generation: he began law school at Ohio State University, and she began a full-time job as a society reporter at the *Citizen*, ostensibly to earn money and help him through law school. He anticipated that after his graduation Charlotte would quit her job and the two could begin a family.

As was true of many aspects of Charlotte's life, appearances were deceiving. Charlotte tried to play the role of the young Bexley wife, joining charity organizations and doing other community work, including teaching a class in narrative writing at the local YWCA. But problems in the marriage soon emerged. She returned from her honeymoon to tell her sister once again that the marriage should not have taken place but that she would "stick it out" because she had promised to help put her husband through law school and wanted to fulfill that obligation.[1] As soon as she started work as a full-time reporter, Charlotte began to absorb the culture of newspaper journalism. That meant socializing with friends in the business — often after work at bars—and discussions that centered almost exclusively on newspaper gossip and the background and complexities of stories they had written. It was a life of coffee drinking, smoking, and, for some, heavy gambling and drinking. Charlotte had been a tea drinker her entire life and rarely if ever drank coffee, and she never developed an affinity for gambling or alcohol. But she was a smoker, a habit she never abandoned, and she blended in well with most of the other reporters as she puffed on Newports. Newspapering at the time was a closed fraternity. Most reporters at the *Citizen* were devoted members of the journalists' union, the Newspaper Guild. Guild members had many organized activities, including writing contests and each year a "Page One Ball," complete with banquet, awards ceremony, and entertainment. It was a generation before political correctness, when the Guild could open its banquet program with a photo of platinum blond actress Jayne Mansfield in low-cut evening gown and exposed legs, accompanied by a description, filled with double entendre, of a "good" newspaperman: "[He] is never satisfied with a surface glance at a story. He wants to find out what's underneath—what's behind it all. . . . He wants to dig, dig, dig until he gets to the bottom."[2] Charlotte became very involved with the Guild and its social events, but Butch Fullerton never fit in. Jane Kehrer Horrocks, the fashion writer at the *Citizen* when Charlotte joined the paper, remembered him well: "Butch hated everyone at the newspaper. He'd stand around [at gatherings] looking glum. He hated newspapers."[3] And Charlotte rarely if ever mentioned her husband at work. "Most of the people she would go out with were bright and funny. He was very stuffy." To Horrocks and others at the *Citizen*, the match was an unlikely one.

Charlotte periodically exhibited a certain conformity to please her mother, although this became increasing difficult as Charlotte grew older. And as worldly as Lucile Curtis was, Charlotte knew she would be devastated if she and Butch divorced. Further, as she told her sister, she felt an obligation to stay with him at least until he finished law school. As Charlotte predicted, when the Fullertons divorced in 1953,

Lucile Curtis was crushed. Mary Davey remembered her mother's humiliation at the news: "Divorcing in Columbus Ohio in 1952? I mean you didn't do it. They [Lucile and Charlotte] had screaming matches, according to Charlotte. She told me about these awful scenes. 'How could you do this to this family?'"[4]

Their daughter's divorce violated the propriety of Curtis family members, who, by the time Charlotte returned to Bexley, were well-known and respected in their community. Over the years, Lucile and George Curtis had become established citizens known for their devotion to their family and to public service. By this time, George had an international reputation as a teacher and researcher, and Lucile's community work and enthusiasm for social causes made her a prominent figure in and outside of Columbus.

"If we had an aristocracy in this city, they were it," said Robert Shamansky, who grew up in Bexley the same time as the Curtis girls. Shamansky believes this status transcended money. Although the Curtises were comfortable financially, he said, "their status was not dependent on their money. Their status relied not on having more money than anyone else, but instead it relied on who they were, what they did in the community."[5]

Lucile held the family together. George Curtis's deteriorating health put an increasing burden on her. She was managing her parents' property during much of the 1950s and sold most of it by the end of that decade, except for her house and the apartment building on Sherwood Avenue. In addition, she arranged rigorous travel schedules for herself and her husband, even after George was wheelchair-bound in the early 1960s. Charlotte's co-workers and friends in Bexley remember Lucile Curtis as soft-spoken and charming—but as a woman with a will of steel.[6] Shamansky said that one word described Lucile Curtis throughout her adult life: the French word *formidable*. "Lucile was a force of nature, a formidable lady."[7]

Charlotte viewed her marriage to Fullerton as an unfortunate accident. Decades later, in several published interviews, she said simply that she had a brief, early marriage to a pleasant man with whom she had little in common. She was not vitriolic about it, nor did she place any blame for the failure of the marriage. In one profile, she said that he "assumed I'd be Mrs. Lawyer and do the canapés. I wasn't deceiving him; that was my assumption, too, but I turned out to like newspapering more."[8]

The demure-looking Charlotte loved the cynicism and roughness of many of her co-workers on the *Citizen*. They helped cultivate her rebellious and unconventional side, and they spoke and acted in ways some Vassar-educated young women might find shocking. For instance, *Citizen* reporter Gene Grove often wrote his stories so that the first letter of the first word of some paragraphs spelled out an obscene word.[9] This prank greatly amused many reporters, yet it went unnoticed by most readers—and, evidently, all editors. One reporter who saw great humor in it was Charlotte—and she soon became attracted to the dark and brooding Grove.

~

The *Columbus Citizen* was one of three daily papers in the city. Its main competition was the family-owned, conservative *Columbus Dispatch*, but it also competed with the *Ohio State Journal*. The *Dispatch*, owned by the wealthy Wolfe family of Columbus, had the largest staff and many more resources than the *Citizen* or the *Journal*, but the *Citizen* was the most aggressive and creative of the newspapers, and its underdog status allowed it to pursue stories the *Dispatch* shied away from because of its owners' close ties to area businesses and the power structure in the city. Like other newspapers of its time, the *Citizen* in the 1950s gave high priority to crime news, particularly stories involving the "beautiful widow" or the "attractive brunette accomplice." But the *Citizen* had a personality of its own, primarily because of its emphasis on columnists with whom readers built up a familiarity and rapport. The theater, sports, gossip, and society columns could personalize their writing in a way unavailable to news reporters because they had license to be subjective.

Although the *Citizen* was the more colorful newspaper, its management was more reluctant than the *Dispatch*'s to employ women to cover hard news. Mary McGarey, who covered news at the *Dispatch* during the 1950s and 1960s, said Charlotte applied for jobs at the *Dispatch* several times during her eleven years at the *Citizen* because she thought she would be allowed to cover news there. She never was hired at the *Dispatch*, even though the Wolfe family lived in Bexley and knew Lucile. "She was too much of a firebrand," McGarey remembered.[10]

But Charlotte was clever, and she had the financial resources and persistence to mold her job at the *Citizen* into something more than conventional society, church, and fashion writing. At her own expense, she traveled overseas to Paris and to Russia and sent dispatches home. The *Citizen* promoted her two series from abroad, and they helped her make a name for herself on the paper. Later, she was given two regular columns and was able to exercise a freewheeling and increasingly caustic writing style.

~

Charlotte had some feature stories on page 1 during her first year as a full-time reporter, but she wrote primarily women's page and religion stories and occasionally personality profiles. As she had done when she was a summer intern, she concentrated on minute personal details of her subjects and their surroundings. She started a technique of capturing the subject through direct quotes, even if they did not portray the subject in the most flattering light. It was a style of writing she used throughout her career.

Frequently, this style led to a brutal honesty in which the subjects indicted themselves through their own words, although Charlotte sometimes gave them a push. This technique is evident in a story she wrote about a French hairdresser who visited Columbus, in which she mimicked his accent. The story begins, "'I do not like zee styles which make zee weemen look like zee bushweemen,' observed a Paris hair stylist Monday in Columbus." She continued: "He smiles ecstatically at the thought of 'zee high-leefted bang.'" And, "in spite of this jealous attention to milady's tresses, the Frenchman insists that a woman is not completely attired without a hat. 'Ah, hats,' he sighed. 'Zay are necessaire comme la lipstick.'"[11]

Charlotte was not content to attribute the hairdresser's quotes with a simple "he said." Instead, by writing that he smiled *ecstatically* and he *sighed*, she made him seem superficial. While the story is informative, Charlotte did not take this hairdresser seriously, and neither should the reader, she implies. Yet because the story is not pure parody, it offers information for readers who take it seriously. As was the case with many of her stories, she had distinct opinions about her subjects, which she subtly imposed upon her readers.

Charlotte's writing was far different from that of other society writers of her era. The conventional role of society pages was to chronicle society events and to serve as purveyor of information rather than to offer opinions of the events, either subtly or overtly. Charlotte, however, revealed in some of her stories that she thought those she covered took their fund-raisers, luncheons, and flower and fashion shows a bit too seriously. Often, she did this by giving nonhuman elements of the stories human characteristics, as she did in a devastating story about a flower show. The story began:

> The heat's on the flower world.
> The Northwest Flower Show will not be held until April 21 and April 22 and thousands of flowers have to bloom on time, or else. Until then, pressure on the posies will take many forms. Apple blossoms will be heated in the living room and daffodils will get a cool treatment in the refrigerator. Shrubs will be stood in a dark corner. And heaven knows what will happen to the pansies.[12]

The theme here, that the planners take the show very seriously, was reinforced with subtle phrases: the flowers must bloom "or else"; "heaven only knows what will happen to the pansies."

Charlotte went on to describe the frenzied activities of the planners, who spent their time hoping everything would work out and devising ways to revive droopy flowers. Some found that keeping records helped:

Mr. R. C. Lichty, the show treasurer . . . has kept a diary since 1948 for the dates when crab apples bloom. He has no record of tulips, but from his figures, the crab apples will be at their best in the middle of May.

"In 1948, they bloomed on April 22," he said. "But it wasn't until May in 1951. Mostly it's in April."

Charlotte implied here that these people had nothing better to do than keep detailed records of previous shows and could recite them at a moment's notice, a meaningless talent.

The tulips, however, worried the planners the most, according to Charlotte: "'Tulips,' said Mrs. Kunkler, visibly moved. 'That's something else again. They have to be hardened. You pick them in the morning while the dew is still on them.'" Mrs. Kunkler, Charlotte indicated, might be overly concerned about her tulips—she expended much emotion on them.

This story, like many others of Charlotte's, prompted calls from readers who were irate that she was mocking the flower show planners. Jane Kehrer Horrocks remembered that so many readers called that *Citizen* editor Don Weaver reprimanded Charlotte and warned her not to write more stories that ridiculed her subjects. But others on the paper thought the story hilarious. The reprimand had little effect on Charlotte, and she kept writing what she wanted to.[13] In fact, the lack of reprisals by *Citizen* editors led Charlotte virtually to ignore complaints about her stories—a habit she would continue when she joined the *New York Times* years later.

Because the *Citizen* prided itself on its reputation of being colorful, editors allowed Charlotte to write in this sometimes snide and irreverent style. In the 1950s, Columbus was still a moderate-sized city, and, though editors occasionally received irate telephone calls about her work, they did not worry about offending large numbers of readers. Only after Charlotte left Columbus for New York City did editors realize that the *Citizen* was ahead of its time in publishing such brutally frank society stories.

~

During her first few years on the *Citizen*, Charlotte, who had traveled extensively around the world with her family, persuaded her editors to let her report from overseas. The *Citizen*, however, did not send her on these assignments. She paid for the trips herself, undoubtedly using resources from her family.[14] She sent stories from the Soviet Union, from Paris, where she covered the United Nations General Assembly in 1951, and from a cruise ship.

Charlotte's zeal to work during her vacations is not surprising, considering the stress her parents placed on the value of taking advantage of time and never wasting it. (Twenty-five years later, she and her husband, a physician, spent Christmas together in a hospital emergency room while he worked: "The patient comes first," she said.)[15] She knew reporting from these locations would offer her opportunities unavailable to most young reporters. These trips also allowed her to follow in the footsteps of a role model—Pulitzer Prize–winning European correspondent Anne O'Hare McCormick, who worked at the *Times* in the 1920s and 1930s.

Charlotte's limited exposure to formal journalism training gave her few role models. Few women worked outside the women's and society pages of most newspapers, and none of them received national exposure. It is not surprising that Charlotte would admire McCormick, who was, coincidentally, a native of a Columbus, Ohio, and a graduate of the private St. Mary's College there. After Anne O'Hare graduated, she joined her mother in Cleveland at the weekly *Catholic Universe Bulletin*, of which Mrs. O'Hare was women's editor.

O'Hare married Francis J. McCormick of Dayton when she was twenty-eight, and because she was planning to accompany him on a European trip in 1910, she received permission to submit stories of her travels to the *New York Times*. Along the way, Anne McCormick endeared herself to Benito Mussolini, who granted her an extensive interview. Using her acquaintance with Mussolini as leverage, she pried her way into diplomatic circles and became known as a writer of interesting and unusual profiles.

Charlotte must have sensed similarities between herself and McCormick. Both women were mavericks who did not conform to conventional women's roles, and both were single-minded in planning their careers. Even more coincidentally, the two apparently bore a physical resemblance. When she was young, McCormick was thin and petite, as was Charlotte throughout her life, and both had red hair. In 1937, McCormick became the first woman to receive the Pulitzer Prize, which she won for her overseas coverage.

Marylin Bender, who worked with Charlotte on the *Times* women's section, said she and Charlotte talked about their admiration for McCormick: "We both aspired to the same place, the pantheon occupied by Anne O'Hare McCormick. I had no doubt that Charlotte would make it."[16]

In addition to McCormick, Charlotte had at least one role model who was closer to home. Charlotte grew to admire *Citizen* reporter Gene Grove, who had an avid interest in the underclass and in the civil rights movement. Grove was a romantic figure, tall and dark with bushy brows and a stubble of a beard. He was a leader of the local chapter of the Newspaper Guild and a professional malcontent. Charlotte had a predisposed sympathy for labor unions and for those less privileged than she, and Grove reinforced these values in her.

Charlotte's admiration for Grove deepened into love, but he was an unlikely object of affection for a woman who had been told repeatedly to love and marry the "proper" type of man. Not only was Grove married with children, but he was a heavy drinker who was once fired for coming to work drunk, only to be reinstated after a battle with the paper's management in which he was represented by the Newspaper Guild.[17] The two began a love affair, the rough but brilliant Grove became a mentor to Charlotte, and many of his interests became hers.

Clearly, Charlotte's upbringing did not condone affairs with married men. But Grove was attractive to her for several reasons: his interests matched hers, and, perhaps most important, she respected him professionally. As would be the case much later in her life, a man's marital status was not as important to Charlotte as his professional stature, his talent, and his intelligence. Charlotte could not love a man whom she did not respect immensely.

Charlotte did not date much after her divorce from Fullerton. Many of the men on the *Citizen* thought her odd because of her education and privileged upbringing, and Charlotte did not believe in flirting with them or batting her eyes to get them to like her. But she was tough, laughed at their jokes, and did not flinch when they made off-color remarks. Gradually her male colleagues came to like and trust her, and Charlotte prided herself on fitting in. Of course, she took active steps to blend in, joining the Newspaper Guild and eventually becoming an officer in the local chapter.

Her role as a union officer was ironic, considering that she also was an officer of the exclusive Junior League, a group of upper- and upper-middle-class young women who did volunteer work for local charities and nonprofit groups. She again was demonstrating the contradictory side of her nature, serving as an officer in a labor union and taking a serious interest in civil rights yet joining an organization whose ranks were made up of white Anglo-Saxon Protestants. But joining the Junior League was what proper young women of Bexley did in the 1950s, and Lucile encouraged her membership in it.[18]

During her first few years at the *Citizen*, Charlotte realized that she would have to use her own resources—internal and external—if she were to do anything unique on the paper. Editors had a set formula for stories that remained unchanged for years. In addition, tight budgets kept reporters from traveling too far from the paper's newsroom. The *Citizen*'s "thriftiness," as Charlotte later termed it, was both a blessing and a curse. It was difficult for reporters to do all the stories they wanted to do, but it was great training in frugality, as Charlotte noted three decades later: "You did everything with bobby pins and old scotch tape."[19]

Charlotte saw tremendous news possibilities in a United Nations General Assembly meeting in Paris in 1951, and she went there at her own expense to cover it for the paper. The subject matter intrigued her because of her interest in history and her love of travel. The trip would also include visits to Lebanon and Istanbul, and it had to seem exciting in contrast to the flower and fashion shows she covered daily.

The *Citizen*, however, treated Charlotte's stories from abroad as "women's" news, and they appeared in the women's section. In editor's notes that accompanied her stories, the *Citizen* was quick to point out that Charlotte was reporting from overseas on "women's interests." Her writing in the early dispatches from Paris contained the same detail as her daily *Citizen* stories, but they lacked the opinion or edge of her society stories. Perhaps she was awed at first by the location of the event, or perhaps it was her respect for history that kept her from becoming too irreverent. Instead, she piled on detail after detail, as in a story about the people involved with the meeting behind the scenes:

> It has cost the U-N an estimated $1,750,000, which has been appropriated in the current year's budget. . . . Approximately 500 tons of equipment had arrived at this historic Palais de Chaillot here. This building, which housed the 1948 General Assembly, is stacked high with packages including pencils, paper clips and carbon paper. Some 160 tons of mimeograph paper and thousands of discs for permanently recording the estimated 5½ million words to be spoken were rapidly dispersed throughout the Palais. Preceding the delegates were typewriters, cameras, interpretation machinery and 200,000 feet of film.[20]

These numbers came as the result of much research. The $1,750,000, for example, comes "from the current year's budget." The building is not merely historic but housed the General Assembly in 1948; the packages include not just office equipment but pencils, paper clips, and carbon paper. To Charlotte, the details told the story, and she went to great lengths to get them.

After a few days, Charlotte's irreverence emerged in a story in which she gently mocked a Russian diplomat. But she spared him the wounds she inflicted on many of her subjects in Columbus. Charlotte believed the diplomat Jakob Malik was grabbing the spotlight at the meeting. Malik, she wrote, "has his picture taken the most often and frequented the speaker's platform more than anybody else. . . . In fact, he rather dominated the afternoon."[21] In a rare first-person story, Charlotte immediately let the reader know what she thought of the diplomat:

> By some standards, I suppose, Malik has personality and good looks. He is tall, dark and not really unhandsome. A Humphrey Bogart of sorts. But he doesn't smile much, and most of the time he has what might be called an expressionless face. But to watch the camera boys go to work, you'd think Jake was either marrying Lana Turner or divorcing Jane Russell. What a play he got.

Charlotte's flip comments, such as referring to the diplomat as "Jake" and comparing him to the husbands of film stars, diminish his importance. The conversational use of the first person implies an intimacy with the reader that allows her to ask conspiratorially who this guy thinks he is. While her style here lets the reader know that she is unimpressed with him, it is more obvious than the style she would employ later, which would have quoted him in an arrogant statement or described an arrogant gesture or action.

Five years later, in 1956, Charlotte again arranged a trip for herself and sent dispatches to the newspaper. This trip to the Soviet Union would be pivotal in her career. It continued in the tradition of Anne O'Hare McCormick and paved the way for a later trip there to contribute to a book about that country by New York Times reporter and editor Harrison Salisbury.[22]

Her first story described Leningrad. Charlotte relied on colors and physical elements to portray a city with a dark, mystical beauty: "From the grey blue of the dawn, which comes early, to well after midnight when the boulevards and squares are dotted with great white globes of electric light, this famous city is wide awake and walking."[23] Still, Charlotte noted, the citizens moved about joylessly, dressed in drab, colorless clothes that created a sense of hopelessness: "One sees the Russian housewife in low-heeled sandals and shapeless drab dresses . . . and black-booted old men with grey beards and mustaches that match the grey of their pants." She continued this theme of darkness, particularly when describing dress and demeanor: "Women of Leningrad don't seem to care. . . . They may wear a wine crepe outfit with navy crowns or chocolate velvet. . . . And it doesn't seem to matter to the men, [who] are dressed in some haphazard fashion."

Charlotte followed a theme here by using colors to describe the drab quality of life, in contrast to the physical beauty of the city. The repetition of the drab colors ("black-booted," "grey beards," "grey of their pants") drove home the feeling of drudgery. In this second trip overseas, she expanded on the descriptive style she developed as a college student writing letters home, but she let the words and phrasing convey the mood and feeling. She had begun to develop sophisticated stylistic themes in some of her stories and had become less preoccupied with using size and scope merely to describe.

Citizen editors were aware that she was a talented and hardworking employee, and in 1952, two years after she joined the paper fulltime, she was named society editor and women's news columnist. The promotion gave her even more autonomy and freed her to write about whatever she pleased. In addition, some of her stories appeared on the front page in the paper's Sunday magazine.

Grove continued to serve as a professional role model to Charlotte and a friend and lover. The two carried on a love affair for much of the decade Charlotte worked on the *Citizen*, although his alcoholism and marital status made the affair difficult and sporadic. Charlotte was intrigued that Grove was a nonconformist who did what he wanted and ignored the opinions of others. But she also admired his empathy for civil rights and for the underclass. Shortly after Charlotte became society editor, wedding announcements featuring black couples began appearing in the *Citizen*, a first for the Columbus newspapers.[24]

More important to her, Charlotte's relationship with Grove cemented her status as an insider in the glamorous world of newspapering—a world that included few women. The few women who worked on the Columbus newspapers in the 1950s socialized and formed tight cliques that met regularly for lunch. Charlotte, however, was not a part of these groups, according to Mary McGarey, who worked on the *Dispatch* then. McGarey said women may have "bored" Charlotte, or she simply did not have the time to socialize with them.[25] Charlotte may have obtained her professional and personal fulfillment from Grove, and she was indeed too busy for these long women's lunches. At a small paper like the *Citizen*, editors often did the jobs of several people. In addition to overseeing a staff of about five, she wrote stories, designed pages, wrote headlines, and wrote a regular column. She also substituted for other editors who were out sick or on vacation.[26] Throughout her life, Charlotte was very selective about how she spent her time and energy—particularly later in her life, when illness allowed her limited amounts of both. As a young *Citizen* reporter and editor, she may have decided to spend her little spare time with Grove rather than making idle small talk with the "girls."

The society/women's pages under Charlotte included many stories on the history of accepted social practices and stories of practical use to women.[27] One of Charlotte's greatest pleasures, however, came from writing a society column, "Mostly About Women," because it gave her an opportunity to exercise her creativity. Puns abounded in copy and headlines: "The Merchant of Everything Except Venison" was the headline of a profile about a local grocer who carried many exotic food items; a headline about a stranded cat that had to be rescued by firefighters read, "The Case of the Ladder-Day Stint"; "Pop Go the Measles," was the subhead of a two-paragraph item about a measles breakout that threatened to cancel a charity event; "Marry-Go-Round" headlined an item about a Columbus family who held engagement parties for their two sons; and she called a formal dance of the Bachelors and Spinsters Club "The Black Tie That Binds."

Citizen editors rewarded her creative column-writing efforts in 1959 by giving her yet another weekly column. Titled "Charlotte's Ruse," a pun on the name of the frilly dessert frequently served at society soirees, this column was less of a compilation of short society items than it was an opinion and humor column. It allowed her further to exercise her playful nature and have fun with puns, literary allusions and other figures of speech.

Charlotte relished the freedom and autonomy the *Citizen* gave her in writing and story selection—freedom that was rare on most daily newspapers of the time. As her career at the paper progressed, she learned how a "women's" story could evolve into a general-interest news story and land on page 1. To get an interview with poet Carl Sandburg, for example, Charlotte rode fifty miles with him in a car from Wilmington, Ohio, to Columbus. And she made sure she was on hand when the mother and wife of the 1960 presidential candidates arrived in town. The result was a series of deadly honest and sometimes devastating profiles.

She began the Sandburg profile with allusions to the poet's own frequent images of snow and clouds, but she described the beloved poet as an irritable and cynical old man: "Poet Carl Sandburg, a snow-capped mountain of a man, crammed his giant, loose-limbed frame into Columbus on Friday, completely unnoticed," the story began. But Sandburg was in a foul mood as he rode from the airport to town, criticizing the numerous billboards he passed—deeming them overly commercial—and even knocking other poets.[28]

Charlotte's portrayal of Sandburg was honest, and she did not sugarcoat his attitude by referring to it as feisty or cute. Instead, he appeared as an irascible old man who resented anything modern. Such frank representation was not unusual in magazine profiles, but it was rarely used in briefer newspaper stories that often recounted pat answers to pat questions. In small and mid-sized newspapers, such celebrities as Sandburg were usually treated in print with the utmost respect and their idiosyncrasies went unreported.

In Charlotte's profiles of political wives, she expanded on the ironic style she had been cultivating during her decade at the *Citizen*. In these profiles, she often mocked her subjects simply by recording their off-the-cuff comments and observations. Most political reporters and candidates were men, so most of the profiles done of wives were light, one-dimensional society page pieces that discussed their clothes and their philosophy of child rearing. Charlotte saw these women as professionals whose job was to help their husbands, sons, or fathers get elected, so she refused to handle them with kid gloves.

Two stories she wrote during the 1960 presidential campaign year are good examples of how she believed candidates' families should be covered. These stories reported on visits to Ohio by Rose Kennedy, mother of Democratic candidate John F. Kennedy, and Pat Nixon, wife of the Republican candidate and vice president Richard Nixon. These stories painted a brutal picture of both women, portraying them as putting on a front of stoicism while they were forced to put up with the indignities of campaigning. In private, they were whiny, with petty complaints.

Charlotte focused on Rose Kennedy's disagreeable state of mind by writing about her desire to control her situation. She claimed that she was too warm and demanded that the air-conditioning be turned on, refused to be photographed without hat and gloves, and would not talk about politics, Charlotte wrote.[29] Charlotte revealed other hidden details, including the fact that Mrs. Kennedy and a large entourage were housed in the same hotel as her son's political opponent: "The small, dark-haired and smartly dressed mother of nine, accompanied by a personal maid and a traveling companion, registered at the Deshler Hilton Hotel, home of the Ohio Volunteers for Nixon-Lodge, and went to bed." Charlotte mentioned the entourage again at the end of the story, along with other trappings of Mrs. Kennedy's wealth. After the news conference, Mrs. Kennedy was given a bouquet of roses, which was promptly turned over to the maid: "The maid took the roses into a bedroom. She got the multi-millionairess's black Persian lamb coat, a pillow and a blanket. National Committeewoman Helen Gunsett escorted Mrs. Kennedy into a rented black Cadillac limousine."

For readers who did not get the message that Mrs. Kennedy was rich and spoiled, the term "millionairess" was inserted for good measure, as were the pillow and blanket, symbols of softness and pampering. These touches were characteristic of Charlotte's "no-one-is-sacred" political profiles and of the understated style she used when digging the knife into her subjects—and certainly uncharacteristic of political or society writing in the nation's mid-sized daily newspapers of the time.

A week before the Kennedy profile, Charlotte interviewed Pat Nixon, and she was prescient in capturing the stoicism for which Mrs. Nixon would be known years later. When Mrs. Nixon arrived at windy Burke Lakefront Airport in Cleveland, she was the picture of composure. Charlotte wrote: "She is a professional, and a shrewd one—a blonde Mona Lisa who sees all, says little and smiles a great deal, and a cool Gretel who won't be caught climbing into any ovens."[30]

But Mrs. Nixon was not cool for long. Charlotte described the scene as the Nixons rode in a motorcade through throngs of people who spilled over the curb to reach the car. Mrs. Nixon, like Mrs. Kennedy, was not too pleased with being manhandled by the adoring crowd and choked by motorcycle and limousine fumes. Charlotte's image of her was one of pain: she smiled a "wifely," mincing smile and had to "extract" herself from those who "yank" her.

Charlotte's articles about these two women showed it was possible to get two readings of her stories: one that could be interpreted as a simple, straightforward profile and one that offers sly, irreverent commentary with inside allusions. Further, these stories show that the fame of her subjects did not intimidate or influence Charlotte and that she viewed herself not as publicist of the candidates or their relatives but as a chronicler of their behavior.

~

Charlotte had worked as a full-time reporter and editor on the *Citizen* for ten years when, in 1960, she began applying for jobs elsewhere. But much had changed in 1959 and 1960. On November 8, 1959, the *Citizen* had merged with the *Ohio State Journal* to become the morning *Citizen-Journal*, a Scripps-Howard paper. Columbus did not have enough readers to support three newspapers, and economics forced the merger. In the summer of 1960, Gene Grove had moved to New York to join the *New York Post*, and these two events prompted Charlotte to realize it was time to move on. By that time, she had won local acclaim for stories and columns, including awards from the Ohio Newspaper Women's Association and other statewide journalists' associations, and service awards from community groups such as the Chamber of Commerce and Lions and Kiwanis clubs. She was particularly proud of one statewide reporting award she received in a contest judged by Anne O'Hare McCormick, and she wrote in a letter of application to the *New York Times* that McCormick "said I wrote the best feature-news story in Ohio."[31]

Decades later, she said she felt at the time that she could go no further at the *Citizen* and had done all she could do there professionally.[32] It is unclear if Grove influenced her decision to seek other jobs, but letters between the two show that he did encourage her to seek a tryout at the *Post*. The two were still romantically involved, and she occasionally visited him in New York.[33] The previous year, Charlotte had applied for jobs at a handful of large newspapers outside of New York, but, by late 1960, she apparently concentrated on seeking jobs in Manhattan, applying at the *Post* and the *Herald Tribune*. The latter paper was known at the time as one of the best-written newspapers in New York, and it attracted the best writers. Charlotte often said the *Herald Tribune* was her top choice when she began applying for jobs in New York.[34] Charlotte sought a job as a news or feature writer, but she heard about an opening at the *New York Times* as a home furnishings writer in its women's news department. She later acknowledged that her letter of application was almost an accident. She had written only two or three home furnishing stories—which she sent to the *Times*—and she had no interest in the subject.[35] But the examples of her writing and her reference to McCormick apparently intrigued *Times* women's editor Elizabeth Penrose Howkins, who responded to her letter immediately. But Howkins had reservations; she believed Charlotte's varied jobs at the *Citizen* would hurt her at the *Times*. Someone who covered such exciting subjects as poets and presidential campaigns might be bored covering fashion and furnishings, she warned.[36]

Charlotte was quick to reassure Howkins that she would not be bored at the *Times* and that her varied work experience prepared her well for a job there.[37] Howkins was persuaded, and she offered Charlotte the job on the strength of two writing samples that Charlotte would later label "godawful."[38] So, in early 1961, the *Columbus Citizen-Journal* society editor who covered events in Paris and Russia, who parodied in print the accent of a French hairdresser, and who reported Carl Sandburg's cynical mutterings about American society became the home furnishings reporter for the staid *New York Times*, where she would stay for the rest of her career. And she could thank her friends at the *Citizen*. That paper had been a great journalistic training ground for Charlotte, and her years there taught her more important lessons: she absorbed the culture of newspaper staff members and gained valuable insights into the "appropriate behavior" that would allow her to negotiate the politics of the newsroom and succeed in the business.

5

"All Brides Are Not Beautiful"

CHARLOTTE SURPRISED few people in 1961 when she announced she was leaving the *Citizen-Journal* to join the *Times*. She was a driven worker and one who always had lofty career goals that did not include spending her life in Columbus. Many staff members on the Columbus papers did not have plans to leave that city, and although Charlotte was raised there and loved the city, she made no secret of the possibility that she might not live there all her life. Like other upper-middle-class young women of her era, she was well-traveled, and, through cultural exchange and other programs, she met people from around the world. So it was no surprise to her friends and co-workers when she announced she was leaving Ohio.[1]

Robert Shamansky recalled that he thought her education was incomplete despite her Vassar degree and ten years as a newspaperwoman. He thought it necessary to educate her in some of the "language" of New York, and as the two sat in a New York restaurant shortly after she moved, he gave her a brief lesson in Yiddish. "I remember sitting there and writing key Yiddish words on a matchbook," he said. "'*Schlemiel*,' '*schlimazel*,' '*schnook*,' words like that. I said, 'I don't think you can work here without this. There are a few words you should know to get the hayseeds out.'"[2]

Charlotte rented a tiny penthouse apartment on 40 East Tenth Street in Greenwich Village, which she bought several years later for $25,000. Although it was too small for entertaining, a terrace ran its length, allowing her to indulge in gardening, which would become one of her favorite hobbies. And she was amused at the history of her new home—it had once been a servants' quarters.[3] The tiny apartment would be her New York home for nearly twenty-five years.

~'

When Charlotte began at the family-owned *Times* in 1961, the newspaper was embarking on a decade of great change. Longtime publisher Arthur Hays Sulzberger, son-in-law of *Times* patriarch Adolph Ochs, who bought the paper in 1896, had had a stroke and was incapacitated. Because women did not hold top executive positions then, it was unlikely that any of his three daughters would be named to the top spot. Sulzberger's only son, Arthur Ochs Sulzberger, known as "Punch," was thirty-five and deemed too young and inexperienced for the job, so the top spot went to Sulzberger's son-in-law Orvil E. Dryfoos.

The *Times*, notoriously slow to change, had had only two publishers in the twentieth century, and Sulzberger's unexpected illness was a great shock to everyone. Little did *Times* readers or employees realize at the time that the naming of a new publisher would be followed by many more upheavals in the next few years.

When Charlotte accepted the job on the paper's "Food, Fashion, Family and Furnishings" section on the ninth floor, her ultimate goal was to work on the third-floor news section. Correspondence between Charlotte and Gene Grove indicates that she had arranged a tryout on the news desk at the *New York Post* at the same time she was offered the *Times* job.[4] Charlotte apparently felt she had no choice but to take the sure thing—the job on the *Times*—although the opening was not in the news section. She had enjoyed covering celebrities such as Carl Sandburg and Rose Kennedy in Columbus, but she still preferred to have no part of society or women's coverage at the *Times*. Her frank style of women's news coverage, however, was unheard-of at most major daily newspapers, although society writer Eugenia Sheppard was pioneering her own style of covering the rich and famous in Manhattan when Charlotte arrived at the *Times*. Sheppard, society editor for the lively morning daily the *New York Herald Tribune* —and a household name in Manhattan—was one of the first reporter-editors to combine fashion and society gossip in New York, creating a type of celebrity "fashion socialite."[5] Sheppard, who was also from Columbus, had a writing style typical of the creative and feisty *Herald Tribune*, a newspaper considered at that time to be the *Times*'s major competitor among New York City's seven daily newspapers.

So Charlotte joined the *Times* women's section with the goal of fleeing it—a goal she shared with many others in the section. "I wanted out. I wanted to cover a fire," said Nan Robertson, who felt she was "sprung" from women's news in October 1959, when she left to cover news.[6] Women's page reporter Marylin Bender, formerly a reporter for *Parade* magazine who later became the *Times*'s Sunday business editor, said the *Times* was reluctant to allow women to cover news: "Most women didn't have a background in news. [It was believed] women should not be subject to the danger, the degradation."[7] When Charlotte joined the staff, the two women quickly became friends, both taking pride in having roots in the "grungy, raw" world of news reporting, according to Bender.[8]

Charlotte was hired to replace Gloria Emerson, who left the "Four Fs," as the section was known, to become a foreign correspondent for the *Times*. She later won numerous honors for her coverage of Vietnam, Africa, and Paris.

Bender, Robertson, and Curtis were quick to admit that while their jobs as women's page reporters did not carry the prestige of a news-writing job, they did have fun. Elizabeth Penrose Howkins, the eccentric women's page editor, gave them much autonomy, and they were free to write in a loose style that was much different from the stodgy *Times* of the era. Robertson said her five years covering women's news "would prove to be among my happiest on the *Times*. We were all young and gifted and full of the devil, and the friendships I made there have endured a lifetime."[9]

The women of the Four Fs had great affection for the eccentric Howkins, whose background as editor of the British *Vogue* led her to treat the section like a magazine. She stressed graphics, photos, and "taste" over words—another departure for the *Times*, which, in the early 1960s, hardly concerned itself with lively graphics. To her reporters, however, Howkins's greatest strength as an editor was that she gave them great leeway. "She brought a love of good writing and visuals [to the section]," Bender said. "She wanted us to capture the essence of the person [in stories]."[10] Howkins had a keen eye for talent and was instrumental in hiring Charlotte, Emerson, and Robertson —all of whom would later make names for themselves on the paper— as well as food writer Craig Claiborne, who would become one of the *Times*'s most famous writers. She also was an odd character whose strange personal demeanor and unconventional professional philosophies amused many of her reporters. Her bearing could not have been more dissimilar from that of the hard-bitten, cynical reporters and editors in news, and her knowledge of how newspapers were run was also limited. Robertson remembered the unspoken policy in the women's section that all major New York retailers be mentioned periodically in stories, a policy that opposed the *Times*'s proud boast of editorial impartiality on all of its pages. The women's section, she wrote, "was the *Times*' dirty secret."[11]

Howkins divided her staff into two parts: the "tastemakers," who were leaders in spotting trends and deciding what was fashionable, and the "ink-stained wretches," the writers whose dreary task it was to report on the tastemakers and their opinions. Of course, the tastemakers were held in higher regard, while Howkins viewed the writers as technicians. She believed that anyone who could write a letter could write a fashion article.[12]

But Howkins brought out the best in her talented staff, and they remember her with great affection for giving them license to write in a bright and bold way that differed from the writing style of most newspapers' women's pages. What stood out in Charlotte's mind was Howkins's outdated and campy appearance, which she remembered in detail twenty years after she met her:

> Mrs. Howkins was one of the great ladies of anybody's lifetime. . . . She would arrive at work in the last word of Paris fashion, or the Orbach's copies of Paris fashions, which were obviously much less expensive. She had at least six fur coats that she would alternate. . . . She was given to large topaz rings, which would be different on different days. . . . She was really rather odd looking. I suppose in the fashion world it would have been considered beautiful. She used to wear silk toque hats, sort of marvelous hats. She never went anywhere without a hat.

Howkins's vivid blue eye shadow was the aspect of her appearance that stood out most clearly in Charlotte's memory:

> She would wear mostly turquoise eye shadow and what would be lovely about the turquoise eye shadow was that some time during the day she would run her finger across her eyes, scratch or whatever, and run it down the side of her face. By five o'clock on any given day, Elizabeth Penrose Howkins had turquoise eye shadow down to the tips of her ears. Of course, no one ever told her about it.[13]

Charlotte was amused by Howkins's appearance but horrified by her journalism ethics — or lack thereof. Howkins saw nothing wrong with altering photos occasionally to flatter subjects, including airbrushing the bangs on a young woman's head because Howkins decided the woman did not look good with bangs.[14] She took similar action in a photo that accompanied one of Charlotte's stories about the Kennedy yacht, the *Honey Fitz*. Charlotte took a photo of the boat's interior, which had several framed pictures on the walls. Howkins did not think the pictures were appropriate and deleted them with one stroke of her grease pencil. The *Honey Fitz* appeared without the pictures.[15]

Howkins's reporters took great advantage of their editor's liberal attitude toward content. She let them embellish their stories with colorful details and snide asides. "You could write something that wasn't flattering as reporting," Bender remembered.[16] In this way, Howkins and her staff strayed from the tight "paper-of-record" style for which the *Times* was known, a rigid style that stressed objective chronicling of events and fact-filled profiles and feature stores. Consequently, Charlotte was permitted to expand on the detail-laden and freewheeling writing style she had cultivated at the *Citizen-Journal*.

In this way, Charlotte was lucky—at the *Times*, she worked for one of the few editors who allowed her and others to write in an unconventional way. She took for granted the permissive and unusual attitude of *Citizen* editors, who also gave her great autonomy. In fact, it never dawned on Charlotte that few if any other newspapers of the era would allow her to cover society in such an unorthodox way. The *Citizen* took pride in its feisty, underdog image in Columbus, and Charlotte benefited from its status as such.

Although she now worked in the big city, Charlotte did not let world-famous fashion figures and designers cow her. She periodically mocked them in stories and let them hang themselves with their own words: "She did the same thing there [in New York] as she did here [in Columbus]," Jane Kehrer Horrocks said. "It made a bigger splash in New York."[17] Her extensive use of quotes high in her stories, literary references, and caustic asides enabled her to paint a detailed and sometimes unflattering picture of those she interviewed. In a story about a New York milliner written four months after she began at the *Times*, she used some of her own asides to illustrate his arrogance.

> He admits he is a genius and the greatest couturier-milliner in the world, and he has tried to forget that he was once a boy from New Rochelle named Hans Harburger.
>
> And when he talks about himself, which is most of the time, he puts up a colorful and audacious smoke screen of clever phrases, shocking tidbits and big names.
>
> "I am Mr. John," he says over and over again. "Mr. John is the dean of the industry. I. Magnin rolls out the red carpet for Mr. John."

Charlotte duly noted his references to himself in the third person and his background, which he tried to hide. But as the story went on, her disdain for him became more obvious when she referred to the fact that he "affects a Napoleonic hairdo and matching complex" and quoted him as saying, "I don't even know how much money I have."[18]

Charlotte enlarged here on a style she had developed in Columbus of using quotations to let her subjects indict themselves—quotes that most traditional women's page reporters ignored because they were unflattering. The subjects of these stories frequently feigned false modesty.

While working on the *Times*'s women's section, Charlotte became more precise in her word choice, and many of her words and phrases took on double meanings. This trait is evident in a profile of one of the trendiest designers of the era, Emilio Pucci, who claimed to love danger. Charlotte wrote:

> His life has become a mosaic of adventure. During World War I he was a much-decorated pilot, and he continues to shadow-box death by skiing down hazardous mountain trails and racing his sports car about the countryside.
>
> "I once terrified four Americans," he explained shucking his dove-gray suede gloves and adjusting his royal blue necktie. "I drove them through Florence. They weren't used to going 120 miles an hour. I wasn't scared. The car can go 150."
>
> These Byronic impulses are tempered, however, by an acceptance of some things as they are. He would never, for example, want to live without a refrigerator or television set.[19]

Charlotte did not mention Pucci's designs until she was halfway through the story, concentrating instead on his quirky and contradictory personality. The "much-decorated pilot" now designs clothes, a profession that carries a tranquil and feminine connotation. This pilot now "shadow-boxes" with death through activities such as fast driving and skiing, hinting that he no longer indulged in life-threatening activities. Charlotte's description of Pucci's "dove-gray suede" gloves further developed this contradictory image and a phoniness—they are adjectives that convey softness and gentleness. As she described these contradictions in his lifestyle, she was able to insert her own personal aside, trivializing Pucci's comments and making them seem ridiculous. Her use of a grand term like "Byronic," in particular, implied that Charlotte thought Pucci was a big talker. Ironically, Pucci's own attempts to impress gave Charlotte the ammunition she needed.

Charlotte's writing style resembled a new form of magazine journalism that was sweeping New York in the 1960s called the New Journalism. A descriptive and subjective style of writing, the New Journalism began appearing in some magazines, including the fledgling *New York* magazine, which was founded in 1968, and *Esquire*. But it was deemed unsuitable for newspapers because of its length and subjective nature. As practiced by magazine writers in the early 1960s, the New Journalism was a blend of fiction and fact; often writers did not take notes when interviewing but instead placed in quotation marks what they remembered was said. This brand of analytical journalism stressed details about the subject, his or her personal characteristics, and the surroundings. Charlotte's writing in Columbus had some elements of this genre, although at that time it had no name. The emergence of this style of writing influenced her when she moved to the *Times*, and it helped legitimize what was then an unorthodox style of newspaper writing.

The term "New Journalism" originated in the days of Joseph Pulitzer and William Randolph Hearst at the turn of the century to describe a new method of news gathering that concentrated on the sensational, often using the play and slant of the news to convey publishers' point of view. When the term reemerged in the early 1960s, it was used by such former *New York Times* writers as Gay Talese and Tom Wolfe and fiction writer Truman Capote.[20] Charlotte had to follow the conventions of newspaper journalism when gathering facts, but her writing had some of the qualities of the New Journalism, and she said she admired *New York* magazine and *Esquire*.[21]

When Charlotte began working on the Four Fs in 1961, women's pages across the country were characterized by fashion stories, self-improvement tips, and service stories—"how-to" articles about successful homemaking. It is easy to see why some women's page reporters of the era were bored. Betsy Wade, who rose through the ranks of the *Times* to become head copy editor on the foreign desk, said the grind of working in women's news inhibited her from having role models: "It was hard for us to get ourselves connected with figures whom we could identify with. We didn't look, feel or taste like Nellie Bly [a crusading reporter in the late 1800s], for instance. And certainly Anne O'Hare McCormick was a good cut above what most of us were doing. Most of us, for heaven's sake, were covering hat shows. It's really hard to see yourself as doing something significant when you are covering a hat show."[22]

Lindsy Van Gelder, formerly a *New York Post* reporter, wrote in *Ms.* magazine in 1974 that she hated women's page assignments in the late 1960s: "I avoided the women's-angle assignments through a maniacally macho willingness to cover train wrecks, riots, anything else, and an unfeigned ignorance of conventional women's-pagey topics. . . . It never occurred to me that anything meaningful could come out of the editorial department whose beat, after all, includes food, clothing and shelter. The women's page was for frivolous, boring, puffy, irrelevant, 86-ways-to-make-tuna-casserole news."[23] Women's pages had a long history of reporting this way, and debate over whether they should change did not come until the late 1960s, when the civil rights and feminist movements gained momentum. As Maurine Beasley and Sheila Gibbons noted in their history of women in the media, "The image of an idyllic home and hearth as a women's main priority—with career achievement as admirable but secondary pursuits—continued in newspaper women's pages through the 1960s."[24] But it is no wonder women were portrayed this way in newspapers: by 1970, men on newspaper staffs outnumbered women by two to one.[25]

Intelligent and accomplished women like Curtis, Wade, Bender, Robertson, and Emerson naturally wanted to escape this environment, and doing so would require planning. Charlotte's innovative and sometimes caustic style of writing may have been self-serving. She realized that a unique approach would get her notice and quicken her departure from the women's section. And her plan worked—but her career took a twist that she never would have predicted.

~

Despite family wealth that allowed her to attend the best schools and travel around the world, Charlotte was on her own in New York, and she earned enough at the *Times* to support a modest lifestyle and return to Columbus periodically to visit her parents. But working forty or fifty hours a week at a new job did not fill all her time, and she knew she had some opportunities in New York that others did not; the extensive library of the *Times* was available to her, giving her access not only to a variety of historical resources but also to all of the *Times* stories ever printed. Further, she had memories of living in the same dormitory room as Jacqueline Bouvier, who in early 1961 became First Lady Jacqueline Kennedy. Shortly after she began working in New York, Charlotte decided to write about her former classmate's life in the White House.

Charlotte's *First Lady*, published in 1962 by Pyramid Books, is a far cry from the sharp, cutting profiles she wrote of political wives for the *Citizen-Journal* and the *Times*. The book jacket capsulizes what *First Lady* had become after editors put their pencils to it: "*First Lady*: the Glowing, Up-to-the-Minute Story of Jacqueline Kennedy's Life in the White House."[26] The 158-page paperback is a simply written, generic account of Mrs. Kennedy's first weeks in the White House ("Mrs. Kennedy's first days included a venture into the business of promoting charity drives, the discovery of a home-away-from-home at Glen Ora, the rambling country house the Kennedys had rented in nearby Virginia);[27] her children ("Caroline, the captivating blonde who added considerable luster to the family image the Kennedy team wished to project during the campaign");[28] and the changes she imposed on White House decor and gatherings ("She systematically and instinctively recreated White House social life so that a new kind of gracious informality prevails whether she and her husband are entertaining nervous teenagers or a knowing chief of state who has already been wined and dined in the world's showplaces").[29] Charlotte did not interview Mrs. Kennedy for the book. The quotes from her and her acquaintances came from previously published sources.

Three pages of notes left by Charlotte's editor at Pyramid, Janet Rosenberg, indicate that the original version of *First Lady* was at times caustic. These notes repeatedly label many sentences and phrases "negative," and they call for either more documentation or elimination of such a portrayal. Unlike most of Charlotte's editors, Rosenberg evidently did not care for her ironic and often cutting style of writing. For instance, Rosenberg noted that "[Curtis] reports what others have said, usually ending up with the negative and thereby leaving *only* a negative impression. Mrs. Kennedy cannot be blamed for her wealth or the society she lives in. . . . The over-all [effect] is far too negative and can serve no useful purpose."[30]

Rosenberg made detailed comments and criticisms of each chapter, most of them dealing with the book's "negative" tone. A comparison of the comments to the book shows that the text was changed in many cases ("Unnecessarily acid—rework paragraph" or "'the colds she seems to have' implies she was lying. . . . Why not have a more sympathetic view on this?"). Rosenberg said another chapter "is much too negative and petty. I would suggest sweetening it considerably . . . emphasizing the praise she has received."

Although *First Lady*, with its bland descriptions and observations, is hardly characteristic of Charlotte the writer, she did manage to convey some irony. In one passage, for instance, she slyly noted that Mrs. Kennedy had no personal sense of style but instead mindlessly copied the experts: "Her tastes are rarely intellectual."[31] This passage is an indictment of the first lady as a trendsetter and tastemaker, implying she had no opinions of her own. This portrayal deeply contrasts the accepted view of Mrs. Kennedy as a young, hip first lady who was not afraid to go against the grain of her colorless predecessors in the White House.

Charlotte in 1933 at age five in Columbus.

Charlotte, age seven, right, and her sister Mary, five, have afternoon tea in the living room of their home on Sunbury Road, Columbus.

Charlotte on the grounds of her home with her pony, Dollar Bill.

Charlotte's school picture at age ten or eleven.

Charlotte, right, and roommate Harriette Moeller, both Vassar freshmen, on the steps of Vassar's Swift Hall of History, 1946.

Mary Curtis, right, and Charlotte celebrate New Year's Day, 1949, at the home of their parents in Bexley, Ohio.

Charlotte and Dwight "Butch" Fullerton on their wedding day,
Columbus, July 10, 1950.

Charlotte and Dwight have a drink with Charlotte's friends from the
Columbus Citizen, 1951 or 1952.

Charlotte at her desk at the *Citizen*, mid-1950s.

For a story about hypnotism for the *Citizen*, Charlotte does some research firsthand. Photo was probably taken in the mid-1950s when she was women's news editor.

Charlotte's sarcastic style, tempered for this book, gives *First Lady* a slightly contradictory tone. Charlotte's writing for the *Times* sometimes displayed irony, but editors at the publishing company must have ignored this and viewed her as a competent writer who could write a fluffy social history of the first year of the Kennedy administration. Or perhaps they wanted the prestige a *New York Times* women's page reporter would give the book.

It is unknown how many of the books were sold or how *First Lady* fared financially, but Charlotte's husband, William Hunt, said she always joked that sales of the book allowed her sometimes to abandon the subway and start taking taxis in New York and that the book gave her a financial boost during her early years in the city.[32] Indeed, Charlotte was frugal during her first few years in New York, and she frequently rode the subway late at night wearing evening clothes after she covered a society event and had to return to the office to write the story.

Charlotte dedicated *First Lady* to the two people to whom she was closest: her mother, Lucile Atcherson Curtis, "L.A.C.," and "E.S.G." —Eugene S. Grove, with whom she was still involved romantically. Grove remained a journalistic role model for Charlotte during her first few years in New York, although letters between the two in late 1960, shortly before Charlotte moved to the city, indicate that their relationship could be stormy. In one letter, Grove wrote that it had not been easy to talk to her during her visit "because you kept yourself on a plane several degrees below your warmest."[33]

The publication of *First Lady* in mid-1962 came at a fortuitous time for Charlotte. She had been working in New York for twenty-one months when members of the International Typographical Union, the printers' union, walked out on the seven daily New York newspapers. They went on strike December 8, 1962, forcing the newspapers to cease publication for 114 days. The walkout was devastating to the countless employees who worked on the newspapers, and it meant tremendous financial losses for advertisers, who had stood to lose millions of dollars in revenue from holiday sales. Those advertisers—

mostly retailers—had few alternatives for getting their messages to customers.

Within a month of the strike's beginning, however, alternative newspapers began springing up in New York. These newspapers adopted specific styles, and each became an unofficial substitute for a specific paper. The "substitute" *Times* was called the *New York Standard*, and it employed many temporarily out-of-work *Times* reporters and editors, including Charlotte, as well as some people from other New York papers.[34] All of the substitute papers were underwritten by local retailers, who used them as vehicles for advertising. The Newspaper Guild, the reporters' union, helped pay the salaries of reporters, and union facilities were used to produce the papers.

The *New York Standard* began publishing on January 6, 1963, and continued until the end of the strike on March 24. It proclaimed in its first edition that it had no intention of permanently replacing any New York newspaper but would publish until the strike was settled. Nor would it take sides in the strike but simply report the news, the publisher pointed out in the pages of the first issue.[35]

The women's section of the *Standard* initially was edited by Marilyn Mercer, an editor at the *Herald-Tribune*. Mercer hired *Times* women's page reporter Joan Cook, who in turn hired several of her co-workers on the *Times*'s Four Fs section, including Charlotte. Cook became the *Standard*'s women's editor when Mercer left.

Betsy Wade, who was also a *Standard* staff member and then a *Times* copy editor, remembered her days on that paper as unique because she worked briefly with people from papers all over the city. "For the first time in my life—and possibly for the first time in the city of New York—you had a copy desk of people who were from all of the newspapers," she said. To the employees, it was a dream come true. They received their usual salaries and then some. They worked six days a week so were paid overtime, or six-fifths of their normal salaries.[36]

As time went on and the strike progressed, the forty-page *Standard* grew in size and complexity. It began reporting from Washington, for instance, and later included letters to the editor, television logs, and late sports scores. It also ran editorials on national issues that had appeared in other newspapers. Eventually, the paper claimed to have five hundred thousand readers.[37] Charlotte at this time was still green, professionally and personally, Wade said: "This was a Charlotte Curtis who was still scraping some of the Ohio out of her hair, who was young and energetic and quick-stepping and bright."[38]

When the strike ended, members of the *Standard* staff returned to their previous jobs. The walkout may have been over, but it left a devastating legacy. It was considered by some to be the costliest and most disruptive newspaper strike in American history. Four of the seven papers never recouped their losses and folded within four years of the strike, altering forever the journalistic landscape of New York City. Journalists and media economists have concluded that the strike was caused by increasing competition from television for the advertising dollar, increasing wage demands by employees who believed that increasing automation would ultimately cost them their jobs, and increasing costs of producing newspapers.[39]

Several weeks after the resolution of the strike, publisher Dryfoos dropped dead of a heart attack after only two years on the job. The Sulzberger family, at a loss again about who would replace him, decided on Punch, who by then was thirty-seven. Still considered too young and inexperienced by many *Times* executives, Punch Sulzberger had limited experience as an overseas correspondent in Paris but none as a manager. He came to rely on the counsel of such *Times* icons as managing editor Turner Catledge and Washington bureau chief James Reston and quickly learned the landscape of the *Times*.[40] Over the next two decades, the amiable and down-to-earth Punch would oversee some of the most dramatic changes in *Times* history.

When the strike ended, Charlotte resumed one of her favorite pastimes: attempting to escape from the women's section. On several occasions she had requested transfers to the third floor for a news or feature writing job, and shortly after the strike ended in 1963, her request was granted. Charlotte was preparing for her move when she had a chance discussion in the hallways with Clifton Daniel, then an assistant managing editor. It would change her life. She had just introduced herself to a man who would be a friend, mentor, and patron for much of her career.

One of Daniel's goals was to pattern some of the *Times*'s softer sections on magazines of the era; he wanted longer, brighter stories that varied from the staid, formulaic structure *Times* readers were used to. It was Daniel who realized the potential of food writer Craig Claiborne, even though Claiborne had never worked for a newspaper before he joined the *Times*. Daniel believed the *Times*'s society section in particular needed a shot in the arm, and he believed its news pages should offer more comprehensive "wrap-up" interpretive stories like those in the *Wall Street Journal*.[41]

In 1963, the paper's women's and society sections were separate. Society consisted primarily of wedding and engagement announcements with some dry accounts of soirees and charity fund-raisers. Daniel, a pharmacist's son from Zebulon, North Carolina, was not born into wealth, but stints as a foreign correspondent in London, Cairo, and Moscow gave him a sophistication and continental manner. In middle age, he married Margaret Truman, daughter of the former president, and the two routinely attended society gatherings and lavish parties. Daniel saw how lively—and ridiculous—these events could be, and he did not appreciate what he saw as dry, uninspired society coverage in the *Times* under the editorship of Russell Edwards. Daniel remembered his conversations with the society editor after he told him to "dress up" society coverage: "I told him society writing could be interesting—lots of multi-millionaires, old families, new ones. He said, 'My staff can't write that stuff.' It was essentially a record-keeping kind of journalism."[42]

When Daniel began reading Charlotte's unusual profiles of fashion figures, he had an idea that he first expressed during that chance meeting with Charlotte: she could work as a full-time society writer under Edwards, reporting primarily on the activities of the upper class. Although Edwards would be her official boss, she would answer to Daniel. And he promised to give her a free hand. Daniel kept sweetening his proposal and made a deal with Charlotte: if she did not like the assignment, she could transfer to the feature desk. He remembered the conversation thirty years later: "Charlotte had no desire to work in society. But I started romancing her as to what you can do in society. My point was, treat it like a sociological phenomenon in this town. It was full of interesting stories—the wealthy, where they came from, where they got their money, how they got to be members of the board of the Metropolitan Club."[43] The job became so tempting that Charlotte accepted it. After all, Daniel told her, the paper had many feature writers, but it would have only one society writer who could follow his suggestions.

Charlotte recalled years later that, as a sociology major in college, she had been trained as a society writer. She could treat the beat as a study of human behavior and mores, and she would report on people's activities in a dispassionate and honest way. She explained her philosophy of society writing:

> Reporting a society story or a woman's news story, or anything, the techniques of reporting are the same regardless of what you do. . . . Something has happened—a wedding has happened, a charity ball has happened, a murder has happened. . . . You answer all the who, what, why, when and where and how and so on, but what you're doing is telling the world it happened. And if you can, you try and tell them what it means, if anything. . . . We were in the business of telling the truth. I mean, the story I used to say in those days is that the notion used to be that all brides are beautiful, and all brides are not beautiful! But it was as though all wedding stories were written, "and the beautiful bride wore, etc." Well, I'm sorry, that doesn't have anything to do with reality.[44]

When Charlotte moved to the third-floor society section, however, she was in for a big surprise. In place of Howkins's open and easy management style she found Edwards's highly structured and rigid one—an office format that brought back images of her days at the Columbus School for Girls. Edwards, she later remembered, had an almost religious belief in the nine-to-five workday, and he expected his employees to share his fervor. Charlotte, never a clock-watcher, was shocked and amused at how he ran the department. Everyone was expected to begin work exactly at 9:30 A.M. and work until precisely 5:30 P.M. At that time, Edwards ordered his employees to stop work and was angry when Charlotte would not quit:

> Promptly at 5:30 in the afternoon, he would say, "Good night," very soundly, loudly and determinedly. At that point, everyone closed his typewriter. It didn't matter whether you were in mid-sentence or what, but you were supposed to close your typewriter and depart immediately, having said "Good night" to the schoolmaster who sat in the corner. My problem, because I've always had problems with authority, I suppose, was that I really had pieces and things that I was working on that kept me after 5:30. . . . But after a while, he got used to the fact that there was no stopping me, and that I might stay for hours and hours. But it really distressed him terribly.[45]

In her new assignment, Charlotte did not write as many stories as she had written for the women's pages, but those she wrote were longer and more in-depth. A typical example is a story originating from London, in which she reported on the financial cutbacks wealthy Britons were forced to make and the high cost of maintaining a castle. Charlotte noted with a wink that many castle owners had turned in desperation to wearing ready-made suits and shirts, and times were so tough that "only a few noble households bother to iron his lordship's copy of the *Times* of London before delivering it to him."[46]

Many of her society stories took on the theme of "poor-little-rich" families, such as the interview with the San Francisco mining heiress who is reduced to employing only five servants—or so she thinks. Charlotte quoted her: "'All I have is a personal maid, a cook, a butler and a cleaning woman,' she said. 'Well no. That's not right, either. There's the chauffeur.'"[47] Memos from Daniel show that some of

Charlotte's early society stories originated with him. In a memo to Edwards, for example, he suggested a story about the rough life of some yacht owners. The tongue-in-cheek tone of the memo resembles Charlotte's writing style:

> I imagine life on a yacht can be very grand, and I can imagine that, depending on the size of the yacht, it can also be a little rugged. One millionaire I heard about the other day said that he escaped from the slums only to find himself living on a yacht. Just like a tenement, there was no room to turn around in the bedroom, you threw garbage out the window and there was only one bathroom at the end of the hall that was used by everybody aboard. He must be a fairly poor millionaire.[48]

Daniel remembered that Charlotte's society stories caught on immediately and that *Times* readers hungered to read her next words about the rich. Edwards, however, was not so enthusiastic. The society editor did not know what to make of his hardworking and irreverent new reporter. "He was horrified," Daniel said.[49]

Other media printed stories about her and her unusual treatment of the wealthy. Both *Time* and *Newsweek* wrote articles about the "sociologist on the society beat," as the *Time* headline stated.[50] *Time* related what it called a typical Charlotte Curtis story—an ironic account of Miami racquet clubs that were restricted to white, Anglo-Saxon members. *Time* summarized the story: "She classified Miami as a 'youthful city . . . with the third largest Jewish population in the world.' Then she proceeded promptly to her point. 'However, there are no Jewish members in the Surf Club, the Bath Club or the Indian Creek and La Gorce Clubs.'" The *Newsweek* article noted that "society seems pleased having Miss Curtis along," and "she doesn't rub people the wrong way."[51]

One person Charlotte did rub the wrong way—at least for a time —was *New York Times* matriarch Iphigene Ochs Sulzberger, mother of Punch Sulzberger. Mrs. Sulzberger's father was Adolph Ochs, and she had been the daughter, wife, and mother-in-law of *Times* publishers. Although she was never on the payroll, she had considerable unofficial clout. Daniel remembered that Iphigene, though wealthy herself, thought it was in bad taste for Charlotte to write derisively about society parties. Charlotte, Daniel said, "was a bit of a shock to the older generation of *Times* management." Iphigene "was very much a lady—a white-gloved lady. She thought Charlotte was making fun of rich people."[52]

In a 1969 profile of Punch Sulzberger, the *New Yorker* quoted Iphigene regarding Charlotte's pages: "'Some of the young ladies who write the social news have more spirit than common sense,' she said. 'We are not the social arbiter of the nation, and it is not our role to hold up anyone to ridicule. You don't get any nearer the truth that way. A casual remark can make a person look awfully silly.'"[53]

Although Iphigene was taken aback by some of Charlotte's stories, she never attempted to censor them, according to Daniel and publisher Sulzberger.[54] But as Charlotte's stories caught on and she became a well-known reporter and editor, Iphigene grew proud of her. The two women began meeting periodically for lunch and eventually became friends.[55]

Charlotte's unorthodox reporting technique was given a stamp of legitimacy when the historian Barbara Tuchman wrote in *Harper's* that Charlotte's meticulous attention to detail made her stories vivid historical accounts. At the beginning of Tuchman's *Harper's* piece about writing history, she praised Charlotte's attention to detail, recounting her story of an opening at the Museum of Modern Art in New York at which Charlotte noted the number of champagne bottles *and* individual drinks. Tuchman wrote that such detail "is the way history as well as journalism should be written."[56]

Charlotte's recounting of this detail and other bits of minutiae in her stories did not come easily. She studied relentlessly about the history and lineage of the places and people she covered, and she read up on her story subjects as if she were taking an exam, as *Time* noted.[57] Her husband, William Hunt, remembered that for her, writing was a painstaking process that involved constant revision and rewriting—and her refusal in the late 1960s to switch from a manual to an electric typewriter slowed the process even more. Hunt described her technique behind the typewriter: "She always wrote from the top. If she had 700 words to do, she'd start on her Royal until she came to a certain point, then look at it, pull it out, throw it out, and start from the top again. Then she'd write until she could go from the opening to the bottom line." Charlotte never used an electric typewriter because she claimed it hindered the rhythm of her writing. Late in her career, she went directly from a Royal to the video display tubes routinely used in newsrooms.[58]

~

During these early years at the *Times*, Charlotte was still very much involved with Columbus and the life there. She liked to say in interviews that she kept her Ohio driver's license current and did much of her clothes shopping at Montaldo's, an exclusive women's clothing store in Columbus.[59] By the time she moved to New York, her father was in very poor health. His medical condition, brought on by several cerebral hemorrhages, forced George Morris Curtis to retire in 1952 after sixteen years as chairman of research surgery at Ohio State University Hospital. During his two-decade career at Ohio State, Curtis continued his research into thyroid physiology, wrote more than two hundred articles, established a residency program, and designed new courses in the medical school's graduate program.[60]

On December 23, 1965, George Curtis died at age seventy-five of gangrene of the gall bladder, peritonitis, and pneumonia. Charlotte flew to Columbus to attend his funeral and to write his obituary. She returned to her journalistic alma mater, the *Citizen-Journal*, to make sure the piece was done correctly. "She said, 'Who could do it better?'" Jane Kehrer Horrocks said.[61] Few people were surprised: it was characteristic of Charlotte to exercise such tight control over something that affected her personally—even during a time of tragedy.

6

The Tiny Person
with the Huge Byline

CHARLOTTE HAD BECOME a phenomenon in New York City by the time she had covered the society beat for a year. She reveled in uncovering the lunacy and hypocrisy of the upper crust, and most of those she covered considered it a badge of honor to have their names in a Charlotte Curtis story, no matter how unflattering the portrayal.

Punch Sulzberger remembered how, during a round of golf, a friend of his "complained" about the way her mother-in-law was treated on the *Times*'s society pages:

> [She] obviously had more on her mind than her putting. After the third hole, she couldn't hold back. "That was a terrible piece Charlotte Curtis wrote about my mother-in-law," she exploded. "Why did she have to write about all those diamonds and furs and the like. I was mortified."
>
> "I'm sorry," I replied. "But what did your mother-in-law think about it?"
>
> "That's the terrible part," she replied. "She loved it."[1]

As is frequently the case with celebrity, Charlotte's fame fed on itself and built momentum. She became increasingly popular. *Women's*

Wear Daily, the New York fashion magazine, devoted two newspaper pages to her in May 1965 — one filled with a four-column, nine-inch photo of her standing next to a page of quotes about her opinions on everything from hobbies to cars to the food of the rich and famous.[2] Charlotte is wearing a simple two-piece dress, gold hoop earrings, and a small bow-shaped pin, her arms are crossed, and in her right hand she holds a cigarette. "Turtle soup turns up seven nights a week on the society beat," she says. "It's the little black dress of social suppers." "The one piece of truffle is like the pearls of fashion." And "A yacht is status — that is, if you don't charter it." *Women's Wear Daily* described her as "[running] counter to the stereotyped society writer. She doesn't run with the Pack. She can spot a phony as quickly as a blue blood." The paper went on to call her "the Boswell of America's social scene from coast-to-coast with her byline gems."[3]

Charlotte's frank reporting about the rich predated the works of such authors as Dominick Dunne and Truman Capote. Capote's biting and often brutal portraits of his rich friends were published in the 1970s, and Dunne did not begin writing until the 1980s. Both, however, wrote "fiction," although frequently their works were thinly veiled portraits of their well-known friends and acquaintances.

As Sulzberger noted, members of the economic upper crust considered themselves slighted only when Charlotte did not write about them: "That was our Charlotte," Sulzberger said at her memorial service. "Skinning them without Novocain, yet they never felt a thing. Focusing a bright light on the foibles of society, yet they never blinked. Pecking at the pecking order, yet wounding only those who didn't make the list."[4]

~

"Making the list" was the name of the game on November 28, 1966, at what was to become one of the most talked-about parties in the history of the Manhattan cocktail party circuit. At Truman Capote's black-and-white masked ball, ostensibly held in honor of *Washington Post* publisher Katharine Graham, Charlotte got her hands on "the list to end all lists," as *Vanity Fair* called the exclusive 540-person guest list thirty years later. It was the society scoop of the year and one of Charlotte's most famous stories.[5]

Details of the Capote party are periodically rehashed in the media. On the surface, the party—enlivened by Capote's insistence that all partygoers wear only black or white formal clothing and masks—was just another excuse by Manhattan's elite to celebrate. But it lives on in popular culture: coming immediately before many dramatic social and political upheavals in American society, it may have represented one of the last times people celebrated with no worries about expense or social responsibility, and it was a testament to the great power of one New York social figure—Capote.[6] Capote's masked ball may have been *the* social event of the year, but Charlotte was not content to cover it as competing news media did—by simply writing advance stories or describing clothes, behavior, and decor at the party. CBS aired live coverage of it, and dispatches about it were delivered by wire services to media outlets all over the country. Many papers ran the story on page 1.

The guest list was secret, and Capote had the invitations printed only a week before the event and distributed them a few days beforehand. And he hired an army of security guards to monitor the doors and check invitations for forgeries. Reaction to the event surprised even Enid Nemy, who had recently started working with Charlotte on the *Times* as a society writer. "I was stunned at the idea that any social event could be so important," she said decades later.[7]

The day after the event, the *Times* devoted an entire newspaper page to it; Charlotte wrote the main account of the party, and Nemy wrote an accompanying story about the guests' preparations. What shocked many readers, though, was not the stories but what accompanied them: a list in tiny agate type of the 540 people who were invited—making liars of all those who claimed they had been invited but were unable to attend, usually because of out-of-town obligations. "The fakers who had fled to the Bahamas or claimed they had 'frugged-with-Kay' were exposed, routed, and humiliated," *Vanity Fair* wrote much later.[8] Charlotte somehow obtained the supposedly secret list, which the *Times* ran in full even in its early edition. Charlotte never publicly revealed who slipped her the list, although Nemy said Capote himself gave it to her.[9]

The partygoers described in Charlotte's story did not fare much better than those who lied about their invitations. As usual, Charlotte made some of them look silly as she detailed the importance to them of one-upmanship. She noted, for example, that Capote spent $13,000 on the party and Rose Kennedy's mask cost "only" $85. Other masks, she reported, cost up to $600. Alice Roosevelt Longworth instituted a sort of reverse competition—the wealthy Longworth, who flew in from Washington, D.C., for the event, wore a 35-cent mask fastened together with masking tape. "Mrs. Longworth's small white mask . . . cost her 35 cents and gave her great glee at having beaten Mr. Capote's 39 cents," Charlotte wrote. In Charlotte's eyes, these partygoers had little else on which to spend their money and nothing better to do than make a contest out of who spent the most—or least. Characteristically, she described partygoers' actions with caustic asides: "Mrs. Anne McDonnell Ford hugged her good friend, the Maharanee of Jaipur, who was invited *at the very last minute.*"[10]

Although the story about Capote's ball and many of Charlotte's society stories indicate a disdain for those she covered, in reality she was ambivalent about the nation's socially prominent. Later in her career, after she published a compilation of her society stories, she said that these people, by virtue of their wealth and status, were pivotal members of American society; they set fashion and social trends, and, more important, they provided funding for important cultural and artistic pursuits. "They own the land, the corporations of America out of proportion to their numbers," she said. "They make decisions having to do with every one of our lives from the clothes we wear, the furniture we buy, the music we hear, the art we see. And in society, we all can't afford to pay for the music and the art . . . the government can't pay for it."[11]

Some of the *Times*'s top news executives did not necessarily share this view of society reporting as sociology. But twenty-five years later, in 1993, executive editor Max Frankel echoed Daniel and Charlotte's opinion that the whims of the upper crust have an indirect effect on most Americans. When hemlines rise and fall, he noted, "industries rise and fall. Why isn't that news?"[12]

~

Charlotte's success as a society writer in 1963 and 1964 had payoffs beyond establishing her well-known byline on the *Times*. In addition to earning the professional respect of Clifton Daniel, the two became friends and she began to socialize with him and his wife, Margaret. The Daniels, in turn, periodically socialized with the Sulzberger family at their country home, Hillandale, in Stamford, Connecticut. Through the Daniels, she grew to know the Sulzbergers socially, as well as the few *Times* people who entered the Sulzberger inner circle, including former foreign correspondent and later assistant managing editor Harrison Salisbury and former foreign correspondent and *Times* vice president Sydney Gruson. Through this social interaction, the Sulzberger family, Iphigene Sulzberger in particular, got to know Charlotte personally and gradually grew more supportive of her irreverent stories. Charlotte clearly fit in with these Sulzberger intimates. After all, she had no trouble selecting the proper fork at formal luncheons, was well-read and well-connected, and held the same left-of-center-but-not-too-radical political views. It was a perfect match and one that certainly helped her career at the *Times*.

So it was little surprise to anyone inside the *Times* when Charlotte was named women's news editor in June 1965 upon the retirement of Elizabeth Penrose Howkins. Daniel by this time had ascended to managing editor, and it was unlikely that society editor Russell Edwards would be named to oversee the section. Further, at the suggestion of Daniel, the society section and women's news section were merged, and Charlotte, who once worked for Edwards, was now his boss. Her situation was unusual at the *Times*. In addition to overseeing the two newly merged departments, Charlotte continued as a society reporter, traveling around the country writing her dispatches. The day-to-day duties of the women's section, including page layout and story assignments, were frequently handled by the assistant women's editor, Joan Whitman.

Daniel's philosophy about the news value of the activities of the nation's socially prominent deeply affected Charlotte, but her own contact with well-to-do classmates at the Columbus School for Girls and Vassar, combined with her naturally cynical nature and disdain for authority, also influenced her reporting and writing. Her views of her story subjects — that they were sometimes ridiculous yet that they played an important role in American society — were paradoxical and typical of her contradictory nature.

To many on the paper, however, her close relationship with Daniel was pivotal to her ever-growing clout on the paper. In his account of the *Times* of the 1960s, *The Kingdom and the Power*, Gay Talese noted the key role Daniel played in Charlotte's ascent in the *Times* power structure:

> Though Daniel would prefer to be identified with several of the *Times'* recent changes for the better — the expanded coverage of cultural news, the more literary obituaries, the encouragement of flavor and mood in "hard news" stories that formerly would have been done in a purely routine way, he is more quickly credited with, or blamed for, the women's page. [Assistant managing editor Ted] Bernstein and other critics say that the women's pages get too much space, and that they particularly oppose the publication of lengthy stories by the women's-page editor, Charlotte Curtis, a five-foot, fast-stepping Vassar alum, describing the activities of the wastrels from Palm Beach to New York at a time when most of America is moving toward a more egalitarian society. Although Miss Curtis is rarely flattering to her subjects, many of them lack the wit to realize this — but what is more important is that Daniel likes to read it.[13]

Talese quoted former foreign correspondent David Halberstam as calling Curtis by the mid-1960s "one of the most powerful men [*sic*] on the paper, since Daniel values her opinions on everything and reads mostly her section." Halberstam's reference to Charlotte as a man is telling. She did, in many ways, act like a man and not like the women men on the paper knew. She worked in a man's profession, was driven professionally and worked long hours, had a cynical nature, and loved talking politics. But the dainty, meticulous Charlotte also had some of the characteristics of a typical woman of her era: she picked her battles carefully, was nonconfrontational, and rarely made waves. But Halberstam's comment was not necessarily a compliment, Talese noted. "Many of the foreign correspondents and 'serious' staff people in those days thought that Daniel's fascination with Society was silly, and that Charlotte Curtis was merely doing his bidding in a way that did neither of them credit."[14] Whether or not they agreed with the value of the expanded society section, few on the staff would disagree that Charlotte at this time wielded great power both in and outside the *Times*. As Roger Wilkins, a friend and colleague of hers, noted years later, "I could not believe such a tiny person had such a huge byline."[15]

Charlotte's most vocal critic on the paper was A. M. Rosenthal, assistant managing editor when Charlotte was named women's news editor. Rosenthal, one of the most famous and feared editors in the history of the *Times*, spearheaded major changes at the paper over nearly three decades. In 1963, the same year Sulzberger was named publisher, Rosenthal, an award-winning foreign correspondent, became metropolitan editor. Sulzberger's appointment of him as metropolitan editor and, later, assistant managing editor, managing editor, and executive editor was a mandate for change. The sly Sulzberger understood that *Times* readers and employees did not adapt to change easily, and he knew that if he asked Rosenthal to make changes, the acerbic editor would not be deterred by negative public opinion, complaints, or criticism. Sulzberger took pleasure in saying during interviews that the *Times* was slow to change, when, in fact, he initiated numerous changes during his first few years as publisher, including the naming of the *Times*'s first executive editor, the naming of two assistant managing editors, a new foreign editor, a new national news editor, new bureau chiefs in Washington and London, and, of course, Rosenthal. In addition, he forced the retirement of longtime Sunday editor and *Times* institution Lester Markel, who with an iron hand ran the Sunday *Times* as a separate entity from the daily paper.

Almost immediately, Rosenthal began to insist on modifications in the way news was reported at the *Times.* The paper had for most of its history taken pride in its reputation as the newspaper of record in the United States, and its reporting was unfailingly concise, comprehensive, factual, and, to some readers, dull and formulaic. As metropolitan editor, Rosenthal insisted that his reporters add explanation and context to their stories; he wanted them to examine the background of news events and provide depth and motivation. The paper was conservative and staid typographically. This, too, began to change by 1969, when Rosenthal became managing editor. Without question, Rosenthal was a major force in shaping the *Times* of the 1960s, 1970s, and 1980s, and it was unlikely that Charlotte would escape his mandate for change. But until 1970, she had Daniel's blessing and could run what stories she wanted most of the time. But even Daniel acknowledged that Charlotte sometimes crossed the line. For example, a brief society page story reporting that millionaire industrialist Aristotle Onassis's son, Alexander, was having an affair with an Austrian baroness violated the *Times*'s policy against "gossip" on its pages, and did not belong in the newspaper, Daniel wrote Charlotte:[16]

> The *New York Times* should not on any page in the paper engage in gossip or scandalmongering unless the circumstances are of the most unusual nature and, even then, a decision to publish should be made at the level of the Managing Editor's office.
>
> The story about Mr. Onassis and Baroness von Thyssen is gossip, and it is, in conventional terms, somewhat scandalous. . . . If an engagement is announced, or we have good reason to believe that they intend to be married . . . I think we could certainly write about it.[17]

Such critical memos from Daniel to Charlotte were few and far between. Rosenthal, however, was not reluctant to state his displeasure with society or women's page stories, particularly when he believed them to be in bad taste or inappropriate for a serious newspaper like the *Times*. In a story about the marriage of an Austrian princess, the reporter, who did not receive a byline but who sounded suspiciously like Charlotte, wrote: "The bridegroom wore a matching Salzburg suit complete with pink silk tie and a dainty rose arrangement in the buttonhole. It is well known that he used to spend up to $100,000 a month playing host to young male friends at Blutenbach —usually seven at a time because, he said, he believed in groups of eight."[18] The apparent allusion to the groom's homosexuality angered Rosenthal, who sent the following memo to Charlotte: "The attempt to make our stories interesting must not violate our own standards of taste and tenor and I think we all agree on that. . . . But in the story of the marriage of Princess Von Auersperg to the Krupp heir, we did violate these standards. That was in the reference to the groom's homosexual proclivities. I think such material really has no place in the story at all."[19]

As long as Daniel was managing editor, however, most of what Charlotte wrote or edited found its way into the newspaper unscathed, and traditionally dull wedding and engagement notices often contained outrageous tidbits. In the wedding announcement of famous impostor and author George Plimpton, Charlotte spelled out in the third paragraph his once active social life: "Mr. Plimpton was married last night, not to Mrs. John F. Kennedy, Queen Elizabeth II, Jean Seberg, Ava Gardner, Jane Fonda, Princess Stanislas Radziwell or Candy Bergen, all of whom he escorted at one time or another, but to Freddy Medora Espy, a wisp of a photographer's assistant whom he met at a party in 1963."[20]

In another wedding announcement, the reporter implied that the bride was not exactly a wallflower: "The wedding, which must have come as a surprise to anyone familiar with the roster of well-known rejected suitors, will take place in Madrid."[21]

Many *New York Times* readers waited wickedly to see who Charlotte would skewer next. A 1969 cover story in the fledgling *New York* magazine noted the powerful punch packed by the petite and demure Charlotte: "Oh, beastly! News is so impolite. Charlotte hung price tags on things that never had them before. . . . All that excruciating detail!"[22] Reporter Julie Baumgold began her story by noting that Charlotte was golden among the top *Times* editors, who left the copy desk directives not to cut her stories: "Charlotte Curtis can be killed but never cut. That's a rule they have on the *Times* copy desk to keep all those anxious lead pencils away from the wit of their women's news editor."[23]

Baumgold labeled Charlotte the "bride of the *New York Times*," a term Nan Robertson repeated in her book about women at the *Times*. According to Baumgold: "Charlotte Curtis is indeed the bride of the *Times*. She is the little woman of the Great Man. Four years ago the marriage was announced and pictured in the *Times*. The bride wore black (she was divorced) and white (two strands of proper pearls) and looked appropriately nervous, as befits a closet radical elected to be women's news editor of the Times—mistress of the home within the House, the food-fashions-family-furnishings page, the Queen of the Hop on the society page."[24] The contradictions in Charlotte's nature intrigued Baumgold. For instance, Charlotte mocked the subjects of her stories, yet she still blended in with them physically: "She insists reporters must remain outsiders, but she changes her clothes. While other reporters appear at parties in dresses disrupted at the seat from a day of sitting, Charlotte is wearing silk. It's as though half of her had left to shake a cautionary finger at the other half—to contradict one interview in a second. Vassar, yes, but the girl who boasted she could drink any of her classmates under the table."[25]

Charlotte's belief in egalitarianism on the job made her uncomfortable with her title as a section editor, and her disdain for personal confrontation made her an unlikely manager.[26] Yet she could still be intimidating because, despite her quiet demeanor, she insisted that her staff maintain her own high standards. One of her employees told Baumgold that her lower lip began to shake whenever Charlotte called for her.[27] Charlotte did not accept editorships at the *Times* for reasons of personal power or fame. She wanted to fill the pages she edited with stories she thought were stimulating and creative and to improve the *Times*, a paper she loved. And sometimes she was single-minded in those goals, according to Nan Robertson, who worked in the *Times* Washington bureau when Charlotte was women's editor. Robertson said that though she admired Charlotte, she eventually took action to circumvent Charlotte's numerous requests for society dispatches from Washington, D.C.: "Charlotte would hound me to cover things for her [in Washington]." Soon, Robertson would work only with assistant women's page editor Whitman. "I got very angry," she said. "I was ambitious. I wasn't going to spend all my time in Georgetown [on the party circuit]." Both Robertson and Charlotte were driven, obstinate, and "very results oriented. We were both stubborn and powerful personalities," Robertson said.[28]

By the late 1960s, Charlotte's fame was growing outside the *Times*, and her power was expanding within the paper. In addition to holding the title of women's news editor and being invited to the Sulzberger family home, she demonstrated her power in subtle ways. In 1966, she was the subject of an extensive *Times* promotion that featured prize-winning and prominent reporters and columnists. One series of promotions featured Charlotte, women's page reporter Virginia Lee Warren, and architecture critic Ada Louise Huxtable in a series of house ads, announcing they had all won awards for excellence in journalism from the Newspaper's Women's Club of New York.

More important, however, was that the venerable Harrison Salisbury—Pulitzer Prize–winning foreign correspondent and now a respected assistant managing editor—selected Charlotte to contribute to a book he was writing about the Soviet Union. The iconoclastic Salisbury had become a respected historian and author, known particularly for his writings about Russia, and his selection of Charlotte as a contributor to his book spoke volumes about her stature on the paper.[29]

Charlotte's dispatches from the Soviet Union a decade earlier when she was a young *Citizen* reporter may have influenced Salisbury's selection of her, but their personal friendship and her entree into the

Sulzberger social circle were also factors. Salisbury said thirty years later that he thought Charlotte "trained herself to turn a phrase" and "was a walking encyclopedia of people and places."[30]

Charlotte wrote twenty-five pages in Salisbury's book about women in Russia, including their views about their lifestyles, their country, and their politics. She gathered the information by talking to dozens of Soviet women, many of whom were professional educators, physicians, and scientists. What stands out in her account is the contradictory nature of many of these women. She wrote about the laborer, for instance, who frequently descended into the bowels of subway systems but who had a passion for flowers, placing them all over her office and home. She noted that many women who were inveterate readers and who studied hard for their education became chronic television viewers after television was first introduced to the Soviet Union.[31]

The most interesting aspect of her chapter about the Soviet women was that it telegraphed her own ambivalence and uncertainty about women's rights and the changing role of women in society. She wrote that the modern Soviet woman "wants to keep right on being equal, but she no longer thinks equality involves opening doors for herself, lighting her own cigarettes, pulling back her own chair at a table. She neither wants nor tries to be coy, helpless or fragile . . . but she wants everyone to remember that she is a woman and that being a woman is a lot different than being a man."[32] Charlotte's own views of feminism, which would emerge as the feminist movement developed, are evident in the piece. She did not necessarily believe "equal rights" meant that women and men should be treated the same all the time—she always believed that the sexes were different socially. In the early years of the American feminism, the definition of the world "feminism" was stringent: "feminists" believed men and women were equal in every way, and a person either supported or opposed the movement. Charlotte had a much more practical definition of feminism that focused on equal rights economically and in the workforce—a view that some early feminists believed was inadequate.

Charlotte admired the Soviet woman of 1967, who, she believed, maintained a pragmatic view of feminism. She wrote that the Soviet woman wanted to marry and care for a family, but she also wanted access to birth control and abortion.[33]

Charlotte described a set of conflicting beliefs that later formed the core of the debate in the ranks American feminism. As she wrote about these Soviet women, she described a loose form of feminism that was not strident or necessarily driven by principle but that conformed to a lifestyle. It is a view of feminism that Charlotte embraced later in her life and one that was evident in her writing and the stories she chose to place on the pages she edited.

As women's news editor, Charlotte had to deal with a variety of content issues outside the realm of society. By the late 1960s, editors at most newspapers began to grapple with how to handle their women's pages and whether the recipes, grooming techniques, and other standard women's page fare were passé. Like Charlotte and Whitman, some women's page editors were downplaying conventional women's page stories and focusing on larger issues that affected women. Lindsy Van Gelder wrote about the changes: "[By 1970] newspapers began covering abortion, rape, child care, alimony, job discrimination, gay rights and other feminist issues, and taking fresh approaches toward their traditional subjects. Some women's sections—notably those at the Washington Post, the Chicago Tribune and the New York Times —are now considered by many in the industry to be the best written, best-read parts of the paper."[34] Interestingly, Charlotte downplayed her role as a trendsetter in changing women's news, saying that other papers may have done that on a small scale, but the *Times* had the personnel and reputation to become a leader: "We opened windows and we brought a news quality to the page that it never had in the *New York Times*," she said much later. "The *New York Times* is credited with leading in that field. . . . But the difference [between the *Times* and other newspapers] is that [other papers] hadn't had the resources, the people, to be able to do it well. But because we had the resources, we could take the framework and we could do it."[35]

In addition to Van Gelder, other journalists credit the *Times* with pioneering a new type of women's page coverage. Charlotte's colleague on the women's section Marylin Bender made the link between Charlotte's society coverage and overall changes on the women's pages, and she believes this coverage was ahead of its time. Bender believes the issues brought up in Charlotte's society stories, combined with the freedom and space she was given, translated into a new more open women's page writing that focused on such topics as feminism, civil rights, and politics. "As time went on there were no holds barred. If abortion was brewing, abortion is what we did. It may have been the [Washington] Post that did 'Style,' but the spadework of reporting and coverage was the *Times*."[36] Robertson, who worked for two decades in the *Times* Washington bureau, agreed that the women's pages under Charlotte served as a model for papers nation-wide: "She was imitated by women's news editors across the country and by the reporters on her own newspaper who were her protégés."[37]

As Charlotte noted, it is difficult to underestimate the power of the *New York Times* as a journalistic trendsetter, particularly during the era in which Charlotte worked. Its enormous resources in the form of money and talent have for much of the century established newspaper trends and customs. To many journalists, the *Times* was the pinnacle, and editors and reporters around the nation were quick to follow its lead. The paper's journalistic influence was enormous, particularly before the explosive growth of television news late in the century. Indeed, when Charlotte initiated her "emperor-has-no-clothes" style of society writing in Columbus, its influence did not extend beyond central Ohio. The same style at the *Times* created a sensation.

Nationally, the most well-publicized departure from the standard women's-page fare came on January 6, 1969, when the *Washington Post* debuted its much-touted "Style" section, a magazinelike section which, under editor Ben Bradlee, replaced the *Post*'s women's section. While women's sections at the time were changing gradually, the *Post* made a big splash because its section changed all at once — one day a traditional women's section existed, and the next day it was gone.

"Style" resulted from a series of changes in journalism and society. The New Journalism made some newspaper editors nervous. Its style was creative and lively, and some editors feared their readers would turn to the magazines that featured it. *Post* editors thought their conventional women's section with its recipes and service stories was outdated. Bradlee said he wanted to print the news "behind the potted palms," and his goals for the page went far beyond merely departing from accepted women's-page fare.[38] He wanted "Style" reporters to exercise a new freedom of expression that was rare in most formulaic American dailies, and he wanted the section to emphasize a human dimension.[39]

The advent of "Style" did not come without controversy. Wedding and engagement announcements were eliminated, and publisher Katharine Graham feared that advertising and subscriptions would drop as a result. Bradlee purposely staffed "Style" with men as well as women so it would appeal to both sexes, and he hired bright and daring young writers such as Sally Quinn and Nicholas Von Hoffman.[40] Quinn's job was to cover parties the way the *Post* news reporters covered political campaigns.[41] These "Style" reporters concentrated on reconstructing dialogue and recounting detail, often making their subjects look foolish: "Dialogue and detail are made integral parts of scene construction," according to the *Post* Writers Group's history of the section. "Mimesis and rhythm of sentence structure all work together to give a gut sense of being present, of watching and hearing live people. . . . Style writers frequently use dialogue as an alternative to standard quotations because such natural interaction offers spontaneous character revelation."[42]

These literary devices were used in some magazines and books of the era, but if they sounded familiar to newspaper readers, it was because Charlotte had been using this same technique for about eight years on the *New York Times*. If the *Times* women's section did not get the credit—or blame—for innovations in women's news and society coverage, it was because those changes on the *Times* came gradually, and they were not necessarily sanctioned by a top editor like Bradlee, who mandated dramatic and sudden changes in the section's content, staffing, and graphics.

Throughout her eight years as women's editor, Charlotte's innovations sometimes met with opposition from editors at the *Times*. Clifton Daniel gave her virtual carte blanche to write daring and unusual stories, but even he had to make sure the stories conformed in a limited way to *Times* convention. And after Daniel was removed as managing editor in 1969 and replaced by A. M. Rosenthal, it became more difficult for Charlotte to impose change.

Charlotte and Sally Quinn sometimes covered the same events, and they became friends. Quinn said that although Charlotte broke down the traditional barriers of women's news before 1969, she did it only sporadically and without the support of the rest of management: "They [the *Times*] continued to have women's coverage for a long time. But Charlotte was an anachronism. Everyone else [on the *Times*] seemed to be traditional." Quinn noted that Charlotte's stories did not depart entirely from standard women's page fare: "It wasn't like she was doing it every day. Every once in a while she'd say, 'The hell with this . . . I'm going to make fun of this.'"[43] The purpose of "Style," in contrast, was to provide this new brand of journalism daily.

Quinn said that with the advent of "Style," she did not compete with Charlotte for stories or fame. "I was always under the impression that she felt we were in cahoots—that we were comrades and partners in crime. She was incredibly mischievous. She always had this sly grin, and loved to think of herself as a bad girl."[44] Charlotte's intense loyalty to the *Times*, in fact, sometimes took a back seat to her loyalty to news; if she discovered a gossipy item she knew the *Times* would not print, she could not resist finding another venue for it—

even if that venue was a competing publication. Liz Smith remembered that Charlotte sometimes gave her news nuggets for her column in the *New York Daily News* if she knew the *Times* would not print it.[45]

Long after Bradlee launched "Style," *Times* editors continued to debate the appropriate content of the women's/society section and how the paper should handle the changing roles of women. Bridal announcements became a political football, thanks in part to a move by the two Houston papers, which, in the late 1960s, stopped running them as editorial copy and printed them only as paid ads, a move publisher Sulzberger considered. Charlotte, of course, opposed it, viewing engagements and weddings as sociological events and therefore news; even Sulzberger was often under pressure from friends and relations to make sure that the bridal announcements of their loved ones were prominently displayed in the *Times*.[46]

The job of Charlotte and her staff would not get any easier in the 1970s. As the role of women changed, so did their views of women's pages. Charlotte would come under fire from two groups: those who felt that the existence of women's sections "ghettoized" women's news and kept it from appearing in more prominent sections of the paper, and those who wanted no changes, comfortable in the knowledge that they could turn to the women's pages to get the practical stories they wanted.

7

"They Hail Planes as Most
People Hail Taxis"

As SHE BECAME a well-known journalist in Manhattan, Charlotte
carved out a satisfying and interesting life there. She cultivated a small
but loyal circle of friends and, as she had hoped, successfully merged
her work and personal life. After her first few years in New York, she
and Grove gradually stopped seeing each other—in part, no doubt,
because she became comfortable by herself in the city. She liked to
say that New York appealed to her because of its eclectic and oddball
nature. Her friend and co-worker Roger Wilkins recalled one warm
Easter day when he and Charlotte sat in Washington Square Park near
New York University. They observed the passing scene, which included well-dressed middle-aged couples, street people conducting
drug deals, young skateboarders with enormous boom boxes, and, on
that day, former congresswoman Bella Abzug and her husband. The
mixture appealed to Charlotte: "She was midwesterner to the core,"
Wilkins said.[1]

Charlotte rarely dated or ventured outside her small circle of
friends for dinners out and companionship. And she rarely if ever
changed her appearance, demeanor, or way of thinking: her friends
could always count on seeing her with the familiar pageboy hairstyle,

simple, classic clothing, and small gold earrings and black and gold bangle bracelets. They kidded her about her "Ohio" twang, although many of them may have simply given that label to the low-pitched, nasal quality of her voice. Particularly distinctive was her deep, throaty laugh.

Charlotte prided herself on her loyalty to her friends on and outside of the *Times*. Once they had established her friendship and respect, her allegiance to them never wavered. But some of the friends she made outside of the newsroom also knew of her loyalty to the paper— her few personal friends on the society beat were aware that anything they said in front of her might later appear in the pages of the *Times*.

Charlotte's forays outside of the newsroom benefited her in many ways. In addition to allowing her to write and see the country, they enabled her to postpone or avoid making decisions about how to cover the women's movement. It was a subject with which she never felt comfortable, yet as the movement gained momentum, the *Times* could not avoid covering it. Charlotte's assistant, Joan Whitman, made assignment and coverage decisions in her absence, although as editor, Charlotte was ultimately responsible for what appeared in the family/style section.

By 1969, Clifton Daniel, her friend and mentor, had been removed as managing editor. By the time he was demoted to head the paper's Washington bureau, Charlotte was so ensconced in the paper's power structure that she could do no wrong. Although Rosenthal, now the paper's managing editor, periodically sent her critical memos about the content of her page, he was little more than a minor annoyance.

How much her friendships at the paper influenced her success there is unclear. Rosenthal said twenty-five years later that it was her writing talent combined with her innovative coverage of society that earned her success.[2] But though Daniel was pivotal in "discovering" her unique style, promoting her, and then giving her carte blanche at the paper, it was his introductions of her to top management that were crucial to her success and rise. Charlotte's close relationship to the Sulzberger family and to Salisbury kept her in the inner circle.[3]

Still, to succeed in the male-dominated world of the *Times* of the 1960s and 1970s, Charlotte needed more than just a few good friends in high places, and she may have cultivated her relationships with men on the paper while sacrificing her relationships with women. Feminist author Gloria Steinem, who knew Charlotte socially, believes that Charlotte felt more comfortable with men than with women: "I think she was a loner. She grew up in an era in which the thing to be was the only woman in a group of men. I think she thought, 'Men are more interesting.'" As time would tell, the *Times* was ultimately unkind to Charlotte—a turnaround that, to Steinem, is typical of that paper, which, she believes, historically has used women and promoted men: "I think of it [the *Times*] as hemophilia. It passes through women and men get it."[4] Columnist Molly Ivins, who worked on the *Times* from 1976 until 1982, said Charlotte succeeded professionally because she was not intimidated by the male egos at the *Times*, and she was smart and clever. "Charlotte was first rate, as bright as she could be and not afraid of anyone," Ivins said. "Even in terms of being women's page editor, I thought of her as someone who was very good at breaking into the old boy's network— she had the guys cowed. She was a lot smarter than they were."[5]

As Ivins pointed out, Charlotte was smart enough not to let the men think she was smarter than they. Charlotte was opinionated but not confrontational, unfailingly polite but not deferential; and her manner was assertive but not aggressive. In these ways, she was, indeed, smart enough to break into the "old boy's network."

When Ivins worked at the *Times*, editors treated women like "delicate flowers," she said. "They hired us and would send us to cover food, fluff and fashion. They'd hire you to do 'safe' things." The outspoken Ivins, who stands six feet tall, circumvented that attitude because of her size: "I towered over every editor I ever worked for. No one ever said, 'Oh, Molly, you petite fragile thing.' It was always, 'Ivins, get your ass out there.'"[6]

Charlotte could not reconcile herself to many of the goals and beliefs of the feminist movement. She did not believe the sexes were equal in every way. She believed they thought differently and excelled in different areas. And she could never abandon the glamour and conventional personal style that feminists of the era abhorred. Still, she was a strong proponent of job and economic equality, and this view formed the backbone of her personal "feminism."[7] Charlotte was asked frequently to give speeches about her job as a society writer, and, by the early 1970s, it was impossible for her to avoid the topic of feminism. The movement raised eyebrows—many people were not sure what to make of it, but they hesitated to criticize it for fear of being labeled unsympathetic toward women. Charlotte, however, had no fear of that label. In a speech she gave in the early 1970s to the American Association of Advertising Agencies in White Silver Springs, West Virginia, she kiddingly denounced the flashy radicals of the feminist movement, noting that most American women were too exhausted by their daily lives to think too much about the principles of "feminism."[8]

Charlotte mocked the prevailing view of women's pages—that they were acceptable to feminists as long as they had the correct name. Women's editors were respectable, she said, as long as they changed the names of their pages "to some euphemism such as Modern Living, Outlook Trend, or Family/Style" and "introduced tough, frankly relevant subjects," she said. This superficiality bothered her.

More revealing, however, are her comments about everyday working women who, she believed, were the real feminists of the era. She denounced Betty Friedan's groundbreaking book *The Feminine Mystique*[9] as missing the point for most women. Most working women, she said, were sympathetic to the plight of women, but, as one middle-aged co-worker—a wife, mother, and full-time newspaper reporter—said at the time, "If I were any more liberated, I'd be dead."[10]

Charlotte viewed some of the leaders in the feminist movement and the rich society matrons she covered as equally frivolous: both were so concerned with appearances and trivial matters that they could not see what was important in their own lives and in the lives of others. Most women were so busy that they did not have the luxury or time to contemplate the often superficial goals or activities of a newly formed social movement, Charlotte believed.

Her fame as a society writer allowed Charlotte to expand into another medium—she became a daily commentator on the *Times*-owned radio station WQXR, offering two- to three-minute observations about events she covered. The role of broadcaster was new to her, and never before had she been permitted to state her opinions publicly so blatantly. Occasionally, she used this forum to tell listeners that the showy demonstrations of some feminists obscured their point.

Her role as section editor, her travels, and her new job as radio commentator took up all of her time. She remained in contact with her mother, mostly by letter, and was determined to keep her close ties to Columbus. All of this kept her at arm's length from her sister, Mary Davey, who now lived in Los Altos Hills in northern California with her husband and three children. Charlotte visited the Davey family whenever business took her to the West Coast, but Mary's children grew up with only a few memories of their aunt. "Geography separated any close relationship," Mary said. "I would say Charlotte was married to her job. That was the all-consuming thing." Mary's oldest son, John, visited his aunt in New York several times as a boy and had vague memories of her when the Davey family lived in Dayton, Ohio, in the late 1950s. To Davey's two younger children, though, Charlotte remained a remote figure, according to Davey.[11]

Charlotte's dispatches from around the world increased as the *Times* began assigning her stories that stretched the limits of society reporting. She was a member of reporting teams that covered the 1968 Republican convention in Miami, the moon launch, and the funeral train of Robert F. Kennedy, and her stories sometimes appeared on the front page. By this time, Charlotte knew what was permissible in the *Times* and what would be vetoed by the editors. And she frequently came very close to crossing the line.

Times editors knew that little was sacred to Charlotte—not even the funeral train that carried the body of Robert F. Kennedy from New

York to Washington in 1968. Charlotte observed in the story that politics was so ingrained in the Kennedy family that Robert Kennedy's son Joseph could not resist using the event of his father's death for politicking. She began her story by describing the young man as he got off the train:

> Down the swaying train he went, putting his hand in 19 of the 20 cars saying, "I'm Joe Kennedy," while outside in the early afternoon sun, the old men of Linden, N.J., stood silently in their undershirts and the women held handkerchiefs to their faces.
>
> "I'm Joe Kennedy," he said to strangers, his pin-stripe black suit not yet a shambles from the failing air-conditioning, his PT boat tie clip neatly in place. "Thanks for coming, thanks for coming."[12]

The details—the PT-boat tie clip and the pinstripe suit—reminded the reader that Joe was, after all, a Kennedy. As was the style of the New Journalism, the details did far more than add color to the story. They took on a life of their own and conjured up the history of the event.

Despite her cool treatment of Joseph Kennedy's behavior, Charlotte was not unmoved by the event, as she later wrote her mother. As was the case with other stories, she hid her sympathies and emotional reaction to the subjects. The contradictory aspect of the train ride appealed to her own paradoxical personality, as she wrote Lucile:

> I rode the train from NY to Washington with the Kennedy casket and all the kids, and it was, predictably, a rare experience in Americana. All those poor people and blacks along the tracks because the trains run beside the homes of the poor. All the inside feeling that this was still California and the campaign and that no one really had been assassinated. And still, an Irish wake of the very rich, 1968 variety, with eating, drinking and laughing on board not so very far from the casket.[13]

Charlotte reported on many of the phenomenal events of 1968 and was thrilled to be covering news and writing history. She once recounted her schedule to Lucile, who was on a trip around the world at the time; it included attending the Republican convention, a trip with Pat Nixon to Texas, and covering the year's political campaigns. Charlotte was prescient in realizing that 1968 was a pivotal year in American history: "All of this will teach you to go away in what has turned out to be one of the world's most incredible years," she wrote Lucile. In her expanded role covering politics and world events, Charlotte was able to experience what every reporter loves: the thrill of the chase. Her job as society reporter gave her fame and freedom, but rarely did it require her to fight for a scoop. In her letter to Lucile describing the Kennedy funeral train, Charlotte described the heady experience of running to a phone to meet a deadline, surrounded by her competitors. At the time, she was traveling with fellow *Times* reporter Russell Baker: "We wrote our stories in long hand and on our knees and then dashed through Union Station to file them. It was a madhouse."[14] Charlotte took great pride in beating most of her larger male competitors to the phone, officially getting the story first.

In addition to covering the Kennedy funeral train, Charlotte reported on the 1968 Republican convention and presidential primaries that year. Although she was now writing in the realm of politics, she spared no one her caustic asides—not even entire states. In a front-page story in June 1968 about the California primary, she delighted in pointing out the quirkiness of the state and its inhabitants. She wrote: "This imaginative state that popularized freeways, supermarkets, swimming pools, drive-ins, backyard barbecues, the bare midriff, house trailers, Capri pants, hot rods, sports shirts, split-level houses and tract living has a former B-movie actor in Governor's chair at Sacramento. . . . In Governor Reagan . . . the citizens have a Republican who was a Democrat. He defeated Edmund G. Brown, a Democrat who was a Republican." California was an easy target for Charlotte. She went on: "California has other realities. . . . It is the state where there are more Nobel Prize winners and muscle-bound Mr. America's than anywhere else in the world. . . . California is also the state where a stripper named Thoroughly Naked Millie can take off most of her clothes in public although it is illegal to read palms or tea leaves."[15] These contradictions appealed to Charlotte, and she was quick to make light of them. The convention itself, though fascinating and flashy, was eerie to her, and its superficiality struck her decades before the advent of all-news networks and cable television. Notes she took while she was there were a barrage of adjectives: "Conventions," she wrote, "A delicious amalgam of cigar smoke, suspense, whisky, noise, multi-denominational prayer, band music and tribal dancing. Hideously sentimental. Splendidly vulgar. . . . Puts party power above national welfare and can mistake mediocrity for revelation."[16]

The lavishness of the convention did not impress Charlotte, and her notes echo the same ironies contemporary writers have observed about the rigidly scripted and manipulative political conventions of the 1990s. She believed the gaiety and earnestness of the 1968 conventions were not simply superficial but frightening: "The Republican National Convention was a handsome affair. . . . But for all its good looks . . . there was something painful and embarrassing about it," she wrote in her notes. "Exposed to these things—mostly peripheral things apart from the basic decisions of the convention—I find myself wondering if there wasn't something a bit sinister about it, too."[17] Her criticism of politics and its emphasis on form over substance continued in her coverage of President Nixon's inaugural ball. Again, she noted the inherent contradictions of the event, reducing everything to a matter of dollars and cents, from the $1,000 admission tickets to the $1.50 drinks to the $25,000 spent on carnations.[18]

Charlotte's stories, a mixture of political and social commentary, were unique among newspaper pieces of the era; biting political commentary was not unusual, but society coverage of political events was usually limited to conventional descriptions of gowns, decorations, and party activities. Such stories certainly did not have the subtle but pointed commentary of Charlotte's dispatches.

~

Charlotte's writing became more daring through her years as a society writer and editor. By the 1970s, she wrote more society stories and fewer political ones, and, because of her wide readership, she had the blessing of her editors. It was hard to believe that these cynical and ironic stories came from the typewriter of the demure-looking and courteous Charlotte. But her close friends remember Charlotte as funny and frequently sarcastic ("She didn't suffer fools gladly," Marylin Bender said), as well as self-deprecating and far from bitter or petty.[19] Bill Hunt said her way of dealing with people who gave her trouble was to avoid thinking or talking about them, and she rarely confronted them. In short, she did not waste energy or time on them.[20]

Charlotte was intrigued by the paradoxical personalities of those she covered. She never hesitated to write about the philanthropic bent of many socially prominent people but was amused that they usually had little interest in charitable causes, simply donating money for tax purposes or to make sure their friends knew they contributed to the latest trendy cause. The rich were oblivious to real-world poverty and "feel neither guilt nor social responsibility," she said.[21] One of her favorite targets throughout the years was the extended family of Henry Ford II, whom Charlotte followed from Boston to Grosse Point to their yacht on the Riviera, chronicling their lavish lifestyle. In one particularly cutting story, she reported on a college graduation party held for Edsel Ford II, the son of Henry Ford II and the first male Ford to graduate from college. The *Times* devoted half a newspaper page to the story and accompanying pictures. Edsel may have received his diploma, but it was no easy task, even though the college he attended was hardly challenging: "After five and a half years of trying, 24-year-old Edsel, as charming a young man as he is well mannered, finally completed the required courses at Boston's easy-going Babson College," she wrote. A wealthy family like the Fords typically demonstrated its gratitude to a college by donating a dormitory or library, but that was not so easy in Edsel's case, Charlotte noted. She quoted

Edsel's brother-in-law as joking that "Edsel had gone to 47 schools, which comes to six dormitories, five football fields and a library."[22]

Her stories of this era also advanced the "poor-little-rich-family" theme she had cultivated earlier. Charlotte learned as a young woman that though most wealthy people were obsessed with money, it was considered *déclassé* to discuss it publicly. She delighted in taking the topic out of the closet and into the homes of readers.

Chronicling a lavish three-day party hosted by ophthalmologist and business leader Jules Stein, for instance, Charlotte noted that he spared no expense, footing the bill for his guests' lodging and plane fare, as well as for food, decorations, and drink. Only a very generous man would spend an estimated $250,000 on his friends, Charlotte implied—until she noted that one of Stein's companies picked up the huge tab and used it as a tax deduction.[23]

In 1973, energy conservation measures imposed by President Nixon gave many of the wealthy an opportunity to exercise the "we-live-simply-with-our-mundane-millions" attitude.[24] Not even the wealthiest Americans could avoid the impact of conservation, Charlotte wrote with a straight face. Cosmetics magnate and multimillionaire Charles Revson, for instance, bemoaned that he would have to confine cruises of his 250-foot, 1,200-ton yacht to the Caribbean or the Gulf of Mexico, and one woman looked at the bright side of the energy crisis, acknowledging that turning down thermostats in her mansion would benefit her furniture. "Now my furniture will have the atmosphere it had in Europe."[25]

Charlotte's subjects gave her ample rope with which to hang them. By the early 1970s, her society stories adopted a sharper edge, and many of them served as forums for her opinions about serious matters. This was at least in part owing to her interest in the civil rights movement and her fascination with the concern the wealthy had for members of the underclass and their glorification of poverty—a term writer Tom Wolfe labeled "radical chic." Charlotte wrote about a variation of radical chic which she called "Mafia chic"—the glorification of Mafia leaders, whom many rich New Yorkers saw as glamorous.

For a brief time in 1972, former Mafia leader Joseph Gallo became the darling of high society after he was released from a nine-year prison term for extortion. Charlotte was clearly unnerved by the attention given to this extortionist and suspected murderer.

In a freelance story for *Harper's Bazaar* written two months after Gallo was gunned down on the street, Charlotte described how actor Jerry Orbach and his wife, Marta, met Gallo after the Mafia leader called Orbach to congratulate him on his role in Jimmy Breslin's parody on the Mafia, *The Gang That Couldn't Shoot Straight*. After meeting him for dinner, Mrs. Orbach became enamored of the convict's charm and knowledge. "It was at that first meeting that he casually asked Mrs. Orbach whether she preferred Camus or Sartre," Charlotte wrote. "As she tells it, 'I almost fell into a plate of spaghetti.'"[26]

The Orbachs' affection for Gallo set off a chain reaction of dinners, theater events, and cocktail parties, all which featured this convicted criminal as guest of honor. The celebrities, actors, philanthropists, and assorted millionaires who hosted these events were impressed by Gallo's knowledge of literature and history, and they adopted him as their social pet. Gallo's rough language and his penchant to tell it like it was greatly amused these pampered philanthropists, Charlotte wrote: "'[Gallo] once told me to shut up,' Mrs. Orbach said. 'I'm Italian and I understand that.'"

In the Gallo story, Charlotte illustrated plainly that she abhorred the attention given to a convicted criminal, and she disputed Mrs. Orbach's contention that Gallo was "misunderstood." After only twelve weeks of fame and attention, Gallo was murdered in the street. Yet Charlotte still had no sympathy for him. "In the end," she wrote, "one of the fascinations Joey Gallo held for this group of people was that he was a gangster, and nobody seems to have come to grips with that."

~

The subjects of Charlotte's stories rarely complained to her or to *Times* editors. But when they did, their criticism frequently egged

Charlotte on. Charlotte knew that most of the people she covered came in three varieties: those who were unaware they were being ridiculed, those who knew but did not care (and sometimes even liked the publicity), and those who were too polite to respond.

Yet she and the *Times* held firm in the face of criticism. For instance, one woman took Charlotte to task at a party for writing that she "was dripping in diamonds." Charlotte recalled the incident: "She was wearing sapphires in pendant earrings, a wide bracelet and a behemoth ring, not to mention two large matched clips. So I did agree that she was not always dripping diamonds, that sometimes she dripped sapphires."[27] Charlotte related how she once complimented a very rich woman on an expensive jeweled necklace. "She said, 'Oh, this old thing,'" Charlotte said. "And to her, that's what they were. Her family had owned them for three generations and she had worn them so often that her friends were used to seeing them."[28] The wealthy were oblivious to their pampered lifestyle, assuming everyone lived as they did. This sense of entitlement amused Charlotte and formed the backbone of many of her society stories, but the stories occasionally infuriated their subjects.

After five years as a society writer and editor, Charlotte could rattle off anecdotes about the rich in rapid-fire style, sometimes offering up to half a dozen examples and aphorisms in one short newspaper interview. "They hail planes as most people hail taxis," she once said of the wealthy. And "In Palm Beach, 11 A.M. is the crack of dawn." Also in Palm Beach, "if someone calls and says, 'Darling, come over for dinner, we're having a few people,' she means a black tie party with its own rock group to entertain."[29]

Charlotte was well aware that the manners and breeding of her subjects frequently prohibited them from giving her a piece of their minds. Once a reporter asked her if she ever got "the back of the hand" from the people about whom she wrote. Charlotte looked the reporter directly in the eye. "The people I write about have the best manners in the world," she said.[30]

~

Charlotte's fame as a society writer led to more freelance writing—
she contributed society stories to such publications as *Harper's Bazaar*,
Gentleman's Quarterly, *McCall's*, and *Town and Country*, and she
wrote political commentary occasionally for *Rolling Stone* and the
Times's opinion pages. Letters she wrote to her mother show a tremendous concern with politics on the national and local levels and
centered particularly on Ohio. Her letters also reveal an extreme liberalism and deepening concern with civil rights and problems of the
poor. She noted, for instance, that she could not vote for Robert
Kennedy, presumably because he was not sufficiently opposed to the
war in Vietnam, and even left-wing candidate Eugene McCarthy
ignored some of her pet causes. Nor were front-runners Hubert
Humphrey and Richard Nixon acceptable, she told Lucile: "We're
all violently against Bobby [Kennedy] here, but McCarthy probably
doesn't even have a chance. I'm not even sure I could stand to vote
for him—peace or no peace. He hasn't said a single word about civil
rights or the urban plight, and frankly he's turning out to be dull,
unimaginative, etc."[31]

If her politics were liberal, Charlotte remained conservative in the
social sense. She purchased her first miniskirt in early 1968, long after
they became a fashion staple. In a letter to her mother she described
her ambivalent feelings about her daring fashion move: "I look about
39 trying to be 5½ years old [wearing it] but I love it madly at $26."[32]
Many of the fashions that arose from the women's movement alienated Charlotte and violated her taste for classic, timeless clothes. The
apparel of the so-called feminists—miniskirts, tight, brightly colored
sweaters, bell-bottomed trousers, and lack of bras—further alienated
her from the movement.

By the early 1970s, her writing was evolving into a combination of
social and political commentary. She enjoyed political reporting the
most, and, fortuitously, the opportunity to do more of it soon arose.
The result was one of Charlotte's most famous stories—and one that
caused her to do a great deal of soul-searching.

8

Panther Tales

WHEN CHARLOTTE COVERED composer Leonard Bernstein's fund-raiser for the Black Panther Party, she never imagined the stir the story would cause.[1] Nor could she have predicted the moral dilemma the episode would present for her. After all, by the time Leonard and Felicia Bernstein hosted the cocktail party in their Park Avenue penthouse on January 14, 1970, Charlotte had been writing about the New York social scene in her frank and often cutting way for eight years. She had suffered no dire consequences short of a few critical memorandums from A. M. Rosenthal, who by this time was managing editor.

The Bernstein fund-raiser endures as part of popular culture in the 1960s and 1970s in part because Charlotte's story reached the country on *Times* news wires. More important, however, Charlotte's story spurred Tom Wolfe's satirical treatment of the event in *Radical Chic and Mau-Mauing the Flak Catchers*, which first used the term "radical chic" to describe how upper-class and often naïve New Yorkers championed the causes of disadvantaged blacks and other minorities, often with hilarious results.[2] Charlotte's story painted a detailed picture of the scene, describing Bernstein and his well-heeled friends munching Roquefort cheese balls and sipping white wine while calmly discussing the overthrow of the U.S. government with a group of black radicals.

The Bernstein story illustrates an important part of Charlotte's nature. She refused to compromise her principles about what constituted news, even though her personal views often conflicted with these professional standards. Charlotte was adamant that news get distributed somehow, even if it was not printed in the *Times* and even if it put her in a precarious position personally.

Her rigid loyalties and principles would cause a conflict for her when the women on the *Times* filed a sex discrimination lawsuit against the paper in 1974. Charlotte was a top editor by that time and felt she could not join the suit. Her failure to participate enraged some of the women at the paper—some of whom were still angry decades later.

~

Charlotte decided to cover the Black Panther fund-raiser because she saw it as yet another ritual of the rich and famous but with an added dimension. It let her view firsthand the mingling of two unlikely groups: the wealthy celebrities who were friends of the Bernsteins and members of the Black Panthers, a militant group of young blacks that formed in the mid-1960s, ostensibly to announce to the world that the status quo regarding race relations, class, and economics was no longer acceptable. Although the Panthers' language was rough and their actions were sometimes violent, some upper- and middle-class whites were impressed by their audacity and their attempts to shake the country out of its complacency.[3] Bernstein and about ninety of his wealthy friends wanted to support some of the Panthers' projects and to raise money for their legal defense fund. The headline for Charlotte's story the next day, "Black Panther Philosophy Is Debated at the Bernsteins," was typically understated, and it seems innocent enough. The story was not.

As Charlotte described the meeting of the two groups, it is difficult to determine who is more ridiculous—Bernstein, in his black turtleneck and black pants, mimicking the dress of the Panthers, Panther field marshal Donald Cox, or the eclectic group of socialites and celebrities who attended the event. Characteristically, Charlotte sat quietly in a corner at the Bernstein penthouse, taking copious notes and remaining silent while the well-dressed guests mingled and quietly chatted. In the story, she wasted no time describing the self-important Bernstein and Cox: "The conductor laureate of the New York Philharmonic did most of the questioning. Donald Cox . . . did most of the answering, and there were even moments when both men were not talking at the same time."

Charlotte captured the most revealing moment of the event when Cox calmly explained that the overthrow of the U.S. economic and class system might be necessary, perhaps using violence, and Bernstein coolly agreed. "'If business won't give us full employment,' he [Cox] said slowly, 'then we must take the means of production and put them in the hands of the people.' 'I dig absolutely,' Mr. Bernstein said."

Bernstein's guests fared no better. Charlotte revealed their hypocrisy by repeating snippets of their conversation with the Panthers and describing their expensive clothing. They enthusiastically agreed that a revamping of the nation's economic and class system was needed and then returned by limousine to their lavish homes.

The Panthers did not escape Charlotte's knife either. They were romanticized in the eyes of the partygoers, but Charlotte let the reader know of their naïveté and of the gulf that separated them from the Bernstein guests:

> Upon meeting Miss Cynthia Phipps, whom he had no way of knowing is a member of the country's wealthier aristocratic families, Henry Miller, a Harlem Panther defense captain, smiled and put out his hand.
> "I hope we can do something to help," Miss Phipps said.
> "What do you do?" Mr. Mitchell replied.

"I work at the Metropolitan Museum," she answered, going on to discuss last year's "Harlem on my Mind" exhibition, which drew the wrath of black and white liberals alike.

Mr. Mitchell listened. Miss Phipps then tentatively raised the subject of Nigeria, which Mr. Mitchell said he really didn't know too much about. She asked if he thought there are any good capitalists and Mr. Mitchell said he didn't think so.

To Phipps, the strain between the races hit close to home only because it became an issue in the art world. Mitchell, meanwhile, displayed his ignorance of current events. Both unceremoniously dismissed all "capitalists" in a few curt sentences.

Charlotte reserved her final dig for the end of the story, when she offered a quick review of the monetary pledges. To one guest, "justice" boiled down to a few well-placed dollars: "'I grew up in France during the rise of Nazism,' said Mrs. August Heckscher, wife of the city's Administrator of Parks, Recreation and Cultural Affairs. 'And I think the one thing we must always support is justice.' She pledged $100."

The *Times* did not take the party at the Bernstein home lightly. Its news wires distributed the story nationwide, and its editors printed an editorial denouncing the event after Charlotte's story appeared. The editorial stated in an obvious way what she conveyed through irony: that the fund-raiser was an insult to both the Panthers and the party guests and that it had serious political overtones. "Emergence of the Black Panthers as the romanticized darlings of the politico-cultural jet set is an affront to the majority of black Americans," the editorial began. "The group therapy plus fund-raising soiree at the home of Leonard Bernstein . . . represents the sort of elegant slumming that degrades patrons and patronized alike." The editorial went on to say that the superficiality of the party undercut the actions and beliefs of Martin Luther King, Jr.[4]

The reaction to Charlotte's story was swift and strong, and the Bernsteins were devastated, particularly considering that the first-edition version of the story was benign and even helpful to the Panther cause. "Mrs. Leonard Bernstein, who has raised money for such diverse causes as indigent Chileans [and] the New York Philharmonic Church World Service . . . was into what she herself admitted yesterday was a whole new thing. She gave a cocktail party for the Black Panthers. 'Not a frivolous party,' she explained before the 30 guests arrived." Clearly this version of the story, which hit the streets at about 10:30 at night, was written before the party began.[5]

This second story was mortifying to the Bernsteins, who began to believe that the *Times* was purposely trying to make them look foolish. And this was the version that was distributed over the *Times* news service and published in newspapers all over the world to, as Wolfe noted, "an international chorus of horse laughs or nausea."[6] As a result of its widespread play, the story launched a chain reaction of events that destroyed the Bernsteins' efforts to help the Panthers and ended with Leonard Bernstein himself criticizing the group. The *Times* ran several letters to the editor condemning the Bernsteins and their friends, and columnists across the country labeled the Bernsteins hypocritical and naïve liberals who trivialized race relations. The Bernsteins also were accused of fueling a growing bitterness in the United States between Jews and blacks, and they began getting hate mail.[7] In Miami, Jewish picketers demanded that a movie theater withdraw a film of Bernstein conducting the Israel Philharmonic in celebration of Israel's victory in the Six-Day War.[8]

Bernstein was hounded by the story all over the globe; United Press International reported that in London several weeks after the event, Bernstein called the Panthers a "bad lot" who "behaved badly" and "laid their own graves." He later said he was misquoted.[9] The Bernsteins tried to quell the fury but to little avail. Felicia Bernstein wrote a letter to the editor, published nearly a week after the party, that pointed out the serious purpose of the event and noted that "the frivolous way in which it was reported . . . is unworthy of the *Times*."[10] And she talked to Charlotte, who agreed that the characterization of the party as "elegant slumming" was unfair but said she stood by the original story.[11]

The furor created by the story, however, had an unsettling effect on the usually unflappable Charlotte. In letters to her mother and in a follow-up story, she indicated she had nothing but sympathy for the Black Panthers and considered them a well-intentioned group in need of help. Indeed, Charlotte and Joan Whitman had once donated office equipment to the Panthers so the group could publicize its accomplishments.[12] In a letter, Charlotte told her mother she regretted the negative publicity the Bernstein story generated and was frustrated by the newspaper's handling of the event: "There is a strong [negative] feeling about the Panthers among our management and they are not getting a fair break on our news pages. But you win some, you lose some and I did get a little story in Saturday's paper which you'll see eventually."[13]

Charlotte referred to her story published nine days after the initial story. This latest story could be considered an apology for the first. It stated that many New Yorkers were having gatherings like the Bernsteins' and that such parties were not unusual. The story recounted the plight of Panther wife Lee Berry, who talked about how her husband, a Vietnam veteran and an epileptic, was mistreated after being arrested.[14] This follow-up story was written in a straight news style, with none of the asides and detailed descriptions of the Bernstein story.

Charlotte's personal views here clashed with her professional standards of news. The gathering at the Bernsteins', with its posturing by both sides, was news by her definition, and she wrote about it without thinking that the story might be viewed as ridiculing a group with which she sympathized. It was this strong journalistic moral sense that prompted Harrison Salisbury to label her a "strict moralist" — one who never compromised her ethics. Her husband, William Hunt, said Charlotte's sense of ethics was rigid: "If something violated her principles, that was it. It didn't matter how expensive it was in terms of convenience or even friendships."[15] Hunt believed Charlotte's single-mindedness and morality could cost her the friendship of those who sometimes thought she could compromise them under certain circumstances, and those strict views did indeed cost her the respect of some women on and off the *Times*. Charlotte was sympathetic with proponents of the growing civil rights and student movements of the 1960s and 1970s, but her views of the newly forming feminist movement were another matter. She was ambivalent, perhaps even apathetic, about the newly formed "women's liberation" movement, although as women's page editor of one of the largest and most influential newspapers in the world, it was difficult for her to avoid the issue. It was a news event, and the paper had to deal with its ramifications in changing language, society, and the work force.

The feminism of the 1960s was controversial in itself. In the beginning, radical feminists, who were primarily college-educated white women, engaged in fiery rhetoric and staged showy events such as boycotting the Miss America pageant. In one particularly ostentatious action, one hundred women stormed the offices of *Ladies Home Journal* editor John Mack Carter, occupying his office for eleven hours to protest what they considered the sexist content of his magazine.[16]

But that was the radical wing of feminism. The movement gathered steam when middle-aged and older women attempted to obtain economic and social equality with men. In 1966, Betty Friedan founded the National Organization for Women (NOW), a group that focused on more practical concerns such as establishing day care centers for working mothers. Its membership included politically and socially moderate women across the country.

Still, the movement remained a battleground, and its participants were not simply divided over the best way to achieve its goals—frequently, they could not even identify those goals. Certainly the women's section of the *New York Times* would take criticism from some quarters no matter what it published. But Charlotte's ambivalence had its ironic elements. For instance, women active in the early feminist movement frequently compared their plight to that of blacks before the civil rights movement and promoted the image of "woman as Negro." (For women, the term "Aunt Tabby" became the counterpart of Uncle Tom.) Charlotte may not have accepted the parallels of the two social movements.[17] Hunt said Charlotte took the civil rights movement much more seriously than the feminist movement, and her feelings about racial inequality were strong and unequivocal.[18]

Charlotte successfully avoided some of the issues relating to feminism because she was often out of the office covering stories. Joan Whitman, who took over the newsroom while Charlotte was away, remembers that Charlotte did not necessarily oppose the goals and views of feminism; she simply had little interest in them: "She was not involved in the women's movement. It just was not something that interested her. She didn't say, 'We should be doing a story on this or that [regarding feminism].'"[19]

When Charlotte's pages dealt with women's liberation, they often treated it in a historical context. On August 27, 1970, the *Times* published several stories about women's rights in response to a celebration in New York of the fiftieth anniversary of women's suffrage. Coverage included front-page play of a March for Equality in Manhattan, a profile of author Kate Millett, an editorial, and, in the women' section, a lengthy story gleaned from interviews of fifty prominent women.[20] Several days later, a story that took up nearly three-fourths of a newspaper page appeared in the women's section outlining in detail the plight for women's rights by the nation's early feminists and their fight for the vote.[21] It was no accident that this story about the early suffragists appeared in the women's section of the *Times* considering that Lucile Curtis played such an active role in the suffrage movement in Ohio. To Charlotte, the contemporary brand of feminism was simply an extension of the suffrage movement. In response to a memo from Rosenthal seeking ideas for in-depth stories, Charlotte mentioned the parallels between the feminist movement and the first "women's liberation" movement: "[It is] an outgrowth of the old feminism with the daughters and granddaughters of the Suffragettes arguing over the goal priorities and how to achieve them and at the same time engaging themselves in everything from street theater and radical rhetoric to serious study," she wrote.[22]

In 1912, Lucile Curtis was one of five thousand women who

marched through Columbus to promote amending the Constitution to give women the vote. Nearly sixty years after the march, Lucile's daughter was in the forefront of a battle for women's rights. But she was a reluctant participant.

~

Charlotte knew she walked a fine line as women's page editor in the volatile 1970s. In interviews, she was cautious when explaining her opinions of feminism, but of course she did not have to be diplomatic in personal communications. In a letter to Hunt, she hinted at the frustration she felt as the *Times* tried to cover feminism and grapple with "correct" terms and labels. To some feminists, the *Times*'s "Family, Food, Fashion and Furnishings" section was too middle-of-the-road in its efforts to avoid controversy: "And the Women's Liberation, which is to say the very feminist (I'm still not sure that's right) younger generation, are up in arms over my women's pages. They're calling us Aunt Tabbies, which apparently is women's lip (I didn't misspell that) for Uncle Tom."[23]

Years later, when she was op-ed editor, Charlotte said she was in a no-win situation as women's page editor in the late 1960s. Some readers wanted a conventional women's section devoted to practical items of interest to women, while others felt that such a section ghettoized and trivialized news of interest to women. They believed that women's sections consigned serious issues such as rape, equal pay lawsuits, and single-parent families to the back pages. "If we ran feminist stories on that page, people would say, 'But you're segregating them by putting them on that page. They belong out in the news,'" she said. "If we didn't run them, and said they should go out in the news section, they'd say, 'You're against us because there should be a page devoted exclusively to feminist problems.'"[24]

Diplomatic when publicly discussing her views, Charlotte in her stories could not resist pointing out that women's attempts for equality could sometimes be ridiculous. She did this in her usual way by letting her subjects' actions and words speak for themselves. As she was quick to point out throughout her career as a society writer, the wealthy found many reasons to hold parties. Usually they were held under the guise of raising money for a cause, and such gatherings, where people wanted to see and be seen, did indeed raise money. But the costs of those parties in clothes, jewelry, food, and extra employees often exceeded the money raised.

Charlotte covered a women's liberation fund-raiser held in August 1970 to honor the fiftieth anniversary of women's suffrage. Admission to the event, which was held on the grounds of a mansion in the Hamptons, was a minimum $25 donation to the cause. The resulting story was déjà vu for readers familiar with Charlotte's account of the Bernstein fund-raiser just seven months earlier.

As was her style, Charlotte got to the point immediately, hinting that the fund-raiser was not exactly flawless: "Everything in the women's liberation party had gone pretty much according to plan. Then Representative Patsy Mink, Democrat of Hawaii, disappeared when she was supposed to speak, and a woman shed her blue jeans and dived into the swimming pool. After that, things were never quite the same." The theme of participants' attire, a common one in conventional society articles, takes a new twist here. In their attempts to ignore clothes and the trappings of glamour, participants unwittingly called attention to them, as Charlotte shows in her description of author and NOW founder Betty Friedan's eye-catching neckline: "She is serious about issues such as abortion on demand, child care centers and equal pay for women. Yet it was her attire, a long red baby dress with teeny white polka dots, puffed sleeves and deep, deep décolletage, that caused comment. 'You've liberated your dress,' said Mrs. (Richard) Coulson, author of How Could She Do That, a crime book. 'You really are liberated.'" Charlotte did not let up, describing Friedan's struggle with her clothing: "'They [women] must be liberated from menial housework,' she cried, hitching up her plunging décolletage.'"[25] The long-term goals of the feminist movement evidently were not as pressing to Friedan as the short-term goal of keeping her dress up.

Charlotte let the reader know that clothes were indeed the focus of much discussion and attention at this party and still were social statements. The women judged each other, for instance, by whether they wore bras, and participants seemed compelled to talk about what they wore and why. Charlotte noted that the aforementioned Mrs. Coulson and her "sisters" in the movement went braless and were, in Charlotte's words, "fashionably liberated." "I chucked bras six months ago," Coulson is quoted as saying. The chaos continued until, in the middle of a speech, a woman reporter stripped, dove into the pool, and began swimming laps.

As in the Bernstein and other stories about fund-raising, a guest is willing to reduce the proceedings to dollars and cents. This time, a donor refers to his $50 donation after learning that the hosts' mansion is closed to partygoers. "'I paid $25 for liberation and $25 to see the Sculls' house,' said Dr. Robert Gould, a psychiatrist, 'and the house is locked up.'" Evidently liberation and a glimpse of this house were of equal importance to Gould—and both had a price tag.

If her coverage of the fund-raiser left any doubts about her views, Charlotte spelled them out in a radio commentary on WQXR. She said the purpose of the gathering in the Hamptons—to raise money —was overshadowed by the chaos. "Many of the women who gathered there are serious about child care centers, equal employment and abortion," she said. "Yet their voices were lost amid the tinkle of cocktail glasses, the spectacle of a woman ditching her blue jeans and diving into the swimming pool." She ended the broadcast with her major point: "Perhaps what I'm saying on this anniversary of woman's suffrage is that if women want to be taken as seriously as they deserve, they will have to get their message across not just loud and clear but logically and simply. Otherwise, nobody's really going to understand how important this movement is." In other words, the attention-getting activities of radicals often obscured the point of the cause.[26]

To Charlotte, radio was a more personal medium than newspapers —though her personality came through in her writing, listeners to her taped radio broadcasts grew to know her more intimately because of the nature of the broadcast medium. But the print medium allowed her to hide behind her words, and its nature emboldened her. Throughout her life, she loathed personal confrontations and arguments and usually managed to avoid them. Occasionally, however, she could not avoid debate with those who disagreed with her conservative views about feminism. In a speech at Harvard University to the Friends of the Schlesinger Library, she drew the ire of some audience members by declaring that it was the poor in the United States—and not women or minorities—who were the most worthy of publicity and public support. Charlotte went on to say that employment discrimination lawsuits filed by women often assumed that women were members of an underclass, which they were not.[27] Charlotte disdained the view of women as victims or members of an underprivileged class, and this view indirectly alienated her from some leaders of the feminist movement. And her disparaging comment about discrimination lawsuits would soon hit close to home.

The social movements of the 1960s and 1970s taught news executives around the country that names and titles often spoke volumes. The women's movement in particular brought about changes in language and attitudes, and *Times* editors found these changes difficult to ignore. By the early 1970s, editors were talking about what to call the women's pages—by this point, "food, fashion, family, furnishings" seemed outdated and alienated some readers. In 1971, assistant managing editor Seymour Topping wrote a memo asking Charlotte and Rosenthal what the *Times* should call the section in the front-page index of the newspaper, noting that "women's news" was unsatisfactory. "What is known as the Women's Page is read by readers of both sexes and covers a variety of subjects broader than the present description suggests. Secondly, an increasing number of our women readers are becoming alienated by the use of the term Women's News."[28]

Nine months later, on September 17, 1971, the *Times* made a change that was hardly revolutionary but that showed the editors were willing to act. On its tiny page 1 index, the *Times* officially changed "women's news" to "family/style." On the page itself, the logo changed from "Food, Fashion, Family, Furnishings" to "Family, Food, Fashions, Furnishings," apparently hinting that the emphasis on food was patronizing to women. What seems innocent today was dramatic for the staid, unchanging *Times* of 1971, and Charlotte received several congratulatory letters and memos about them. It was not until 1986 that the *Times* started using "Ms." as part of its editorial style, although editors began discussing its use in the early 1970s. A decade after its entry into the *Times*, Punch Sulzberger joked about its long-awaited debut: "We were dragged kicking and screaming into Ms.," he said.[29]

Rosenthal and some other editors strongly opposed the use of "Ms." in the pages of the *Times*. To some women, however, the unwillingness to incorporate the abbreviation was symbolic of bigger problems on the paper. "That unwillingness bespoke other, more complex rigidities," journalist Kay Mills wrote. "The men at the top at the *Times* simply could not envision women in many of the key jobs, and, worse, didn't recognize their own blindness."[30] To some reporters, the use of "Ms." was simply a practical issue, as Sulzberger noted. They were forced to ask the marital status of the women they interviewed: "All the reporters hated it [use of "Miss" and "Mrs."]," Sulzberger said. "They hated to call people up and ask if they were married."[31]

Charlotte was among those who initially opposed the use of "Ms." She told Hunt in a letter that "Ms." had a negative connotation and therefore had no place in the paper. Further, she thought it would be difficult to use it in stories uniformly:

> This afternoon, the managing editor is going to have a meeting to take up the matter of Ms., pronounced miz, the new title for ladies. The liberated ones want to be called Ms. I don't. I like being Miss. When we did a story about Betty Friedan, the feminist, we called her Ms. and her mother, who appeared in the same story, we called Mrs., because she doesn't want to be Ms. either.
> It's going to be like blacks. In the transition days of black libera-

tion, there were blacks, Negroes, and colored people. There still are. It will probably be the same with women. Women will aggressively want to be Ms. Some will equally aggressively insist on Miss or Mrs. Anything that's pronounced miz sounds like poor blacks in the South, and that's very distasteful to me.[32]

Her phraseology, "the liberated ones want to be called Ms." and her use of the verboten word "ladies" show her alienation from those labeling themselves "feminists."

Fourteen years after this 1972 meeting about the use of "Ms," the *Times* finally adopted the term. Gloria Steinem, who for years hounded her friend Rosenthal to incorporate its use, remembered well June 20, 1986, the first day it was permitted in the *Times* as a courtesy title. The previous day, Rosenthal mailed her a copy of his memo to staffers approving its use, which she framed. It read:

> The following will appear in the paper tomorrow: Beginning today, the *New York Times* will use Ms. as an honorific in its news and editorial columns. Ms. has not been used because of belief it had not passed sufficiently into the language to be accepted. The *Times* believes now Ms. has become a part of the language and is changing its policy. The Times will continue to use Miss or Mrs. when it knows the marital status of a woman in the news unless she prefers Ms. Ms. will also be used when a women's marital status is not known or when a married woman wishes to use her maiden name professionally or in private life.[33]

Steinem was amused by the sentence stating that "Ms." had not been used earlier because it was not sufficiently accepted in the language. "They'll never admit they're wrong," she said.[34]

The first day "Ms." appeared, Steinem and several other women went to the *Times* building to present Rosenthal with a bouquet of flowers in appreciation. His reaction was telling, she said: "We took him flowers, and he said, which made me want to kill him, 'I've had so many women come and want to say thank you to me that if I'd known it meant so much to you, I would have done it sooner.'"[35]

The personal friendship between Steinem and Rosenthal, a man who has been perceived by some women on the *Times* as sexist, might seem like a strange one. But both had a love of India and professional and personal ties there, and this interest brought them together and was the basis of their friendship. Steinem believed that Rosenthal's strong feelings over the years against the use of "Ms." were not necessarily based on sexism but on his passionate, almost obsessive, love of the *Times*, the only paper on which he had ever worked. "I'd write him a letter of some kind of what I'd hope was constructive criticism, whether it was about the use of Ms., coverage of abortion, or whatever," she said. "And I'd get back this three- or four-page, single-spaced letter of defensiveness. I remember writing Abe, 'We criticize the *Times* because we hold it to a high standard and because we love it. Don't be so defensive.'"[36]

While grappling with the use of "Ms." in the paper, top *Times* officials became engaged in a bigger and more costly fight by the mid-1970s. During this time, surveys indicated that women in the work force were underpaid compared to their male counterparts, and women were filing lawsuits seeking equal pay and equal treatment. Media organizations seemed particularly susceptible to these lawsuits, and organizations such as *Newsweek, Newsday, Readers Digest,* and the Associated Press were targets of complaints or lawsuits. Women at the *Times,* too, met frequently to discuss what they felt was discrimination, and in 1974 they filed a class-action sex discrimination lawsuit against the newspaper. Decades after its 1978 settlement out of court, it still evoked strong emotion from both sides.[37] Charlotte's role in the lawsuit—or lack thereof—in some ways illustrates the "strict morality" that Salisbury and Hunt talked about.[38] Hunt said Charlotte would not violate her principles even if it meant sacrificing personal friendships. In the case of the women's lawsuit, she made those sacrifices—perhaps unwittingly.

The suit was spawned after art writer Grace Glueck wrote a letter to Sulzberger in 1970 asking him why only men at the newspaper had been promoted to top editorial positions. Sulzberger, who seemed taken aback, wrote Glueck to say he would consult "key manage-ment executives" about the issue.[39] Evidently, Sulzberger never had those consultations, but the letter prompted other women to look at payroll and personnel records.[40] They found that women earned an average of $59 a week less than men and that key women on the newspaper—such as economics reporter Eileen Shanahan and health writer Jane Brody—earned less money than men with less seniority and visibility. Further, in 1970 and 1971, only 7 percent of the reporters and editors hired were women.[41] Many women on the newspaper saw irony in the situation: the *Times*, which often took a liberal editorial stance, had over the years been a strong proponent of civil rights and frequently editorialized in favor of equal rights for minorities.

After four years of discussion and negotiation, seven women—including four editorial employees—filed a class-action suit under the name of Betsy Wade Boylan, who was then a copy editor on the newspaper. Members of the initial group, known as the "women's caucus," knew they were putting their jobs on the line by placing themselves in an adversarial position with people with whom they worked forty hours a week. Talking about filing the suit and taking action to do it were two different things, but they took the plunge, and the litigation occupied a large portion of their lives. By 1977, a U.S. District Court judge ruled that all 550 women employees at the *Times* could be represented in *Boylan* vs. *the New York Times*. Absent from the plaintiff list, however, were the two most visible women on the *Times*: Pulitzer Prize–winning architecture critic Ada Louise Huxtable and Charlotte.

Nan Robertson remembers how disappointed and angry caucus members were at Huxtable and Charlotte. They felt that as two of the most powerful women on the newspaper, they could have lent clout to the suit. Charlotte, however, seemed to bear the brunt of the anger. And some women who participated in it, like Wade, would never for-give her.[42]

As Robertson pointed out, Huxtable and Charlotte were similar in some ways. Both were opinionated, competitive, and ambitious in temperament and tiny, well-coifed, and dainty in appearance. But Huxtable, who joined the *Times* at age forty-two, was not "married" to the newspaper as Charlotte was. Although Huxtable worked hard and was tremendously successful, she considered herself an outsider to the politics of the paper and never aimed for a top editorship.[43] That was not the case with Charlotte, whose prim demeanor and self-deprecating manner could be deceiving. Her co-workers knew that the little endearments she tacked on to the names of both male and female friends (co-workers Roger Wilkins and David Schneiderman were typically, "Rogey-poo" and "Davey Dearest") and her insistence that she was "just a little girl from Ohio" were smoke screens for a steely determination and toughness.[44] Charlotte may have had a self-deprecating sense of humor and an easygoing manner with her friends, but her job and her career were the top priorities in her life.

The leaders of the women's caucus considered Huxtable an outsider, Robertson said, but they did not forgive Charlotte for not participating in the lawsuit.[45] Twenty years later, Wade called Charlotte a "quisling," which she defined as a label for a Hitler collaborator meaning a "sell-out," "a rotten bastard," and "[one who] usually gets shot." Wade recalled an incident when Charlotte was scheduled to appear on a local late-night talk show to discuss the case. It enraged Wade that Charlotte would speak about the lawsuit because she had taken no role in it. Wade remembers sitting at her desk when Charlotte approached her to tell her of her appearance on the show. Charlotte said she could help the women because of her position on the paper. Wade was enraged: "I said 'You will not speak for the women's caucus. You will not speak for the women's caucus now or ever. You are not part of the women's caucus. . . . You could have given us money. We use money. We need money. . . . It's an insult to all of the women of the *New York Times.*' I was really screeching. And the word 'fuck' was not used in those days but I was giving it to her in just every way I knew how." Wade told Charlotte that if she spoke on the show, Wade would call in and tell the audience that Charlotte had never offered financial or moral support to the women. "I said, 'I will cook your goose because you are a hypocrite.' And she said, 'I guess you win,' or words to that effect. I was horrified."[46]

Robertson is more sympathetic to Charlotte than Wade is and believes that Charlotte honestly felt she could help the caucus from within by using her influence with top *Times* executives to help them understand the plight of the women and make them understand they were underpaid. But the women did not trust her sincerity, and they believed Charlotte's allegiances were first to herself and second to the men who promoted her. They felt that the women's caucus ran a distant third in her heart.[47]

The women's lawsuit eventually was settled out of court. The newspaper was never found guilty of sex discrimination, but it agreed to place women in one in four of the top news and editorial jobs by the end of 1982 and to provide $233,500 in back pay for the 550 plaintiffs. Still, there was little question that the lawsuit had forced both sides to play out a dirty game of accusations and countercharges. Each plaintiff had to spell out in detail her specific grievances and describe her criticisms of the company; the company had to detail why it felt each of the plaintiffs was treated fairly, based on her job performance.[48]

Charlotte's close friends and Hunt remember her role in the women's caucus far differently than Wade. Many of them—including former managing editor Clifton Daniel, Rosenthal, and Sulzberger—say she could not have taken part in the lawsuit because, as women's editor and later op-ed editor, she was part of the management group that was the target of the suit. Hunt was angered by the idea that Charlotte might have participated in the lawsuit. "She did what she could behind the scenes," he said, adding that she was a strong supporter of labor unions and had been active in the Newspaper Guild when she worked in Columbus. "She talked to Punch [Sulzberger] and did what she could, but would not sign off with the group because she was management."[49]

Twenty years after the suit was filed, Sulzberger did not remember if he had any specific conversations with Charlotte about the issue, but "she must have worked behind the scenes, knowing Charlotte." He also said Charlotte was in a no-win situation: she sympathized with the women but was a part of *Times* management. "I suppose there was resentment [toward her]. But anyone who thought about it for thirty seconds would have known she was in an impossible situation."[50]

Rosenthal, whose actions and attitudes about women were targeted by some members of the caucus, thought the plaintiffs "had some justification." He said: "In the newspaper business generally and probably everywhere there was certainly not enough attention paid to women. When I became editor, there were practically no women on the staff. Of course, as I feel I promoted a lot of them and brought them on the paper, I was not happy being the target." Rosenthal agreed that Charlotte could not have joined the suit as a news executive. But he also believed—and Charlotte's public comments back this up—that Charlotte never thought she was discriminated against in the work force.[51] She had said in some magazine profiles that she had been fortunate in her career never personally to have experienced discrimination.[52] Of course, whether Charlotte was a member of management at the paper may be a moot point; executives usually do not participate in employee strikes, but any person can file a lawsuit against another person or organization. The women's caucus believed that Charlotte's managerial status had no effect on her failure to be a plaintiff in the class-action suit.

Wade, Shanahan, Glueck, and the other principals of the lawsuit were not about to forget their legal battle with *Times* management. In 1988, they held a tenth-year reunion of the lawsuit's settlement that featured nineteen speakers—many of them women on the *Times* who had been hired after the suit was filed. Members of the original women's caucus wanted to keep its memory alive for fear younger women would be unaware of this history of the women on the paper.

Throughout her career, Charlotte displayed the rigid loyalties and principles Hunt and Salisbury described, so it is likely she felt she could not join the women's caucus. But the reasons why she left her name off the plaintiff list might be more complicated. Perhaps her personal friendships with people like Sulzberger and Daniel prevented her from taking an adversarial role against them. While Charlotte had a strict sense of fairness, she also had a strong sense of loyalty to her friends. But she had to suspect that active participation in the lawsuit could hurt her own career. She tried, unsuccessfully, to have it both ways: she could not help the women in a discreet, underground way; she had to be open with her support or risk being considered a traitor. Gloria Steinem, who knew Charlotte but was not a close friend, speculated that her refusal to join the caucus may have been a symptom of ambivalence about the women's movement overall and a sign of her insecurity as a woman in a man's world. Steinem said insecurity may have led Charlotte to support the civil rights movement vocally throughout her life but to remain silent about women's rights. "She didn't like herself enough to unite [with other women] on issues of gender," Steinem said.[53] Steinem has written essays stating that sometimes women, who are raised in a male-dominated society, support only "masculine" rebellions such as civil rights or antiwar efforts because they believe a male focus gives legitimacy to a movement. Some women do not consider themselves part of the "oppressed" minority they believe feminism represents so they shun it.[54] And Charlotte's comments that women who file sexual discrimination lawsuits may be placing themselves in underclass roles may give credence Steinem's views.

It will never be known if *Times* executives would have punished Charlotte for participating in the lawsuit. While the women were in court, however, Charlotte was further consolidating her power at the paper by aligning with one of the few women at the *Times* with influence: Iphigene Sulzberger, the publisher's mother. Charlotte had met Iphigene when she was a society reporter and found she had much in common with this freethinker. Iphigene had always been a progressive politically, and she kept active until her death in 1990 at age ninety-seven. Charlotte genuinely enjoyed Iphigene's company, and the two had in common a privileged and genteel upbringing, liberal political views, and, of course, a passionate love for the *New*

York Times. Still, despite her role as the grande dame of the paper, Iphigene did not get special treatment from Charlotte when it came to the content of the women's pages. In late 1969, Charlotte ran a series of fashion articles about furs. The series drew criticism from Iphigene, a conservationist who believed women had no right to wear animal skins and the paper had no business writing about those who did.

In a courteous letter to Charlotte, Iphigene explained her point of view, saying she "had no luck in persuading the Advertising Department of the *Times* to refuse to carry ads of garments made of skins of endangered species. The only way we can persuade women and men not to bedeck themselves in the skins . . . is by making them feel they are not fashionable." The usually demure Mrs. Sulzberger had strong feelings about the subject: "My reaction to a woman in a leopard skin coat is that I wish I had a gun to shoot her."[55]

Charlotte, also a conservationist, held her ground, defending the series and holding to her definition of news. She wrote Mrs. Sulzberger that as long as women wore furs, furs were a topic that should be covered: "Inevitably some of the developments in fur fashions, like developments in the political scene, are not very attractive or are even immoral . . . or tasteless. But the women's news pages report such developments because a responsible newspaper is expected to report such news, whether its staff approves of what's happening or not." Charlotte was careful, however, to thank Mrs. Sulzberger for her concern and her "consistent and constructive interest in the women's pages and for the friendship. I value your friendship very highly."[56] Charlotte did not bend her views or her ethics to conform to those who happened to be in power, and her treatment of Iphigene Sulzberger was no exception.

9

Changing Times

THE RELATIONSHIP BETWEEN Abe Rosenthal and Charlotte was a
curious one; professionally, they clashed during much of Charlotte's
career at the *Times*. Memos he sent to her indicate he was relentless
in his criticism of her pages, and their philosophy of what constituted
society coverage would always be at odds. But on a personal level,
Rosenthal and Charlotte tiptoed around each other. Although Rosenthal's memos could be cutting, and Charlotte held her ground in response, correspondence between the two was far from malicious or
bitter in tone. In fact, both relented even as they disagreed.

When Charlotte traveled to Columbus in July 1972 for breast cancer surgery, an upbeat telegram from Rosenthal greeted her shortly
after she arrived: "I think you ran away just because I was finally going
to win one argument. All us Panthers miss you. Love, Abe Rosenthal."[1]
Ten years later, Rosenthal had surgery in New York and received a
plant from Charlotte. A thank-you note from Rosenthal found in her
papers indicates he was genuinely pleased and grateful: "The plant
and I are looking at each other with pleasure. It's a lovely rich red. I
love the plant and your sending it, Charlotte."[2]

This sentimental aspect of Rosenthal, the hard-bitten and sometimes brutal newsman, is discussed by Nan Robertson, who related stories of his Jekyll-Hyde personality in her anthology about women and the *Times, The Girls in the Balcony*. Though Rosenthal was an outspoken and bitter opponent of the women's lawsuit against the newspaper and some of the women considered him sexist, she recounted how warm and helpful he was to her after her husband, Stan Levey, suffered a crippling heart attack while the two were vacationing in Istanbul. Robertson said that Rosenthal worked tirelessly to transport the two home and communicate with them. She remembered Rosenthal sobbing over the telephone after Robertson told him her husband had a relapse.[3] Nearly a decade after Charlotte's death, Rosenthal spoke warmly about her and said he respected her talent and drive.[4]

When Clifton Daniel was managing editor and Rosenthal his assistant, Charlotte received an occasional critical memo from the assistant managing editor. But by the early 1970s, after Rosenthal had served several years as managing editor, he became more than just a minor annoyance to her. He was not nearly as enamored with Charlotte's news judgment as was Daniel, and Charlotte knew the day would come when Rosenthal's disdain of her section would become a problem. In 1969, after Daniel was removed as managing editor, she spelled out her fears in a letter to her mother: "As of this weekend, Clifton Daniel is to be made an associate editor of the *Times*, an upgrading that actually is a downgrading. . . . He's actually being pushed upstairs and out of the way and those of us who adore him are sad. His replacement as managing editor is Abe Rosenthal, a rat whom my group hates. . . . My group includes Harrison Salisbury, [foreign editor] Sydney Gruson, [theater critic] Clive Barnes, [food writer] Craig Claiborne and [assistant managing editor] Emmanual Freedman."[5] Charlotte predicted in the letter that there would be a "repressive time artistically and journalistically" at the paper and "a reversion to some of the stodginess, lack of humor and whatnot that characterized the paper when I arrived here." She went on to call Daniel "en-

lightened," while "Rosenthal is not. . . . He's also a liar with little social conscience."

And Charlotte's view proved prescient. Rosenthal frequently criticized Charlotte's pages. Mainly, he opposed many of her efforts to
extend the subject matter of the pages beyond "service" or how-to articles, and he frequently asked Charlotte to copy the style of some
other publications, including the newly formed New York magazine,
which specialized in practical stories. He also frequently questioned
the taste and level of sophistication of the pages' content.

In a two-page memo, Rosenthal criticized one entire page as "a
pretty good example of a page I did not care for" and one that could
have had "a more immediate relationship with the reader." The
main story on this page was a lengthy piece by feature writer Lisa
Hammel about a group of Carmelite nuns who abandoned their
cloistered monastery to start a self-supporting craft-manufacturing
colony.[6] Rosenthal complained about the story's length and lack of
what he called a "service function": "A paradox arises from the fact
that the page is supposed to be geared to a service to the reader, and
such a length . . . makes the service function more difficult. The page
becomes predictable and it tends to weaken its more important aspect, its special character." But Rosenthal also slipped in compliments: "Despite the fact that the page is generally so excellent, there
seems be certain shibboleths that stick in the mind of critics," and
"the very fact that it is a page of special character demands more attention to be paid to maintain that character."[7]

In another memo, he asked Charlotte to look at the current issue
of New York, which ran a story about what to do with children over
Easter week: "I find this kind of service feature enormously interesting. . . . New York has the knack, which I devoutly hope we can develop, of figuring out what type of service material people are
genuinely interested in." He asked Charlotte to come up with a list
of ideas for service—the kind of stories she hated.[8]

Many of Rosenthal's memos focused on stories that he believed
were of questionable taste or ones that challenged his political or so-

cial views. In one, Charlotte had reporter Georgia Dullea interview blacks in Westchester County to see how they viewed their social lives in this suburban region that was 90 percent white. Some of the respondents were brutally frank, like the woman who said she was invited to parties because "they wanted to see if we knew how to use a fork or if we slurped our soup." Others said they were not invited to social events at all or were invited as tokens.[9] The negative picture drawn by those interviewed may have been reverse discrimination, Rosenthal thought. He wrote Charlotte that the story was an "Amos and Andy" piece in which the whites were the Amos and Andy: "They did everything that mean old white liberals always do. . . . They were insensitive, stupid, graspy. . . . Beyond that, there was a . . . lack of sophistication. The story goes beyond what the black couples think of their neighbors. The real story has to do with changing attitudes towards blacks of whites as well as the other way around." Again, he ended on a complimentary note: "I do not mean in any way to discourage this type of story. I think few papers in America do it as well as you do. . . . Carry on to even greater heights!"[10]

Rosenthal and others on the paper were not always so diplomatic when it came to violations of "taste" on the pages of the *Times*. Charlotte once wrote an account of a fund-raiser with a "great lovers" theme in which participants were asked to come dressed as one of history or literature's great lovers. A photo accompanying the story depicted a male partygoer straddling the back of a female partygoer. "Robert Sinn came as a cowboy and Mrs. Fern Tailer Denny was his horse," the caption read. "To show her strength, Mrs. Denny jumped up and down with him in the saddle."[11] Rosenthal, unamused by what he saw as the racy content of the photo, fired off a memo to photo editor John G. Morris, who in turn sent a memo to Curtis: "The Managing Editor has asked me formally to reprimand you for the caption under the society picture on page 46 of today's Late City Edition."[12]

Rosenthal was notorious for reading the *Times* cover-to-cover and word-for-word each day, and much of his criticism focused on seemingly minor details. But his views regarding Charlotte's pages were often echoed by other top news managers on the paper, most notably assistant managing editor Seymour Topping. In one story, an aging Russian princess discussed her book about etiquette "in this permissive age." Sex was a recurring theme in the book and the interview with Princess Beris Kandaouroff, whom reporter Judith Weinraub described as "a cross between Mae West and Emily Post." The princess pulled no punches in the interview, relating how her book discussed such topics as ways women could hide extramarital affairs and common foods that could be used as aphrodisiacs.[13] The views of the princess and the *Times*'s willingness to print them apparently shocked Topping, who wrote Charlotte that it "lowers the standard of sophistication of your page" and "the story reads as if we used the Princess as a framework for getting a number of cracks in the paper. . . . It is the sort of device commonly used by tabloids."[14]

Sometimes Rosenthal's memos were short but vitriolic: "Please pass on a sour word from me to whoever selected the picture of Mr. Valentino in Saturday's paper. It was a stroke of genius to select a picture about a hair stylist that concealed his own hair style."[15]

While Clifton Daniel considered national magazines the *Times*'s competition, Rosenthal was obsessed with what other daily newspapers were printing, worrying that it would be better and more stimulating than what ran in the *Times*. "Personally, I found the picture in the *Daily News* today on the Muskie wedding entrancing and I wish we had it," he wrote Charlotte. "I thought it was far better than the pictures we ran on the society page of the Toronto races."[16] Or, "Would you do me a favor and take a look at the *Washington Post* Style section for a few days? Is it any good? Is there anything they are doing that we ought to do?"[17]

The gulf between Charlotte and Rosenthal ran deeper than their disagreements over suitable content for her pages. The conservative Rosenthal and the liberal Charlotte were worlds apart politically. As she told her mother, Charlotte sympathized with the Columbia University students who staged a sit-in in 1968 in the university president's office to protest the Vietnam war. "The Columbia students continue to harass their administration and rightly," she wrote. "The children, universally decried as dirty, bearded and wearing beards . . . are really very nice looking and nicely spoken."[18]

Rosenthal was passionately opposed to the Columbia students and became so angry at the sight of the violence that he ran to the scene of the sit-in and wrote an emotional account of it, condemning the students.[19] According to his friend Gloria Steinem, student unrest at Columbia "was such a sore spot and a turning point for Abe. Mentioning those riots was like lighting a fire under a haystack with Abe."[20]

Rosenthal's deep preoccupation with the content of the *Times* came in part from his overall obsessiveness regarding the paper. But he had other reasons during the early 1970s to micromanage. At this time, American newspapers were in a near-crisis state and news managers nationwide realized that something had to change. By 1969, circulation was declining, advertising lineage was down, and papers were folding. Even the good gray *Times* couldn't seem to buck the trends.

The typographers' strike that crippled the New York newspapers early in the 1960s triggered a decline from which many papers never recovered. The *New York Herald Tribune* and the *World-Telegram & Sun*, considered by some two of the best papers in the country, folded. While circulation of morning papers increased slightly, evening and Sunday circulation dropped, leading to an overall decline in circulation.[21] Between 1969 and 1975, daily circulation of the *Times* dropped nearly 12 percent and advertising lineage shrunk by 21 percent.[22] During one month in 1971, daily circulation of the paper dropped from 845,000 to 814,000.[23]

Whether the problem was caused by a poor economy overall, the growing influence of television news and news magazines, poor newspaper management, or just an overall apathy on the part of readers, Sulzberger and Rosenthal knew things had to change. Although papers like the *Times* and the *Wall Street Journal* took pride in their consistent and unchanging format and quality, readers seemed to be getting bored. Rosenthal, in particular, had the feeling that top editors would have to begin watching the bottom line. Shortly after he was named assistant managing editor, Rosenthal remembered, Harrison Salisbury gave him a warning: "You're going to be the first managing editor of the New York Times who will have to worry about money."[24]

After two years as managing editor of the Times, Rosenthal began to let Charlotte know he wanted a change in the tone and theme of her pages to revert to the way the pages were in the early 1960s. He told her he wanted fewer of the "long, long stories," a somewhat light mix of "sociology," and a "lighter tone." And he suggested that Charlotte might be forcing her personal views of news on her staff: "It may also be, Charlotte, that your own disinclination and even distaste for fashion news has had an effect on your staff and they are not presenting the fashion news that they might be if you were really enthusiastic about the subject."[25]

Charlotte reacted by doing things as she always had done them. Some of their disagreements stemmed from the natural political factions that always exist in the workplace—but many ran deeper than that. Daniel, Salisbury, Charlotte, and some other top news managers became friends in part because of their liberal political views and their vision of the Times as a national newspaper. Rosenthal believed the paper should focus on issues of local interest. Because of Rosenthal's stature on the Times, it was clear that Charlotte could not ignore him. Yet Hunt maintained that her determination and steely will allowed her to work around him.[26] But Salisbury remembered that it was not easy to work with Rosenthal. Many years after he retired, he said that Rosenthal severely hampered Charlotte's career at the Times—so much so that near the end of her career, Salisbury routinely urged Charlotte to quit the paper and get a job on one of the New York–based fashion magazines. Her loyalty to the paper and her refusal to work at a publication that did not have the stature and reputation of the Times were too strong to allow her to leave, he said.[27]

Twenty-five years after he worked with Charlotte, however, Rosenthal remembered it differently, saying that he supported and admired her: "There were people at the *Times* who thought society should not get that kind of [heavy] emphasis and who felt it was a waste of space. I thought [Charlotte's section] was very revealing of life in New York. You can say the plain old society story . . . was a bigger waste of space because you didn't learn anything you couldn't learn in a telephone book. But she told you a lot and it was amusing and it was well-written." As for their differing political views, "I certainly regard myself as different from Charlotte," he said. "As a matter of fact, different from a lot of people [on the *Times*]. I had a different outlook than Harrison Salisbury and several other people. . . . I have no problem if people are farther left than me—and many are farther right. As long as they don't take it out on the paper."[28]

The internal politics at the *Times* were complex and relationships were not easy to define. But Charlotte's relationship with Daniel was clearly more than a professional one. His mentorship made it possible for her to establish herself as part of the *Times*'s inner circle, and this status would help her thrive during most of her years at the paper. Daniel's loss of much of his authority hurt Charlotte politically and emotionally—his presence and encouragement were invaluable to her. The two developed a deep friendship, as evidenced by a letter he wrote her shortly after he was removed as managing editor. The letter illustrates the depth of their friendship and the pain and ambivalence Daniel felt about his new job as head of the paper's Washington bureau. The forty-person bureau was for a long time an autonomous arm of the paper, considered by some in the main newsroom as difficult to control.[29] So Daniel's new assignment was daunting to him, as he wrote Charlotte: "It may be that, professionally speaking, I appreciate you more than any man in the world. It may be? Hell, there is no doubt about it. But you are troublesome. You play a very irritating role in my life: You are my journalistic conscience. You tell me what I ought to be, what I ought to do. But, unhappily, I am not young enough, strong enough, resolute enough to do all the things you admonish me to do." Daniel went on to say that of everyone giving him advice about his new assignment, Charlotte's was the most rational:

You are the only one who tells me I must take the hard and rocky road of being a tough, unremitting, unrelenting editor. I know you are right. I will try. But it won't be easy. I will do it more gradually, more gently than you would do it. . . .

In any case, I am grateful for your good advice. I do respect your integrity and your wisdom—and I like your sass, as we used to say so long, long ago when I was a boy in North Carolina. Thank you.[30]

Charlotte held her ground and kept her close friendship with the Sulzberger family, which she cultivated after she became a successful women's page and society editor. Harrison Salisbury and Clifton Daniel said that publisher Punch Sulzberger's mother, Iphigene, and his three older sisters were at first shocked by Charlotte, but all soon became good friends.[31] But it may have been Iphigene's three daughters and not Iphigene who took offense at Charlotte's writing style. Sydney Gruson, former *Times* vice president and longtime close friend of the Sulzbergers, remembers that Iphigene was far too worldly to be taken aback by Charlotte's stories.[32]

Some memos among her papers indicate that Charlotte's unconventional coverage did bother Punch's sisters. For instance, coverage of a designer fashion show for middle-class shoppers did not please Punch's sister Marian Heiskell, who objected to reporter Enid Nemy's description of a certain designer as recovering from "both a hangover and several show seasons." The same story quoted several women shoppers as admitting they attended the show not to buy but to get ideas so they could sew them on their own.[33] Heiskell wrote to Charlotte to tell her it was unfair and in bad taste to quote women at fashion shows who openly admitted they had no intention of buying: "The article, to me, is just filled with snide remarks and far from covers a fashion show," she wrote.[34] Charlotte was diplomatic in defending her news judgment and defining the realities of fashion shows to Heiskell. She pointed out that many women went to fashion shows not to buy clothes but to get fashion ideas. "Bergdorf's knows this," she wrote, "They are used to it." Furthermore, she said, the purpose of the story was to report about the atmosphere of such shows rather than to report on the clothes themselves. And, she implied, she could not control what story subjects told reporters: "The business about the gent recovering from the hangover is another matter. It isn't necessary to the story, although he apparently told this to the reporter himself."[35]

Charlotte was successful in part because she was not afraid to stand up for herself, but she did not do it in a shrill manner—that was not her nature, and she believed it would accomplish nothing. One of the contradictions in her personality was that while her writing was frequently controversial, she shunned confrontation and considered herself shy.[36] But she was more than willing to defend herself and consolidate her position on an issue if she believed in it.

Indeed, to take on the powerful and unpredictable Abe Rosenthal, even in a quiet way, was not the act of a timid person. David Schneiderman, who worked with Harrison Salisbury and, later, Charlotte, on the op-ed page, believed that the powerful correspondent and editor Salisbury respected Charlotte because of her fearless attitude toward Rosenthal. "He [Salisbury] liked anyone who stood up to [Rosenthal]," Schneiderman remembered. Salisbury believed that Charlotte's seemingly fearless attitude angered Rosenthal and drove a wedge in their relationship. "There was no way she could maintain a non-aggressive relationship with Rosenthal," he said. "He couldn't dominate her. He only liked people he could dominate."[37]

~

Confrontations with Rosenthal over the content of her pages were not the only battles Charlotte fought in the early 1970s. She was to take on one of the biggest fights of her life in 1972, although few of her friends would know the gravity of it. She was diagnosed with breast cancer that year and, after returning to Columbus that summer for a mastectomy at Ohio State University Hospital, was given a grim prognosis. Doctors told her there was a 95 percent chance the cancer would recur within five years in a fatal form.

By this time, Charlotte had been dating Dr. William Hunt, a surgeon at Ohio State University, for about four years. He suggested that she see specialists in London. Charlotte spent several weeks there before returning to work, silent about the diagnosis and eager to get on with her work. Her mother was distraught about it—cancer was an all-too-familiar subject to Lucile Curtis, who had suffered through breast cancer and cervical cancer.[38] Charlotte told her co-workers and friends about the operation but kept mum about the prognosis. Schneiderman believes public acknowledgment of any illness was a sign of weakness to Charlotte, and illness of any kind was something she normally did not talk about.[39] But the main reason she kept it from co-workers was that she believed it would prevent further promotions at the paper.[40] Charlotte's sister, Mary Curtis Davey, believes she kept the prognosis to herself simply because she had no intention of succumbing to the cancer: "There wasn't much hope given, but then you come back to that spirit. That of course is what kept her alive all those years. She had a terrific outlook. She wasn't going to let it get to her."[41]

Davey said Charlotte's alliance with Hunt contributed greatly to her ability to overcome her illness and to prove doctors wrong. "She had Bill at the time. If she had been by herself, I think it would have been different. Bill is equally strong. He was strong for both of them. It was a remarkable team."[42] Sadly, Hunt's knowledge of breast cancer would go beyond what he learned about it as a physician: years later, he, too, would contract cancer and survive it.

~'

Charlotte first met Bill Hunt when she was a girl, although both had only vague memories of these meetings. Hunt, a medical student then, frequently was invited to the home of his teacher and mentor George Morris Curtis. Hunt's relationship with the Ohio State University School of Medicine continued throughout his life; much later he worked on the staff there and eventually headed the division of neurological surgery.[43] Charlotte's friends agree that the match between her and Hunt was ideal; both concentrated on their careers yet respected the other's job. And both had the same liberal political views and the same interests: current events and politics, a love of words and medicine. Charlotte, the journalist, was an "amateur" physician, while Hunt, the surgeon, dabbled in politics and journalism.

As the daughter of a physician, Charlotte had more than a passing interest in medicine and in her own health and the health of those she loved. She had spent much of her childhood years listening and observing while her father entertained and conversed with physicians and medical students, and she absorbed the mentality and the jargon of physicians.[44] At her memorial service, Schneiderman recalled how Charlotte took charge when his fiancée was rushed to the emergency room with acute appendicitis. She demanded the best doctor, asked for his credentials, and barked orders in medical jargon.[45]

Until 1967, when she and Hunt became reacquainted, dating and romantic relationships were low on Charlotte's list of priorities. Until then, the loves in her life had been the dark, handsome Gene Grove, whom she followed to New York, and Dwight Fullerton, her college sweetheart whom she married shortly after their graduation. Both romances ended, and through most of her thirties, Charlotte was not involved in a serious romantic relationship.

Nor did close women friends play a key role in Charlotte's life. She counted as friends fellow journalists Sally Quinn, Liz Smith, and some others, but these women were professional acquaintances and not close friends to whom she would speak regularly and confide in. Lucile Curtis served the role as confidante in some ways, and Charlotte kept in constant contact with her by mail or telephone. Many of her close friends with whom she socialized were couples: Richard and Shirley Clurman, Joan and Alden Whitman, and the group that socialized with the Sulzbergers: Sydney Gruson, the Daniels, and the Salisburys. When Bill Hunt entered her life, he was one of the few people outside of journalism who would become an intimate friend and sounding board.

Not unexpectedly, it was politics and journalism that reunited Charlotte and Hunt after Hunt wrote a controversial editorial for the

October 1967 issue of the *Academy of Medicine Bulletin of Franklin County*. The article said that "poverty and racial inequality are the two most important challenges to [the nation] today" and advocated a middle-of-the-road approach to remedy them. The editorial, which seems innocuous by modern standards, so outraged the conservative medical community of Columbus as to prompt a news story in the daily *Citizen-Journal*. Most of the doctors who responded declared that Hunt exaggerated the severity of poverty in the United States, and one called his view "intellectual buffoonery."[46] Hunt sent a copy of his editorial, the responses, and the related newspaper article to Charlotte after the two had met socially a few weeks before. "Don't laugh," he wrote her. "As you pointed out, all surgeons are frustrated journalists."[47] Unlike many of his colleagues in Columbus, Hunt was liberal, or as he termed it in a letter to Charlotte, "radical center." He was far more liberal than many of his colleagues, although he insisted to Charlotte that the conservative reputation of physicians was inaccurate: "I keep insisting Columbus physicians aren't reactionary. Occasionally the radical center raises it head and draws a little fire from the far right."[48] The editorial and resulting brouhaha drew the two together. After a few more cordial letters, Curtis and Hunt began a romantic relationship.

By 1968, Hunt's life was tumultuous. He was still married to his wife, Virginia, and had three children: Ginny, a teenager, Will, in his early twenties, and David, in his late teens and a leader of the antiwar movement at Amherst College. Will had recently been drafted, and David was threatening to burn his draft card, which greatly upset his father, who encouraged him to take the more conventional and law-abiding route of claiming to be a conscientious objector. Hunt was worried about both of his sons, and he voiced his concerns repeatedly in his correspondence with Curtis.

Hunt was born in California and attended Culver Military Academy in Indiana and Ohio State. A quirk of fate sent him to Columbus in 1939. An uncle who died in the early 1930s left a trust fund for Hunt and his sister; he was given the choice of attending public school and the college of his choice or Culver and Ohio State. Once he moved to Columbus as a young man, he never left. In 1995, he won Culver's Man of the Year Award.[49]

Because Charlotte lived in New York and Hunt in Columbus, their romance was conducted primarily by letter or over the telephone—much as the romance between Lucile Atcherson and George Curtis had been forty years earlier. Letters between the two reveal that while they enjoyed each other's company and found each other intellectually stimulating, both thought the relationship was doomed because of Hunt's familial obligations, the unwillingness of his wife to agree to a divorce, and distance. "We kept saying, 'This is foolish and childish and we shouldn't do it,'" he recalled nearly thirty years later.[50] But the letters between them grew more passionate as time went on. Hunt was more willing than Charlotte to open himself up and admit his feelings and the conflicts he felt. Hunt wrote in his nearly illegible scrawl, often on airplanes or hotels when he attended medical conferences. These letters often contained little drawings of animals and other doodles—sometimes they contained his scrawled illustration of the "Mouse," his pet name for Charlotte.

In contrast, Charlotte's letters were typed neatly on the eight-by-ten-inch newsprint "stationery" she used for nearly all her correspondence and memos. Letters written by both of them are rational and intellectualized, and it took Charlotte longer than Hunt to allow herself to be free with her emotions. Often her letters were breezy and light with commentary on current events and politics. Hunt's were far more introspective and emotional. Overall, the many letters between the two in the late 1960s reflect the ambivalence and schizophrenia they must have felt about conducting a clandestine affair. In one letter, for instance, Charlotte, back to Manhattan from a trip, tries to sound cheery:

> And so from the emerald green pastures of heaven with miles of dogwood, apple trees, tulips and wooded carpets of violets back to big town and cement. . . . From a litany of spring's natural wonders to a catalogue of urban blights. . . . And this morning you sounded

so—displaced? Depressed? Uncertain? Tired? Disappointed? . . . I feel very useless. Helpless even. . . . And all the letters, phone calls and positive thoughts in the world will never, never equal one moment when you have your arms round me and the world is a joyous place.[51]

Many of the letters between the two were analytical, trying to assign logic or reason to their feelings. Charlotte wrote the following on Christmas eve of 1969, which Hunt spent with his family:

> And for Christmas? I will try to be what you want me to be, where and when you want me for as long as there's more joy for you than sorrow, and although that does not banish uncertainty, it should assuage it considerably. It should also assuage the longing.
>
> I cannot make the longing go away, nor would I if I could. Only apathy can do that, and although apathy is a form of peace it is also a form of living death, and I couldn't in conscience want that for you. Or me. Unless it involved your survival.
>
> My destructive and/or analytical feelings are not . . . based on hostility, but my sense of reality, my sense of inevitability, my essential cynicism and my sure knowledge of what human beings are like. Arrogant? Of course, but perceptive, too, and based on facts, knowledge and truth.[52]

In one letter, Charlotte was uncharacteristically morose and makes the rare admission that she has trouble coping:

> Dear Bill,
>
> It is strangely sad to be reminded of New Year's. Next to Christmas, it is perhaps the most awful day of the year. And while coping with utterly untenable situations seems to have become one of my questionable specialties, even I cannot quite cope with New Year's Eve. This last one or any other one I can ever remember in the last million years.[53]

Hunt's letters could be deeply philosophical as he attempted to reconcile his affair with Charlotte with his "other" life. He wrote in November 1969:

It is not depressing to want something very badly that you can't have. It is only sad, maybe very sad, often distracting. It is only depressing not to want anything.

It is too strong, or mature, to be able to want what you can't have. . . . It is only strong to be able to handle the wanting. . . .

It is a thing of infinite value to me, whether I can, ultimately, afford it or not. . . . I have never, repeat never felt my life interlaced with another personality. This is you as you point out.

You give the impression, dear woman, that only I was taking risks for this—that you were the tough one. I do not think this is true. . . . But we must continue to cope. . . .

I am trying very hard not to write Charlotte, I love you, because it is so goddam banal. But probably true. But I shall not write it because I don't know what it means and I hate clichés. But I have written it.[54]

Hunt's letters to Charlotte reveal much about why she fell in love with him. Her nature was far more rational than emotional, and she, too, could discuss highly emotional issues with a detached logic. But Charlotte clearly felt strong love and a deep respect for Hunt, and she frequently wrote to her mother about the joy she experienced when she was with him: "Bill is coming to New York this weekend and on Wednesday we go to Barbados," she wrote. "Yippee! All we're taking are bathing suits and books to read and with any luck we'll come back very tan."[55]

By the summer of 1970, Hunt was making progress in obtaining a divorce, and for the first time, he and Charlotte thought they might be together permanently. Lucile had hoped they would marry—she adored Hunt, and she was not too pleased that the two were living together outside marriage when Charlotte visited Columbus on many weekends.[56] So she was delighted when Hunt wrote her an upbeat letter:

I can write to you my feelings, facts, big events or trivia, I guess. First, and most important, is the continuing joy and growing confidence in the relationship between Charlotte and me. I think you know that we two hyper-rational beings committed ourselves quite non-rationally (I do not say irrationally) to each other with the conviction that all was right with us, would remain right indefinitely, and that the details would simply have to arrange themselves. . . . It seems that we were right. I think we are both as happy as we have ever been in our lives. I continue to be surprised by this.[57]

Pivotal to the relationship between Charlotte and Hunt was the fact that work and professional success were central to both, and they had great professional respect for each other. Her reputation and devotion to her job delighted him, as he wrote Lucile after he accompanied Charlotte when she covered a story in New York: "Enjoyed watching C. in action. Also sense the respect she generates in her own people and the public . . . I am very proud to be loved by this little woman."[58] Mary Davey believes the match was perfect from the start: "I think she found her match in Bill. A totally secure man, not afraid of her power and her influence. He had his own kind of experience and credibility."[59]

Charlotte, who was then forty-four, and Hunt, fifty-two, were married in a brief ceremony on June 15, 1972, in Pasadena, California, the home of Hunt's mother, and the two moved into Hunt's penthouse apartment in a Columbus high-rise apartment building. Brief stories about the wedding appeared the next day in the *Columbus Dispatch*, the *Citizen-Journal*, and the *New York Times*.

~

The one constant throughout Charlotte's life was her mother, Lucile. Her frequent letters to her mother, from her college years through her years as a professional on the *Times*, varied little. They served as a sounding board on current events and politics, work, or school and gave running commentary about her own activities and those of her friends and colleagues. Charlotte used these letters to Lucile as a way to sort out her own emotions and feelings. Although she may have held back some things from her mother, the letters were surprisingly candid, written in a light, newsy, and sometimes humorous style.

Charlotte sometimes "signed" the letters with a girl's smiling round face, hair flying in the background. Other times, she addressed her mother in affectionate terms in the salutation "Dear Lucy Birdlet" (apparently in reference to Lyndon Johnson's daughter Lucy Bird) or other diminutives. Other times, it was simply "Dear LAC."

Charlotte's desire to please her mother did not wane as she rose through the ranks of the *Times* and became a key editor at the paper. Lucile was not easily impressed, even by her own daughter's accomplishments. As Charlotte's fame grew, old friends and acquaintances in Columbus often praised Charlotte to Lucile. Mary McGarey, a longtime Columbus resident who interviewed Lucile several times for the *Columbus Dispatch*, recalled that a woman once came up to Lucile and mentioned how proud she must be of her daughter. "Which daughter?" was the reply. "I'm proud of both of them."[60]

After the death of her husband in 1965, Lucile embarked on a heavy travel schedule that took her out of Columbus for much of the year. Charlotte's letters to her went all over the world: to Bangkok, Cambodia, Rio de Janeiro, and even the Orient Express. Because of Lucile's frequent forays overseas, Charlotte often apprised her mother of current events in the United States, and sometimes she seemed so eager to get to the news of the day that she began her letters with it. For instance, in one 1970 letter, she addressed fashion and feminism, making it obvious that she was a little shocked that professional women had adopted the midi-skirt and were wearing trousers to work: "[The midi-skirt] is here, and a lot of silly people—including some ladies in women's news—are wearing them dripping down to the ankles, with boots and velvet bands around their throats and it's to throw up. And some ladies are picketing stores and fighting the midi, and wearing pants to the office and the whole thing is utterly out of hand." Parenthetically, she noted that more women were filing lawsuits for equal pay: "Women's liberation continues. The ladies are going to the courts to get equal pay. Airline stewardesses are mad because male pursuers [*sic*] are paid more for doing the same job. So they went to court to get the whole thing straightened out, and they'll probably win. Isn't that fun?"[61]

In the next few years, the issue of equal pay for women would become to Charlotte more than just a news tidbit. Usually the social and political commentary Charlotte provided Lucile was cheerfully liberal in nature and, at times, even naïve. In a letter to Lucile about the Black Panthers, Charlotte recounted incidences of what she called violence against some incarcerated Panthers, stating twice that such violence would not have occurred in Columbus. Furthermore, she defended some criminal activity:

> When you hear and see and find these things [police and prison guard brutality], you can understand why the blacks are so hostile. In fact, you can understand why [activist Eldridge] Cleaver gets up and talks violence and guns. From their point of view it may be the only way. . . . I honestly feel that if the Panther 21 were in Columbus, despite its conservative and very racist feelings, they would have a fairer trial and a better chance. The good people simply wouldn't have let them be beaten, jailed for six months and what not.[62]

Because she frequently traveled around the country—and because of her genteel upbringing in Columbus—she may have had an idealized view of life in the Midwest.

Charlotte's letters to her mother were always upbeat and cheerful, and she rarely if ever agonized over weighty personal issues. Although it was Charlotte's nature to mask her problems, there may have been another reason her letters to Lucile were unfailingly cheerful or simply informational. Charlotte and her sister, Mary, worried most of their lives about their mother's bouts with depression, and although Lucile traveled and kept busy well into her seventies, her illness remained a cause of great concern for both of her daughters. In some letters, Charlotte made fleeting, veiled references to it ("Please, please take care of yourself and if it's too cold or too hot, or you are even slightly sick, please don't sit on some silly ship or in some silly country and suffer. Please come home—either to New York or Columbus"),[63] but in most it is not mentioned. In late 1969, however, their fears were realized when Lucile tried to commit suicide by taking a drug overdose. Mary Davey remembers that Hunt, in particular, was immensely helpful in finding Lucile doctors she trusted and that Charlotte immediately raced to her side.[64] Letters to Lucile from Charlotte indicate that Lucile, who was hospitalized in New York, may have been a difficult patient in a hurry to return to her home in Columbus. In one such letter, Charlotte pleaded with her to stay in the hospital: "Dr. Terner feels strongly that to leave now would be exceedingly premature, that you are in what amounts to mid-treatment with drugs that must be carefully administered and carefully controlled, and there's still important progress to be made within the institutional setting. . . . I see no reason to rush back and cope with meetings and Christmas when you're taking strong medication."[65] In another letter, Charlotte is more blunt: "Please try to look on the hospital as a very temporary resting place, a place to get your bearing, to get help for the problems that you and I both know have been building up over the last few years. I know it must be terribly difficult for you to face these problems, mother, but I think dealing with them is important —not just for you but for all of us."[66]

Lucile Curtis's battles with depression continued throughout her life. Her suicide attempt came as a shock to Mary Davey but not to Charlotte, who knew her mother well and had feared for a long time that Lucile might try to kill herself.[67] It was Lucile's great strength and character, Davey believes, that kept her from more suicide attempts. She remembered that sometimes during a bout of depression, Lucile would try to intellectualize her feelings: "She'd say, 'I know what this is and I'm going to fight it and I'm not going to let it overcome me.'" Davey believes Charlotte had this same strength in her battle against breast cancer and the grim prognosis. It helped her carry on day after day as she lived in the shadow of a death sentence.[68]

10

Leaving the Champagne-
and-Caviar Beat

By 1973, CHARLOTTE was spending much of her time in Trans World Airline departure gates in Port Columbus and LaGuardia airports — but she did not complain about her weekend trips between Ohio and New York. After her marriage to Hunt, she played dual roles as reporter-editor and wife. For the first time, she had someone with whom to share the success of her life. Charlotte and Bill Hunt spent every weekend together, usually in Columbus, and they enjoyed vacations and holidays in various locales around the world. "They had some marvelous magic," Charlotte's sister, Mary Curtis Davey, recalled. "You could feel the chemistry. They were devoted to each other." Davey said Charlotte and Hunt loved the unconventional living arrangement that gave them time together only on weekends. It allowed them both to do their jobs and posed a challenge they both enjoyed: "She had her life in New York and he had his life in Columbus. They had the weekend to look forward to and the switching from one world to another was a great challenge." This double life and its paradoxes were particularly exciting to Charlotte. "To go off and interview the Shah of Iran and then go home and make brownies — it was exhilarating," Davey said.[1]

In Columbus, the two lived in a penthouse apartment in the exclusive high-rise Summit Chase. A balcony with a view of much of the city encircled their apartment, which was decorated beautifully with antiques, art, and memorabilia gathered from their vacations around the world.

Sally Quinn remembered that Charlotte's style of conversation changed after she and Hunt began dating: "She got very soft when she talked about him. I wouldn't say she got all gooey and giggly, but she talked about him a lot. It was, 'Bill says this or Bill thinks that,' invoking him but not telling about what they did personally. Clearly they were very involved intellectually."[2]

Marriage to Charlotte provided an education for Hunt, whose layman's interest in politics and media made way for a new life as an insider in the world of newspapers. He had a front-row seat in viewing how news was processed at one of the nation's largest newspapers, quickly learned the nuances of story placement and news selection, and was privy to the grumbling and complaints of reporters and editors.[3]

Although Charlotte felt healthy during this period of her life, her serious medical prognosis no doubt concerned her. But she rarely discussed it because few of her friends knew about it. She and Hunt knew too much about medicine to discount it, although she was determined to prove the doctors wrong in their prediction that her cancer would recur within five years. And she did prove them wrong.

While the frequent critical memos from Rosenthal to Charlotte continued, they were joined by praise from other quarters. Periodically, publisher Sulzberger sent complimentary memos to Charlotte about the content and look of her pages, and her concern that blacks and minorities receive balanced coverage would pay off to a small extent.[4] While *Times* editors were still debating the use of "Ms." in the paper, coverage of minorities was also the subject of much discussion. The paper was criticized by those who thought it covered blacks only in connection with violence and crime. In 1971, a story that appeared in Charlotte's section earned kudos from the *Times*'s in-house evaluation sheet, "Winners & Sinners." The story, about day care and new night care programs in the Harlem area, was well done, according to a line in "Winners & Sinners": "Black and White: ["Winners & Sinners"] observed that if we are to avoid having literate members of our black communities say, 'That's whitey's paper not mine,' we must concentrate more on the nonconfrontation news of those communities. Gratifyingly that is being done. Charlotte Curtis' page has been a leader. See, for example, the take-out on day care centers and night care centers by Virginia Warren."[5]

The early 1970s were not an easy era for the *Times*. In addition to financial downturns, the paper was regularly criticized by some nontraditional sources. The *Village Voice*, Manhattan's well-known alternative paper, had always been quick to point out what it considered mistakes and errors of news judgment in the *Times*. Now, in addition to the *Voice*, a little journalism review called *More* appointed itself a watchdog of the local New York media and took delight in knocking the region's most prestigious newspaper. *More* printed gossipy and anecdotal items about *Times* personnel and content, and these items were seldom flattering. They often enraged top news managers of the paper — particularly Rosenthal — but they encouraged other *Times* staff members to take a hard look at the paper and at themselves. A hiring boom in the 1960s had brought with it many personnel changes at the paper — and many of those hired then were young, well-educated reporters and editors who were now seasoned veterans at the paper. Some of these reporters and editors now had the confidence and seniority to question the way things had always been done.

By 1973, Charlotte was a twelve-year veteran of the paper. Her rise in the company had been rapid. In those years she had been promoted from reporter in the women's section to editor of one the paper's largest sections, but she belonged to the ranks of the new breed of reporters and editors who were not always content with the status quo. Charlotte was one of a handful of *Times* editors and reporters who met occasionally to talk about problems on the paper.

Jokingly calling themselves the "cabal," members of this group included theater critic Clive Barnes, reporters Joseph Lelyveld, Martin Tolchin, William Ferrell, and J. Anthony Lukas, and Charlotte. "They took in people who needed taking in," according to Sydney Gruson, a *Times* vice president and assistant to Sulzberger. "Wherever there was rebellion, you would find her [Charlotte's] hand. But there was usually was good reason for her to take up a cause. And God knows there were enough causes."[6] Barnes had been angry about what he felt was censorship by Rosenthal in a review he wrote about *Inquest*, a play about Julius and Ethel Rosenberg. Lukas thought his hands were tied by *Times* editors in his coverage of the 1968 Democratic convention in Chicago. And Charlotte still felt the newspaper was covering the Black Panthers unfairly. Aside from the Panther coverage, though, it was natural for Charlotte to be drawn to a dissident group.[7] Meetings of the "cabal" would not have attracted much attention among *Times* staff members because cabalists simply discussed issues, took no action, and made no demands. But the group's meetings infuriated Rosenthal, who looked upon participants as traitors to the newspaper. And he would not soon forget who participated in these informal meetings.

Ironically, one of the complaints of cabal members was that Rosenthal's temperament and heavy hand might force talented *Times* news people to leave the paper, or word of it might alienate prospective employees and keep the *Times* from attracting new talent. Sally Quinn—who once agreed to take a job at the *Times*—was once the target of Rosenthal's notorious rage and never did become a *Times* staff member.

Charlotte asked Quinn several times over the years to apply for jobs in her section. Quinn, who was a popular writer on the *Washington Post*'s revamped women's section, "Style," repeatedly turned her down because she did not want to leave Washington. By 1974, however, she had left the *Post* to join CBS and its morning news show but left that job later that year. She was living with her future husband, *Post* editor Ben Bradlee, by that time, so she felt she could not work again at the *Post* because of a possible conflict of interest.

Rosenthal offered her a job in the *Times*'s Washington bureau writing the same type of stories she had done for the *Post*'s "Style" section. Quinn accepted.

Several months before Quinn was to begin her new job, she had been writing on a freelance basis for the *Post* and had agreed to do a profile of the outspoken Alice Roosevelt Longworth on Longworth's ninetieth birthday. Because she was a future *Times* employee, Quinn checked with *Times* Washington bureau chief Clifton Daniel for approval to write the *Post* story.

The Longworth profile appeared and characteristically portrayed Longworth as outrageous and controversial, addressing such topics as men's anatomy, lesbianism, and other risqué subjects. The unconventional profile drew many comments, pro and con, from *Post* readers, and it killed the prospect of Quinn becoming a *New York Times* reporter. Quinn remembers an angry Daniel calling her on the telephone, furious that a future *Times* reporter was writing for the *Post*. "Clifton Daniel called me up and said, 'How could you do this, you're not loyal to the *Times*. . . . You'll never fit in and even if you work for us it's going to be a disaster.'" She learned later that after the Longworth profile was published, Daniel received a call from Rosenthal, who was livid—not only was a future *Times* reporter writing for the *Post*, but her story fell far below what he considered minimum standards of decency. The episode sent a chilling message to Quinn. "Here was this piece that caused such a sensation and I knew I could never do that for the *Times*," she said. Quinn eventually returned to the *Post* and realized that her early hunches about working for the *Times* were correct. Quinn was never sure her writing could conform to the *Times*'s standards of "good taste" and she mentioned her fears to Charlotte several times when Charlotte offered her a job. "Charlotte basically admitted to me that I'd never be able to do what I did [for the *Post*] for the *New York Times*," Quinn said. "She didn't come right out and say it, but I told her they wouldn't let me write what I write for the *Post*. She said 'you're right.' She understood that."[8]

But the paper's main problem during the early years of the 1970s was making it more readable. A report among Charlotte's papers indicates that in 1973 the paper commissioned a "traffic" study to determine how many people read each section. Called the "Simmons Traffic Study," the sixteen-page report, complete with charts and graphs, asked 1,036 people to read the Times for a month and answer a battery of questions, including how many of them regularly read the front page and section fronts; how many read stories that continued off the front page; what kind of news got the highest readership; what columnist attracted the most women readers; and many others.[9]

The study found that 92.4 percent of the readers read at least one story on page 1, but only 19.7 percent followed through to read front-page stories that were continued inside the paper. The study also found that the editorial page was the most popular section in the paper; nearly half of all readers said they read one or more items on it. Items that frequently ran on Charlotte's pages, such as "Notes on People" and "Health/Medicine," were also popular. The study found that Charlotte's pages received higher readership from women than men and that a low percentage of readers were interested in wedding announcements. About 40 percent of Times readers read at least one story in what the study called the "Family Page." Twenty-six percent of male readers read at least one article on the page, as did 55 percent of female readers. In addition, the study found that those in the age group thirty-five to forty-nine provided most of the readership of those pages—about 30 percent read at least one story in the family/style section. One of the most interesting findings for Charlotte, however, was that a very low percentage—only about 9 percent—said they read "weddings/society" news.[10]

The study was commissioned as part of an effort to beef up readership. During that era, Times editors began questioning their own news judgment. For example, in one memo, Rosenthal asked section editors why they believed readership was the lowest on Saturdays and "what we can we do to make the Saturday paper more compelling to people who do not buy it now, but buy the paper the rest of the week? . . . Are there any . . . leisure time activities or other features that have journalistic validity and might make the Saturday paper a better one?"[11] Charlotte responded with several ideas: a temporary Saturday editor should be appointed "who'd go about goosing all departments to do something bright for Saturday," and there should be more planning. The Saturday paper, she wrote, needed larger investigative, enterprise, and interpretive stories.[12]

Times news executives also did much soul-searching in an effort to reduce internal costs, and executives warned news managers to take their efforts seriously. In a memo issued in early 1973, Peter Millones, Rosenthal's assistant for personnel, chastised department heads for ignoring previous edicts to cut costs and restated a policy calling for department heads to seek approval from Rosenthal's office for all "unusual" items: "Recently, a number of major cost items have been brought to our attention only after the fact. I am obviously not talking about $25 items, but rather things such as retaining an outside consultant to work with a reporter, assigning five people to work on a project on an overtime basis, etc."[13] Two weeks earlier, Millones told department heads that cutbacks in 1973 would require a reduction of seventeen people in the paper's news department.[14]

A tighter fiscal environment may also have forced *Times* news managers to take a hard look at policies of the paper regarding such topics as printing corrections in the paper, questionable language in stories, and public statements to the media by the newspaper. Memos among Charlotte's papers indicate that all these issues arose in 1972 and 1973, the time of belt-tightening. It is likely that the beginning of labor negotiations prompted a two-page memo by Harding F. Bancroft, executive vice president for administration, about "procedure for handling statements to be made by the publisher or other spokesman on behalf of the Times." The memo—written in the same bureaucratic language that reporters routinely were forced to translate—noted that no policy existed for handling statements issued by the newspaper, but now one person would be responsible for all such statements and "[consultation] with the executives familiar with the situation." Sulzberger would sign off on all statements to the press.[15]

As news executives tried to entice more readers to the *Times* during the early and mid-1970s, some of the most dramatic content and graphics changes in the paper's history were made. One of the first, in 1970, was the introduction of a new kind of page—new for the *Times* and for any other paper in the country.

Because of his age and personality, it was unusual for Punch Sulzberger to select the sixty-one-year-old Harrison Salisbury to launch the op-ed page, a forum for public opinion that would appear daily opposite the newspaper's editorial page and feature guest commentaries. Considering Salisbury's autonomy on the paper, he might not have been the choice of some publishers. David Schneiderman, who worked with Salisbury and Charlotte as an assistant op-ed editor, said he and Salisbury never figured out why the latter was appointed editor of the new page: "I'm surprised they gave Harrison the job. They [*Times* management] had no control over him. He wasn't going to take orders from anyone. I once asked him why he thought he got the job. He didn't know."[16]

The op-ed page was a long time coming. Such a page had occasionally been suggested by editorial page editor John Oakes, but over the years it had become a political football. Editors debated its jurisdiction and place in the paper. Would it be under the supervision of the news desk, the Sunday desk, or the editorial page editor? That issue was avoided until 1970, when Sulzberger decided to initiate the op-ed page despite opposition from the *Times* news department. And it was an innovative move—other papers occasionally printed a page featuring outside columnists, but none published one daily.

As op-ed editor, Salisbury was in a rare position. He would, on paper, report to editorial page editor Oakes, although in fact he reported only to the publisher. The *Times* had always taken great pains to ensure that its opinion pages were separate from its news pages. To maintain objectivity in its reporting, *Times* officials thought it vital that the paper's news operation be unrelated to its political or opinion section. Salisbury described the page's purpose and mission: "It was to be opposite in the true sense. If the *Times* was liberal, the op-ed articles would be reactionary or conservative or radical or eccentric. The page would offer a window on the world, particularly that scene which for one reason or another (usually the parochialism or timidity of editors) the *Times* was not presenting in its news pages or editorial comment."[17] The four-person op-ed staff handled hundreds of unsolicited submissions a week and decided which ones to publish, as well as commissioning submissions. The debut issue, on September 26, 1970, ran three opinion columns on the pros and cons of legalization of some drugs, including a column advocating legalizing marijuana written by author and historian Gore Vidal. The content of the following day's op-ed page was a bit more eclectic: an author wrote of the joy of riding New York subways, and a federal communications commissioner panned the new television season.

David Schneiderman was a copy clerk on the foreign news desk when the op-ed page was formed. In his early twenties at the time, he was a favorite of Salisbury's, who named him his assistant when the page was created. Schneiderman remembered that with few exceptions, Salisbury had virtual carte blanche over the content of the page, paying little attention to Oakes, although Oakes rarely tried to influence what ran on op-ed. "Harrison couldn't quite do whatever he wanted," Schneiderman said. "He was respectful of *Times* traditions. But he pushed the envelope." Often, "pushing the envelope" meant printing a column by a public figure or journalist that was critical of the *Times*.[18] *Times* news executives hated all criticism of the *Times*, no matter how and where it was aired. They were particularly irritated when that criticism was played out on the paper's own pages.

To Schneiderman, working with Salisbury was a heady experience. Salisbury feared no one and enjoyed rocking the boat. Schneiderman was awed by Salisbury's power and reputation: "I could call anyone I wanted in the world. I was a nobody, but if you're from the

New York Times. . . . It was fun." Few people could match Salisbury's knowledge of historical and political details—details that were frequently obscure, Schneiderman said.

Salisbury was a democratic manager who sought input from his employees—to a point. Schneiderman recalled that Salisbury always passed around to the op-ed staff submissions he was considering printing. He wanted everyone to have a voice about whether the submission was appropriate for the page. One day, however, Schneiderman learned accidentally that Salisbury had made his decisions before the submission was distributed to the staff. As a joke, the op-ed staff decided to design a gag gift for their boss to use: "We had a rubber stamp made up that said, 'Please read this and tell me what you think I should do to see if it coincides with what I've already decided to do—Harrison Salisbury.' Then it had a box that said 'yes' or 'no.'" Salisbury loved the gift, Schneiderman said, and used it all the time.[19]

Salisbury knew when he initiated the op-ed page that he would soon have to give it up. The *Times* required its top-level employees to retire at age sixty-five, and Salisbury would turn sixty-five in 1974. As op-ed editor, Salisbury was an associate editor of the paper, and he was listed on the masthead as such, so the job carried the added cachet of being identified publicly each day as one of the paper's top editors. Also, the *Times*'s opinion sections were considered the most intellectual part of the paper, and they were highly respected. To head op-ed, and particularly to succeed Salisbury, was a plum assignment.

Sulzberger asked Salisbury for names of those he thought could succeed him on the page. Salisbury said much later that Charlotte's was the only name he gave Sulzberger.[20] Others say the publisher was considering three people: Charlotte; Bill Moyers, former broadcaster, presidential press secretary, and *Newsday* editor; and Roger Wilkins, a U.S Justice Department official who then worked as an editorial writer for the *Washington Post* and was later to write editorials for the *Times*.[21]

The job went to Charlotte. Salisbury said that she was perfect for it: "She could capture a character in a few phrases. . . . She had the quickest eye of any reporter I've seen. She was a walking encyclopedia of names, people, places."[22] Sulzberger remembers that it was important to Salisbury that the op-ed editor be capable of stirring things up, and Charlotte certainly fit that description: "Charlotte liked to poke holes. She was perfectly delighted to deflate people and to deflate institutions if she thought they were pretentious."[23]

Charlotte's energy, talent, and unconventional outlook appealed to Salisbury and Sulzberger, and those qualities no doubt led to her op-ed appointment. This big promotion, however, did not come simply as a result of her hard work and sharp mind. For about a decade, Charlotte had cultivated the friendship of Salisbury, publisher Sulzberger, and Clifton Daniel, and she did so in a subtle and clever way. These men found her not just talented but amusing, intelligent, and urbane; even more important, they found her personality a pleasing blend of masculine and feminine. Charlotte was not flirtatious, nor did she dress provocatively. But at five feet tall, she was tiny, dainty, and pretty, and she was always impeccably dressed in stylish, classic clothes. This softness, combined with her sly sense of humor, cynicism, and deep, throaty laugh, appealed to them. She was street smart, well-educated, and well-traveled, and she could converse comfortably about many subjects. Unlike many women of her generation, she was single-minded in her dedication to her job and did not allow herself to be distracted by romance or children. Charlotte's drive and intellect—considered "male" attributes—combined with her prim and elegant demeanor—her "female" attributes—earned her the friendships and loyalties that propelled her career at the *Times*. In short, her male superiors found her attractive yet nonthreatening. They felt she was one of them.

When she was named to the op-ed page, the women in *Boylan* vs. *Times* were preparing their case against the paper. The plaintiffs never commented publicly about whether they felt that Charlotte's promotion came indirectly as a result of her nonparticipation in the lawsuit, but Wade and some others thought Charlotte's top priority was her career and that she would do what she had to do to promote herself with *Times* executives. Now, as an associate editor, she was one of the leading news managers at the paper.

~

If *Times* reporters and editors were surprised that the newly named op-ed editor was the tiny society editor who traveled around the country covering parties, they didn't show it. The editorship of the family/style section was a key spot on the *Times*, but Charlotte aspired to more, and most people on the paper knew it. "If I recall, I thought it was an interesting choice," Rosenthal said more than twenty years later. But it did not surprise him that Sulzberger named Charlotte as op-ed/associate editor of the *Times*. "It's one of the most important jobs on the paper, and she had a political outlook," he said. "Charlotte was a very political animal and she had her eyes larger than society work. And she was close to Harrison. They were friends and had the same political outlook."[24] Sydney Gruson, who had always been keenly attuned to the politics of the *Times*, was more blunt: "She and Harrison were thick as thieves."[25]

During the time she edited the society pages, the current media-created "cult of celebrity" was not widespread, although Charlotte practiced it in her writing. Television had not yet merged show business, sports, politics, and society into one entertainment form. Charlotte was ahead of her time in covering the activities of the wealthy in all those fields, and she believed that not all celebrities lived in Hollywood. In her own way, she *had* covered politics for the *Times*—the politics of class, culture, and wealth.

About a decade after Charlotte became op-ed editor, another *Times* journalist employed a similar style of writing. White House reporter Maureen Dowd used details and her story subjects' own words to illustrate their personalities and to make them look foolish. A 1992 story in *Washington Journalism Review* called her one of the hottest journalists in the country and hailed her "innovative" style: "Her colleagues like to say she has 'perfect pitch in words.' . . . Dowd has a novelist's eye for quirky detail and a laser wit that she uses to dissect the nation's most powerful. . . . Her dispatches from the White House —equal parts mocking wit, literary flourish and class criticism—have shaken up the data-fed Washington press corps."[26] Interestingly, the writer uses many of the same adjectives here as were used to describe Charlotte's cutting style of society writing. Like Charlotte, Dowd was quick to inject class criticism into her reporting—even though it appeared on the news pages and not the society section.

Charlotte became the darling of the media when she was named op-ed editor. Magazine reporters loved the dichotomy of the petite, well-dressed society editor filling the shoes of the gray, lanky, intellectual Salisbury. In addition, it was news that a woman would finally hold one of the highest editorial jobs at the *Times* and become its first associate editor. Nearly a dozen magazines carried profiles of Charlotte or offered news of the appointment. "Curtis, 44, has come a long way covering caviar and its consumers," *Time* wrote. "When she moves into the *Times* editorial offices . . . she will be the highest-placed [female] editor in *Times* history. That will not stop her from taking along her pink evening gown."[27] Reporters outside the *Times* were amused that Charlotte was not simply a female version of Salisbury: "A first look at [Curtis] is something of a surprise. You might expect, perhaps a modern-day Joan Crawford, complete with steely manner and severe business suits. Instead this is a petite woman, five feet tall, 95 pounds, a size six dress, perfectly groomed. . . . She doesn't threaten—she assures," *Harper's Bazaar* wrote.[28]

The appointment represented everything Charlotte had worked for, and it thrilled her. Still, Charlotte's professional ambitions were not to head a large department and have power over dozens of people. Instead, she wanted to earn a limited amount of prestige doing something she found enjoyable. She treaded lightly when reporters interviewing her discussed with her the "power" accompanying the new job: "Power isn't the point," she told a reporter for *Quill*, the magazine of the Society of Professional Journalists. "I'm not interested in power except in terms of writing about it, as a reporter."[29] A *Harper's Bazaar* writer asked her a blunt question in a 1978 profile: Did she think she had the heavyweight credentials needed for the job? She responded: "I think perfectly intelligent and legitimate questions were raised about my qualifications—and not just because I was a woman. It's quite debatable whether anyone can truly replace a Harrison Salisbury. He created a standard of excellence that is very difficult to achieve."[30]

A reporter for *Viva* magazine asked her if she was "frightened" to assume the job as editor of the *New York Times*'s lofty op-ed page: "People say the job sounds so frightening. . . . Why would it frighten me? Just as I'm not frightened by the city of New York, I'm not frightened by presidents of the United States, either. I'm just not frightenable."[31] Her new position immediately elevated her to being one of the most influential women in the country. Each year, several news organizations and magazines compiled lists of the nation's most influential women. Charlotte was named to these lists repeatedly beginning in 1974, and she was in the company of women such as Congresswoman Shirley Chisholm, First Lady Betty Ford, and publisher Katharine Graham.[32]

Hunt said Charlotte was truthful when she said she was rarely frightened or intimidated. Fear drove her to study harder and do even more homework to overcome negative feelings, he said. Power, to her, was not direct authority over others but something more subtle: "Her definition of power was, when you talk, who listens. That was something she always came back to."[33] In other words, instead of her own "power" or influence over others, Charlotte wanted respect from others in positions of power.

The publicity that came with her appointment to op-ed allowed Charlotte to explain why it was not a big leap from the society pages to op-ed; both jobs, she said, required her to examine the "politics" of everyday life: "To ground everything in terms of reporting is absolutely essential. We define ourselves by everything we do. Our clothes are our political statement. We have chosen this way over another way because we think it makes us beautiful, because it makes us look like Marie Antoinette, because it's the way everyone's wearing her hair. There's a reason for it."[34]

Despite its power and prominence inside and outside the paper, the four-person op-ed page staff was tiny compared to other *Times* departments, and they worked closely in its tenth-floor headquarters. When she started editing the op-ed page, Charlotte assured the staff in her self-deprecating way that although she was taking Salisbury's job, she was just "a little girl from Ohio" out to do the best she could. Schneiderman, who shared an office with her for four years, laughed at the memory of Charlotte's words: "I heard it over and over again and I didn't believe it. I told her so. Charlotte used to like to play word games and I never took her seriously — this poor little girl in this big job." Although Charlotte would say such things half-kiddingly, Schneiderman believes this attitude helped her deal with her unique position as the most powerful woman on the *Times* staff: "I thought a lot of that self-deprecation was her way of dealing in a very male world. After all, she was the only visible female executive in the entire company."[35] As Schneiderman noted, Charlotte's flighty comments and coyness about her job were a smoke screen. Her easygoing demeanor camouflaged a tough and highly motivated personality. She was driven and very goal-oriented, but she knew any obvious outward display of her ambition would only hold her back; she would be perceived as too pushy. Besides, she was raised to believe that such outward displays of ambition were unattractive. Part of her power lay in her ability to surprise those who did not take her seriously — and she frequently took advantage of that element of surprise to get what she wanted.

Charlotte's immediate goals were to lighten the content of the op-ed page and to print more contributions from everyday people rather than government officials, academicians, and other "experts." *Cosmopolitan* magazine pointed out the vast differences between

Charlotte and Salisbury by describing how she swept his copies of the Russian newspaper *Pravda* out of the office and replaced them with her collection of *Town and Country* magazines. That anecdote, though, may be apocryphal. "She didn't replace the so-called stodgy with the so-called Town and Country," Schneiderman said. "What she did do was to de-emphasize the 'official' quality of that page. Charlotte tried to take what Harrison pioneered—the first-person piece. She wanted to do more of that."[36] Despite the variety of columns run by Salisbury, Schneiderman acknowledged that Salisbury's love of Russia was evident even on his op-ed page: "He ran [columns from] a lot of Russian dissidents. We'd joke if you had a Russian name or were a Russian dissident, you'd get published."[37]

Under Charlotte's direction, the op-ed page ran columns by world leaders and former presidents alongside those of people like Yoko Ono and author Erica Jong. Columns could be political, intellectual, funny, and even poignant. Once she published a first-person account of the sadness one woman felt about having an abortion. Another time she ran a column by a corporate executive about the joy he derived from eating at McDonald's.

While Salisbury's breadth of knowledge extended to literary, historical, and political figures, Charlotte was able to incorporate onto the page her wide knowledge of the nuances of culture and class systems. Schneiderman remembered an incident when he, Salisbury, and J. C. Suarez, another op-ed staff member, traveled to France because the French government was holding an exhibit of art from the *Times*. Vineyard owner Phillipe de Rothschild invited them to Bordeaux for dinner, and the three men worried that they would commit some culinary faux pas. Schneiderman, who consulted Charlotte about table etiquette, remembered her detailed response: "'Let me tell you all you need to know.' She's sitting at her desk, she takes out a paper plate, and puts it in front of her desk, and then she takes pencils and says, 'okay, this is where the fish knife is, this is where the knife and fork are going to go, this is the order in which you use your

Charlotte as *New York Times* society editor, mid-1960s.

On assignment aboard the *Charay Mar II* in Newport, Rhode Island, 1964. In the foreground are story subjects the Wiley Buchanans and, in the background, Mrs. George Vanderbilt.

Charlotte interviews the Duke of Marlborough in Southhampton, 1964.

Charlotte in evening clothes on assignment as a *Times* society reporter, mid-1960s.

Charlotte, with unidentified canine companion, writes a dispatch
about Palm Beach society from her hotel room there, 1969.

Charlotte Curtis, 1972.

Lucile Curtis with daughters Mary and Charlotte, early 1970s.

Lucile Atcherson Curtis in her eighties.

Charlotte's husband,
Dr. William Hunt,
late 1970s.

Charlotte and William
Hunt, late 1970s.

Charlotte and William Hunt, early 1980s.

silverware.'" Charlotte then explained the intricacies of doilies, finger bowls, and the dessert course, telling about the time she attended a dinner at which an uninformed guest failed to remove a doily at the proper time and embarrassed himself when his dessert landed on top of the doily. To Schneiderman, the story was amusing—and characteristically Charlotte: "She had an incredible eye for detail. And she would see a situation and notice things that other people didn't."[38]

Charlotte's years as women's page editor during the growth of the feminist movement may have taught her to be concerned about political correctness—to a fault. Schneiderman remembered a scene in Charlotte's office during the Arab-Israeli conflict. After getting numerous calls from both Arab and Israeli sympathizers accusing her of bias, she sat on the floor and counted the number of op-ed contributions the *Times* had published that year by Israelis and Arabs. Schneiderman remembered: "After about twenty minutes of counting, Charlotte lifted her head and said, 'It's twelve–eleven in favor of the Jews. Are we okay?' Frankly, I wasn't sure."[39]

Charlotte's influence as op-ed editor extended far beyond simply selecting and soliciting the *Times*'s daily op-ed columns. She regularly attended what were called "publisher's luncheons" in the *Times* executive suite—high-powered luncheons at which the publisher and editorial writers met and talked with top cultural, political, and literary figures to help determine the paper's editorial policy. It was this part of the job that Charlotte enjoyed the most—she loved meeting powerful and well-known persons and conversing with them. She frequently took copious notes describing the comments and personal characteristics of these luncheon guests so she would not forget the meetings.[40] It was evident to Sulzberger, too, that Charlotte loved this part of her job and usually participated enthusiastically: "My recollection was that she took part but of course never embarrassed anyone. You always knew when Charlotte was in the room. She didn't take a back seat to anyone."[41]

Notes she took on these visits indicate her attention to the personal characteristics of the visitors. Her notes about outgoing Israeli prime minister Moshe Dayan indicate his demeanor as well as his thoughts and ideas:

> He outlined his plan for the west bank[sic]/Jordan. . . . He makes Arabs sound like Ahabs. His English has a slight British accent. . . . His suit must have been Italian—a little too big, his shirt a little too big around the collar. His tie a little too large. What is remarkable about him besides a delicious sense of humor about himself and all else, is of course, that eagle-bright eye and his workman's hands. They are brown and knarled [sic] like a farmer's hands with a badly twisted index finger (he did not use a finger bowl). . . .
>
> It troubles him to be so severely criticized by some of the Israelis now. "I did not like it when they called me a 'murderer,'" he said.

Curtis noted that editorial page editor Oakes, evidently a fan of Dayan's, "lighted up in Dayan's presence. I don't think I've ever seen him so obviously in an admiring, warmly affectionate mood about anything or anyone before. But that doesn't mean he didn't ask his usual hard questions," Charlotte wrote in her notes.[42]

In another publisher's luncheon in May 1974, the Democratic governor of Georgia, Jimmy Carter, then an obscure figure, indicated that he might run for president. After the lunch Charlotte was one of the few people present who predicted that he might actually have a chance.

Charlotte also had lunch with William Saroyan, one of her favorite authors, who told her that he was not fazed by rejection letters:

> William Saroyan came by today. My hero. . . . His book, "The Daring Young Man on the Flying Trapeze—10 Years or is it 20 Years Later," is coming out in about six months. . . . He won't do the book tour to sell it. "I don't like to do that," he said. "A writer writes. An editor really can't help, but you can learn from book critics, but not much. You can only do what you do yourself by doing it." Rejection slips don't bother him. "I don't pay attention to them," he said. He was wearing a red turtleneck and talks loud.[43]

Charlotte had said that the one aspect of the op-ed editorship that she disliked was that she no longer wrote for the paper on a regular basis.[44] But she enjoyed the fact that the job allowed her to meet and talk with some of the most famous people in the world and that, indirectly, she had a hand in determining the *Times's* editorial stance. It also must have appealed to her sly sense of humor that she wielded power over some of these well-known figures. Schneiderman remembered how, as a woman, she could serve as her own "secretary" and screen her own calls. One such call came from Henry Kissinger, who ran into a brick wall in the form of the fictitious "Miss Wilkinson": "I vividly recall the time Miss Wilkinson would not let a call from Henry Kissinger go through, and Charlotte was delighted of course with this ploy. There was no reason, of course. She just enjoyed it."[45]

Although the new job may have taken some getting used to, Charlotte grew to like it and the perks that came with it. Her lofty spot in *Times* top management, however, did not keep her from making waves. The same old Charlotte piqued her bosses with the content of her page and her quietly rebellious attitude.

11

The Best of Times

CHARLOTTE LOVED TO TAKE pictures of the unusual and interesting places she visited, and her photo album filled up quickly after she began editing the op-ed page. She and Hunt traveled across the country, as well as to Asia and Barbados. The appointment brought with it some unexpected and pleasant lifestyle changes, including the chance for her to travel and write more.

When she took over the op-ed page, she assumed she had given up writing on a full-time basis. Little did she realize that her writing career would continue in an altered form. She continued her free-lance society writing projects, but now she was beginning to write political and current events commentary for magazines like *Harper's* and *Rolling Stone*. During this time, Charlotte published a compilation of many of her society articles in a book titled *The Rich and Other Atrocities* (1976). In addition to vacation travel with Hunt, she embarked on an extensive publicity tour for her book, giving talks about politics and American culture and society. The dedication to that book is telling—she dedicates it to her friends and mentors Punch Sulzberger, Clifton Daniel, and Harrison Salisbury, who she believed were vital to her professional success.[1]

Charlotte was living a tranquil but busy life during this period while many around her had entered into an unproclaimed revolution. The women at the *Times* were in the middle of their lawsuit, *Boylan* vs. *Times*, and the litigation was taking its toll on both sides in time, money, and tension. Meanwhile, women journalists at other large media outlets were filing similar sex discrimination lawsuits and complaints against their employers.[2] And although the women's movement had been gaining momentum in support and respectability, women were failing to make strides in the nation's newsrooms; only a handful of women held executive positions on newspapers, and only a few were bureau chiefs. Indeed, women would not become part of the power structure at newspapers until the mid-1980s—a full decade after Charlotte became associate editor of the *Times*.

∼

The *Times*, meanwhile, was about to initiate one of the biggest changes in its history—the expansion from two sections to four and the introduction of new daily sections that differed each day of the week. These themed "C" sections, which were engineered by Rosenthal, were designed as a daily "magazine" to attract upscale readers and boost circulation overall. Over a period of about three years, the "Sports Monday," "Science *Times*," "Living," "Home," and "Weekend" sections appeared—coinciding with sharp increases in circulation and advertising. Readership rose by 2 percent and advertising linage by 12 percent during the two-year period in which the new sections were introduced.[3]

It took years for the paper's new themed sections to come of age, but readers could see immediately that they differed from *Times* style. These sections represented dramatic changes in graphics and story content. Graphics were big and bold, with large photos and drawings that sometimes occupied nearly half a page. Topics included the "wonders of the Cuisinart," the joys of hand-painted wallpaper, and profiles of the grand hotels of the world, and they carried the Rosenthal stamp, focusing on consumer issues and other "news-you-can-use" topics. While the writing was breezy and bright and headlines often full of puns, the stories bore little similarity to the irreverent style Charlotte initiated, and the subject matter was the kind Charlotte had resisted despite Rosenthal's hounding. Such dramatic changes on the stable and static *New York Times* naturally created controversy. Although the new sections proved to be financially lucrative, many outside the paper said they showed the paper was growing increasingly elitist, reporting aggressively on the world and nation but neglecting news in its own backyard. The paper was specifically targeted for its renewed attention to upper- and upper-middle-class New York suburbanites and accused of ignoring the poverty in New York City.

Harper's, for instance, noted satirically that the problems of women living alone were portrayed in the *Times* by an article about the heiress to the Agnelli/Fiat fortune. And, the magazine claimed, the paper dutifully reported that rents for foreigners were rising in Moscow while editors turned a blind eye to burned-out tenements in South Bronx. *Harper's* summed up what it decreed the "typical" article in the paper's new sections: "An article about an overpriced restaurant in which women dressed in the latest fashion may sit at antique tables and prepare their own slimming dishes with a Cuisinart provided by a waiter whose film about the matriculation of nasty children at Yale has just closed at an Off-Broadway theater."[4]

These changes in the paper brought about some controversial personnel changes as a result of reshuffling, retirements, and internal politics. But Charlotte, by the mid-1970s, was in the right place at the right time. Her position was secure, despite her usual propensity to rock the boat. Other longtime and established *Times* employees, however, did not share this secure position in the mid- and late 1970s. But Charlotte was busy, happy, and as healthy as could be expected, and she may not have seen the writing on the wall.

By this time, Charlotte was firmly ensconced as a regular at many New York premieres, parties, and receptions. Her personal papers are filled with invitations to these events from such people as millionaire philanthropist Brooke Astor, journalist Barbara Walters, actresses Shirley MacLaine and Liv Ullmann, author Betty Friedan, and others.

Letters in her personal papers also show she occasionally corresponded with a former Vassar classmate, Jacqueline Kennedy Onassis. By 1980, Onassis had been a book editor for five years—first at Viking Press and then at Doubleday. Despite her enormous wealth, she balanced a full-time job with motherhood. Charlotte's attitude toward her former classmate had been ambivalent over the years. The first draft of Charlotte's 1963 book, *First Lady*, had been critical of her. Although most of her comments were never published, Curtis wrote that the first lady was not a fashion trendsetter in the White House, nor was she as sophisticated as was widely believed. In his biography of Onassis, Lester David recounted the *Times* story that said Onassis, as first lady, was a spendthrift. He noted that Charlotte had written that she spent the enormous sum of $50,000 for clothes in the sixteen months after Kennedy's election.[5]

To Charlotte, marrying into wealth or social position was not the same as earning it oneself—even if one had been clever enough to marry a United States senator and future president. Although Charlotte liked many of the society wives she covered, her true respect was reserved for women whose own accomplishments earned them fame or wealth. When Onassis had become a respected book editor who went to work each day without fanfare, she finally earned Charlotte's admiration and respect. The two had a casual but warm friendship and saw each other at book parties and literary gatherings.

Charlotte was certainly a well-known and sometimes feared figure when she was society editor, but her power as op-ed editor was greater, although more subtle. Her four-person staff was smaller than that of women's news, but she and her staff determined what more than eight hundred thousand readers saw on the op-ed page each day, and her frequent presence at the publisher's luncheons gave her a voice in shaping editorial policy.

As op-ed editor, Charlotte no longer was pressured to report on what she may have seen at these receptions even though she may have been "off duty." But her friends maintain that she was never without her notebook at any event and guests knew their silly or superficial comments might appear in the *Times*.

The mid-1970s preceded the years of the "celebrity journalist," when many reporters and editors who have regular columns become familiar fixtures on television news and talk shows, offering commentary; certainly journalists like Charlotte, Barbara Walters, and Eugenia Sheppard were known names in New York and made frequent speeches and appearances, but they did not get the exposure received by today's celebrity journalists, who appear on dozens of shows via cable television and whose faces are as well-known as their names.

Nonetheless, Charlotte walked a fine line when she attended events as both a guest and a journalist. In his chronicle of New York society, *Chic Savages*, *Women's Wear Daily* publisher John Fairchild noted that in the 1970s some journalists mixed with the society figures they covered. He wrote that Walters, *New Yorker* writer Renata Adler, and Charlotte frequently appeared on guest lists: "Charlotte Curtis and . . . Eugenia Sheppard, among others, began to mix printer's ink and after-hours pleasures at society's table tops."[6] Charlotte's new role enabled her to mingle with the people she used to cover. She no doubt had mixed feelings about those with whom she rubbed elbows —for more than a decade, she had skewered them in her writing. Yet she took New York society very seriously.

Leslie Wexner, chairman and chief executive officer of The Limited Corporation, was in a situation similar to Charlotte's when his chain of women's apparel stores experienced explosive growth in the early 1980s. A Columbus native who said he would never leave Ohio, he spent much of his time in Manhattan because of the success of his stores and his retail empire. It was inevitable that their paths would cross, and Charlotte became a friend and confidante, in part because they both were ambivalent about Manhattan "society." Charlotte sometimes ridiculed its excesses, yet she believed the wealthy had a deep influence on the nation's economy and culture. Wexner was a giant in retailing, a business that made him dependent on the nation's wealthy and well-connected trendsetters, yet he did not have time for their superficial cocktail gatherings and idle conversations. Charlotte stressed to him, he said, that it was an important part of both their jobs to mingle with members of New York society and to take them seriously. He enjoyed observing her at such gatherings because she did not take them lightly: "I think she was always processing. And she wasn't glad-handing. That wasn't her. . . . I might have said some critical things about New York social life and the artificiality as I saw it, but her point of view was that 'you don't understand it.' She would defend it and say 'There are some serious people here, some good people, some major institutions.'"[7]

Charlotte's background as a society reporter and editor and her role as op-ed editor put her in a very public position. She now had the reputation as being one of the nation's leading opinion shapers, and she was on the A-list for many Manhattan social events. During her tenure as op-ed editor, she received numerous awards and honorary degrees, including the annual Ohio Governor's Award presented to outstanding Ohioans; the Carr Van Anda Award for excellence in journalism from Ohio University; a Headliner award for outstanding journalism from the Ohio Press Club; and a Distinguished Achievement award from the Society of Professional Journalists. She received honorary degrees from St. Michael's College in Vermont and Denison University in Ohio, and she served on advisory boards in humanities and sociology at Princeton University and the University of Chicago. She gave so many speeches at professional gatherings that she began to keep a file of them.

Charlotte also became a respected figure in Washington, where she attended one of the breakfast meetings President Ronald Reagan held for journalists at the White House to discuss economic issues.

As part of this event, Charlotte also attended briefings by Secretary of the Treasury Donald Regan, Budget Director David Stockman, and Murray Weidenbaum, chairman of Reagan's Council of Economic Advisors.

It is ironic that Charlotte, an outspoken liberal, would end up having ties to the Reagan White House. Her best friend from college, Selwa "Lucky" Showker Roosevelt, formerly a reporter for the *Washington Star*, had become chief of protocol in the Reagan White House, and the two remained friends over the years although they lived in different cities and held vastly different political views. Periodically, when Charlotte visited Washington or Roosevelt visited New York, the two would meet. In the late 1970s, they occasionally met with their spouses—Charlotte with Hunt and Roosevelt with her husband, Archibald Roosevelt. Hunt remembers those times fondly, joking that "even though she was a Republican," Roosevelt and Charlotte were close and that gatherings of the four were fun and frequently raucous.[8] Although she vociferously opposed their politics, Charlotte had great respect for the Reagans' sophisticated social outlook. Shortly before her friend Lucky took the job as White House chief of protocol, Charlotte wrote her to compliment the Reagans: "The Reagans are delightful people even though they are Republicans and I think you'll enjoy them if not the people around them. Furthermore, they are great hosts, which will be a very nice change from Nixon, Ford and Carter."[9]

The Roosevelts had a dinner party for Hunt and Charlotte during one of their visits to Washington, and the occasion allowed Archibald to indulge in one of his favorite pastimes: writing doggerel. In an eleven-verse ode to Charlotte and Hunt, he recounted some of the history between Charlotte and Lucky:

> And next came Charlotte, guest of honor.
> We've gathered to heap praise upon her.
> At Vassar—not so long ago—
> She shared a room with Lucky—so

She saw me dance the mating dance
And suffered all through our romance.
In time she fell, this red-haired runt,
Caught by the brilliant Dr. Hunt.

We both found out what married life
Would be with newshens for a wife.
Of course, I knew it when I caught her
That Lucky was a born reporter.
Her life became the *Evening Star*,
While I just worshipped from afar. . . .

Now each here who recalls our life
In every stage as man and wife,
Can see why I appreciate
Bill's choice of such a feisty mate,
A brave and valiant man to wed
The tiny tyrant of Op-Ed.
So raise your glass, high as you can,
and drink to Charlotte and her man.[10]

Roosevelt remembered that she and Charlotte differed on everything from politics to journalism to fine cuisine. She recalled specifically that she did not always agree with what she considered
Charlotte's cold-blooded approach to reporting, recalling a conversation they had when both covered the 1968 Republican convention
in Miami: "I was the type of reporter who would never hurt anyone.
I didn't like working on deadlines. I remember being shocked when
Charlotte said to me, 'Oh, Lucky, I'd walk over my own grandmother
for a story.' She apparently thought that was perfectly legitimate.
That's the attitude these days. I simply don't belong in that world."[11]

Still, in keeping with Charlotte's often paradoxical personality,
close personal friendships were ultimately more important to her
than getting a story. "We were always good friends whether we agreed
or disagreed," Roosevelt said. "No story was worth it to me. . . . But to
care more about a story than a friendship or a love or a family—that

to me was inconceivable. But she was a good friend and she never wrote anything about me. She would never have betrayed me because we were very very good friends."[12]

Throughout her life, Charlotte's heart was in Ohio, but she enjoyed some of the luxuries New York offered—particularly the food. Charlotte had always been a picky eater, and she enjoyed the variety and high quality of the cuisine in the city's restaurants. Roosevelt, however, did not share her culinary sensitivity. She remembered an offer by Charlotte to take her to dinner in New York after Roosevelt returned from a long trip overseas. Charlotte took her friend to the elegant Oak Room in the Plaza Hotel. But Lucky was not interested in fine cuisine: "The waiter almost fainted when I said I want a hamburger and banana split. I don't think they had ever been asked for that. It probably amused [Charlotte]. I thought we'd go to the equivalent of a McDonald's, but, no, she wanted to take me to a grand place with her expense account."[13]

Charlotte could not invite a large number of people to her apartment in Greenwich Village because it was too small—and that was frustrating for her because planning parties was one of her favorite activities. Hunt said she considered such planning an art form, and she spent hours considering the proper food, decorations, and seating arrangements. Thus her appointment to the op-ed page came at a fortuitous time. The *Times* wanted to celebrate the fifth anniversary of the page, and, Charlotte believed, who better to plan the event than the section editor? The party was held during the cocktail hour on the *Times*'s fourteenth floor, and guests included leading political, entertainment, and cultural figures such as playwright Arthur Miller; writers Lee Radziwill, Calvin Trillin, and I. F. Stone; former attorney general Ramsey Clark; Israeli ambassador Chaim Herzog and Iranian ambassador Ferydoun Hoveyda; photographer Richard Avedon; and a variety of *Times* writers and editors. Notes in her papers indicate that Charlotte painstakingly arranged seating plans and guest lists to include a properly eclectic group of people.

Charlotte's zeal for arranging special gatherings was more than just a hobby, and she believed strongly that a successful party was the result of a combination of the right details. Parties were serious business to her, and she took great pains to plan them—even taking charge of her own memorial service.

∼

As editor of one of the most prestigious sections of one of the most prestigious newspapers in the world, Charlotte lived in a fishbowl. The publisher appointed in-house *Times* columnists, but she was ultimately responsible for the selection and editing of the outside contributions that appeared on the op-ed page. But though Charlotte met with little interference from Oakes or Sulzberger, she would never have the stature of her predecessor, Harrison Salisbury. Salisbury hand-picked Charlotte to succeed him because of her iconoclastic personality and news judgment; and, indeed, Charlotte's goal was to feature unusual and offbeat contributions.[14]

But she knew that in stature and reputation, she was no equal to Salisbury, despite the success of the op-ed page under her leadership. In fact, Charlotte's toughest critics were not from outside the paper but from within. In a 1974 article about innovations at the nation's leading newspapers, *Time* praised the op-ed page as "a model forum of contrasting ideas and attitudes. . . . The section is now edited by Charlotte Curtis, 45, who previously transformed the *Times'* routine women's page into a sophisticated mini-daily on modern living styles."[15] In an overview of the emergence of op-ed pages nationwide, *Los Angeles Times* media critic David Shaw hailed the new attitude of the page under Charlotte, calling the emergence of puns in headlines, bold illustrations, and the sometimes quirky nature of guest columns as "an effective antidote to the stolid, somber quality of much of the *New York Times*." He added that "most editors speak of the *New York Times* op-ed page with considerable envy and enthusiasm."[16]

Charlotte's willingness to take chances on the page did not please everyone. Shaw's article quotes her as saying that her boss, Oakes, sometimes labeled her page frivolous: "He calls my softer pieces 'True

Confessions' or 'Readers Digest' pieces," she told Shaw with characteristic candor.

Her friend and patron Salisbury was not, ultimately, pleased with her page. Fifteen years after she was named op-ed editor, and after her death, Salisbury said Charlotte was not daring enough in her selection of op-ed pieces. Salisbury said he was disappointed: "She probably didn't run as good a page as I thought she'd run. It wasn't as feisty. She didn't challenge the *New York Times*." Charlotte's bold treatment years earlier of the Bernstein Black Panther party became a symbol of her daring writing style and news judgment, and Salisbury referred to that story as an example of Charlotte's iconoclastic news judgment: "She didn't have a Black Panther writing on the page," he said.[17]

Some of Charlotte's former colleagues believe, however, that she could never fill Salisbury's shoes no matter what she ran on the pages for one simple reason: he was a legend at the *Times* and she was not. This rare stature gave him license to do whatever he wanted. Roger Wilkins, an editorial writer for the *Times* when Charlotte was op-ed editor, said few *Times* editors would interfere with Salisbury: "Harrison may have wished for greater risk-taking [by Charlotte]. Harrison was a riverboat gambler. He was a risk-taker. Charlotte was not bold in that sense. She was careful."[18] David Schneiderman saw Salisbury as a paternal figure who had impossibly high standards: "He expected his so-called children to be as good as he was—without realizing his special stature."[19] Both Salisbury and Schneiderman offered the same example of an op-ed piece that ran under Salisbury but would not have been published under Charlotte: a reprint of a column by a Mississippi physician who was so incensed at student rioting against the war in Vietnam that he wrote that he would want his own son shot if he were involved in student demonstrations. The column naturally created a big controversy—one that Schneiderman believes Charlotte would have avoided. "Harrison could absorb an uproar like that. He had the stature to take it," Schneiderman said. "So Charlotte's pages did not have as many pointed edges."[20] Charlotte may

have been cautious during the beginning of her tenure as op-ed editor
—but, characteristically, she did not always spout the company line.
Shortly before she was named to the job, she created a hubbub on
the staff—and the ire of Sulzberger—for agreeing to take part in a
"counter" convention of journalists held by *More* magazine, the
journalism review that frequently criticized the *Times*. The magazine
was the sponsor in the spring of 1972 of a journalism "convention"
that it claimed in advertisements would be more meaningful and honest than those held by the American Newspaper Publishers Association (ANPA), a group in which Sulzberger was active. Advertisements
for the event labeled the yearly ANPA conferences "circuses" and
claimed theirs would be a radicalized, more honest version of the
one held by the publishers. Not coincidentally, the counterconvention was scheduled to take place at the same time as the publishers'
conference. The publishers met at the posh Waldorf Astoria Hotel;
the counterconvention would take place across town at the Martin
Luther King Labor Center.

Sulzberger was not amused at the irony of the conference dates,
nor was he pleased that Charlotte and the paper's Washington bureau
chief Tom Wicker were participating in it. He sent two uncharacteristically harsh letters informing them that their participation put him
in an awkward position with the ANPA and asking them to withdraw:

> Whether or not you are in agreement with the philosophy of the
> American Newspaper Publishers Association, your participation in
> this "counter convention" puts me into an embarrassing position.
>
> Obviously, I have no desire to censor your activities, but I do feel
> it fair to point out that you, as an editor, are more than a reporter on
> the paper, and that you bring with you the authority of the entire or-
> ganization. I would truly hope that you would reconsider your deci-
> sion to attend the meeting, conclude that it is not in the best interest
> of the company, and that you withdraw.[21]

Charlotte sent an apologetic reply to Sulzberger, but she did not
back down. Instead, she explained that *More* might be guilty of exag-
gerating the radical nature of what could be a meaningful event: "My

impression is that the meetings themselves are going to be far less controversial than they have been billed," she wrote. "Except by implication, they have nothing to do with the publishers. . . . Nor are the publishers on the agenda." Charlotte told Sulzberger that she would not moderate a panel about women's news pages because she did not want to talk publicly about a section in the *Times*, but instead she agreed to moderate a more neutral panel of news subjects called "How They Cover Me." "If this still troubles you, and I hope it doesn't, I would be happy to discuss it with you at any time," she wrote.[22] Sulzberger later reconsidered, writing Charlotte that the paper might be embarrassed if she and Wicker withdrew. But he also admonished her: "Please, though, in the future bear in mind my reservations about the wisdom of participation in this kind of thing by you and other executives of The Times."[23]

The *Washington Post's* "Style" section gave extensive coverage to the counterconvention. Sally Quinn called Charlotte's panel one of the biggest draws of the convention. The panel was an eclectic mix that included historian and writer Gore Vidal, motion picture director Otto Preminger, hippie Abbie Hoffman, Marvin Miller, an attorney who represented striking baseball players, Representative Bella Abzug, and actor Tony Randall.

Quinn noted with a wink that participants on this panel that was moderated by a *New York Times* editor had no qualms about knocking the *Times* and other papers. As she knew, nothing irked *Times* executives more than public criticism. She wrote: "Gore Vidal had a few testy words about the *New York Times* and reporting in general. 'There is a trivialization in our press and everything is personalities. The only publications worth reading are the *New York Review of Books* and *Screw* magazine.'"[24]

A memo she sent to Clifton Daniel indicated that Charlotte enjoyed participating in the event. She described its chaotic atmosphere to Daniel, telling him it was "alternately fun, boring, exciting, long-winded . . . so awesome as to bring tears to the eyes . . . overloaded with rhetoric and clichés and studded with idealistic calls for very high goals. It was like an urban country fair of ideas, the shoddy all mixed in with the superb." Charlotte could not resist describing to Daniel what she considered one of her personal highlights—the criticism of Rosenthal: "One high point . . . was [former *Times* reporter] David Halberstam's personal (and vitriolic, but that's an editorial comment) denunciation of Abe Rosenthal. Apparently several others who had better be nameless willingly seconded that motion."[25]

Sulzberger knew of Charlotte's radical tendencies when he named her op-ed editor eighteen months later. And she did not disappoint him. She viewed the op-ed page as the stage for debates about journalism regardless of whether the *Times* was the target of criticism. In one incident which Schneiderman remembered clearly more than twenty years after it happened, Curtis once again ruffled Rosenthal's feathers, much to the delight of *More* magazine.

The *Times* had had an uneasy relationship with *More* since the journalism review was founded in 1971. One of the articles in *More*'s first issue was a recounting of an editorial reshuffling at *Harper's* in which its beloved editor, Willie Morris, resigned, along with the rest of the staff. The author of the article was none other than the women's editor of the *New York Times*, one of *More*'s favorite targets of criticism. Charlotte's participation in the launching of the magazine did not please Rosenthal, who, *More* pointed out later, "stormed into her office . . . and ranted loudly about how she was giving aid and comfort to the enemy."[26]

In 1974, *More* was pleased to report on what it portrayed as another of Rosenthal's tantrums—this one over a column that appeared on the *Times* op-ed page by Roger Morris, a staff member at the National Security Council under Henry Kissinger. The column, a reprint of an article that appeared in the *Columbia Journalism Review*, chastised the press for being soft on Kissinger and for blindly accepting whatever he said, despite what Morris claimed was evidence to the contrary. He used as an example of this blind acceptance stories that appeared in the *Times*.[27] Rosenthal had denied Morris's charges in the *Columbia Journalism Review*, but the reprinting of the charges on the op-ed page reignited the dispute, and it began to take on a life of its own in the national media. Morris appeared on the *Today* show to discuss the matter, and a *More* reporter called Rosenthal to ask why the newspaper reprinted the column if Rosenthal had already denied Morris's claims.

An annoyed Rosenthal sent memos to Charlotte and editorial page editor Oakes reminding them to tread lightly because *More* reporters loved conflict with the *Times*: "From vivid past experience I know what he [the *More* reporter] and others will be after is any indication of dispute among the editors of the paper. I know you both agree that we should do everything possible to avoid feeding this."[28] But it was too late. In a blurb in its next issue, *More* reported on Rosenthal's enraged first reaction to Morris's op-ed column: "Rosenthal went into a mega-frenzy. Furious over Morris' criticisms of the *Times*, Rosenthal called Curtis (new op-ed editor) at 3 A.M., woke her out of a sound sleep and berated her for half an hour for, among other things, trying to do him in. When we called the Times to discuss the tantrum with the managing editor of the world's best newspaper, we were told he was in Alaska. Cooling off, we hope."[29]

Schneiderman remembered that some other *Times* news managers supported Charlotte's decision to run the column—Washington bureau chief James Reston, who, ironically, was specifically targeted by Morris, called to give his approval.[30] The usually affable Sulzberger, however, was not so supportive. In stern memos to Oakes, Rosenthal, and Sunday editor Max Frankel—and in a separate memo to Charlotte—he let them know he was not pleased with the Morris column. He told Oakes, Rosenthal, and Frankel that he was "distressed" by the column, and "to avoid repetition, I want to spell out the ground rules as I want them played in the future." Sulzberger continued, clearly alluding to Charlotte's contributions to *More*: "I do not wish to use the pages of the *Times* for attacks upon the integrity of our news gathering process or our employees. There is a clear difference between this type of attack and a difference of opinion that we always welcome in our letters columns."[31] In his memo to Charlotte,

Sulzberger was less severe and even slightly encouraging: "If you ever needed evidence on how sensitive the [op-ed] page is, you have just had it. But everyone makes mistakes at one time or another, and this is just to let you know that, above the disappointment, this fan of yours remains a wholehearted fan. Now let's close the book and return to tomorrow."[32]

It was unlike Charlotte to let controversy force her to back down on any issue, and Sulzberger was benevolent and forgiving. Rosenthal, however, was a different story. As op-ed editor, Charlotte was able to circumvent Rosenthal during her day-to-day activities, and her superior, Oakes, supervised with a light hand. But Rosenthal, as managing editor, read the newspaper from cover to cover each day and took a passionate interest in all aspects of it. He was so passionate, in fact, that he sometimes may have been too quick to point a finger at someone he felt had wronged the *Times.*

Wilkins, the first black person on the *Times* editorial board, does not mince words when he discusses Rosenthal's temper and strained relationship with some *Times* employees—particularly Charlotte: "He was insecure. Anyone who rose to stardom diminished him."[33]

Wilkins, Schneiderman, and Charlotte became good friends during Wilkins's short and often tempestuous tenure on the *Times.* The nephew of civil rights leader Roy Wilkins, Roger Wilkins had worked as an assistant attorney general in the U.S. Justice Department and was an editorial writer for the *Washington Post* before he joined the *Times.* He and Charlotte were a natural match; they had similar liberal political views and shared a deep interest in civil rights. Wilkins indicated that he became friends with Charlotte for a more important reason: he appreciated her warmth and openness. After his first day as an editorial writer, Schneiderman, Charlotte, and Charlotte's assistant Muriel Stokes came to his office with champagne and balloons to welcome him. It was a gentle gesture that stood in contrast to his grave surroundings and position, Wilkins said: "I'll never forget that. The editorial board [on the *Times*] was not a place that was warm and fuzzy. There were eleven men and one woman [architecture critic Ada Louise Huxtable]. Most took themselves very seriously. Their role in life was to be a member of the *New York Times* editorial board. Charlotte knew being the first black wasn't going to be easy."[34]

Charlotte often absorbed Rosenthal's wrath silently, but Wilkins could not. He remembered Rosenthal's anger when the *Times* ran an editorial about Africa that broke news as well as stating an opinion. Rosenthal was outraged that the editorial conveyed news that was previously unpublished in the *Times*, apparently feeling the editorial page had infringed on the news pages. Without checking to see who wrote the editorial, he blamed Wilkins, the newspaper's only black editorial writer. Wilkins remembered his own reaction: "My phone rings. It was Abe [Rosenthal]. He started yelling at me. He's upset about the editorial because it broke news. I said, 'Shut the fuck up.' No one ever talked to him like that. He said, 'What?' I said, 'You're an asshole.' Instead of calling the man who's head of the page, he called me. He assumed it was a black man who wrote the editorial. Well, I didn't. I slammed the phone down."[35]

Wilkins admired the fact that Charlotte was not willing to allow Rosenthal to force her to compromise her news judgment. Shortly after Wilkins left the paper, he realized that some editors there were angry that he had the audacity to quit, he said. But Charlotte valued his opinions and admired his writing, and she repeatedly tried to persuade him to write a guest op-ed column. Wilkins finally relented and wrote the column, much to the chagrin of some editors, who became angry with Charlotte for publishing anything by Wilkins. But she was unfazed.[36]

Much of the history of the *Times*'s opinion pages in the 1960s and 1970s focuses on the activities and beliefs of John B. Oakes, editorial page editor from 1961 until 1977. Oakes, a cousin of publisher Sulzberger and nephew of publisher Adolph Ochs, was an ardent conservationist and supporter of many progressive causes. He also held passionate and unshakable views about some topics and people.[37] One person who stirred strong emotion in Oakes was William Safire, the former Nixon speechwriter who, in 1973, was named by Sulzberger as an op-ed columnist for the *Times*.

Safire's appointment came as a surprise to many people inside and outside of the *Times* because of his affiliation with Nixon and his job as a Nixon speechwriter. The *Times* gave editorial support to Nixon's opponent George McGovern in the 1972 presidential election, and the paper's op-ed columnists frequently criticized the former president. Safire's unlikely appointment as columnist shows how the newspaper's opinion pages frequently served as a battleground for top editors. *New York* magazine gossip columnist James Brady reported that Sulzberger hired Safire under pressure from some family members who felt the page needed balance to counteract its liberal tone. Brady also said Oakes was very angry about the decision to hire Safire.[38] There was little he could do about it, however, because Sulzberger was the only person on the *Times* who had jurisdiction over the hiring and editing of op-ed columnists. Safire was hired a year before Charlotte became op-ed editor. But Sally Quinn remembers that Charlotte was among a large group of journalists inside and outside of the *Times* who criticized the hiring, telling people, "'Over my dead body will Bill Safire ever come to work at this newspaper.'"[39]

Oakes's opposition to Safire's hiring did not end with protests to Sulzberger. After Safire began writing his column, Oakes sent many highly critical memos to the publisher about the column's content and writing. Charlotte, meanwhile, grew to enjoy Safire's column and was frequently complimentary of it despite the political differences of the two. Sulzberger, ultimately, probably considered the former speechwriter a good hire—five years after the *Times* hired him, he won a Pulitzer Prize for his columns.

~

John Oakes may have used up some of his political capital at the *Times* opposing Safire. Three years after Safire was hired, Oakes was asked to step down from his editorship as part of an extensive shakeup in the staffing of the *Times* opinion pages—a shakeup that was announced after a controversial *Times* political endorsement.

The behind-the-scenes story of the *Times*'s endorsement of Daniel Patrick Moynihan in the 1976 Democratic senatorial primary in New York is legend—it is one of the most widely told tales in recent *Times* history.[40] Of all the inner-office *Times* anecdotes Charlotte told Hunt over the years, this one stands out in his mind because of its serpentine twists and turns.[41] The story of Oakes and the endorsement is ironic and funny, but it illustrates how seriously *Times* employees took their positions, and it may have launched a rightward political turn by the paper.[42]

In 1976, it was widely believed that the winner of the Democratic senatorial primary in New York would be elected senator, in part because of the negative effect of Watergate on the Republican Party and in part because of weak support for incumbent Republican James Buckley. Oakes, Sulzberger, and others on the *Times* realized the paper's endorsement of the Democratic candidate could be pivotal in determining the result of the September 14 primary and the general election. But Sulzberger and Oakes were divided on whom to endorse: Oakes wanted the liberal congresswoman Bella Abzug, a left-leaning liberal from Manhattan who was a leader in the women's movement. Sulzberger wanted to endorse Moynihan, the centrist and former official in the Nixon administration. The liberal wing of the party opposed Moynihan, who was seen as insensitive to the plight of minorities and oblivious to many social issues.[43]

As a compromise, Sulzberger and Oakes agreed that the *Times* would make no endorsement in this primary but would do so before the general election in November. Satisfied, Oakes left for a vacation to Martha's Vineyard.

After a few days' vacation, Oakes opened the *Times* and found a James Reston column praising Moynihan. Four days later, he received a call from *Times* vice president Sydney Gruson, who informed him that an endorsement of Moynihan would appear the next day. Livid, Oakes composed an eight-paragraph column that was sharply critical of Moynihan and dictated it via telephone to the *Times* for publication next to the endorsement. The next day, *Times* readers found the endorsement of Moynihan—but no column by Oakes. Instead, appearing as a letter to the editor was one paragraph by Oakes claiming to disagree with the endorsement.

This endorsement and watered-down version of the Oakes column set off a chain of events that was widely reported on. Wilkins, furious that the paper would endorse someone he thought was blind to the needs of blacks, wrote an op-ed column knocking Moynihan that was scheduled to run the day of the primary. Sulzberger ordered the column published *after* election day, prompting Wilkins to step down as an editorial writer and concentrate his efforts on an ill-fated urban affairs column.[44] Moynihan, meanwhile, won the primary with 36 percent of the vote, compared to Abzug's 35 percent.

The Moynihan debacle may have helped accelerate the retirement of Oakes, who was due to turn sixty-five in 1978. The *Times* had a mandatory retirement age of sixty-five for its top executives but was very flexible as to the month of retirement. Oakes made it clear that he was not anxious to leave, and he was expected to stay in the job as long as possible. Sulzberger may have had enough, however, of editorial page intrigue. He announced a major shakeup of the paper's editorial page, replacing John Oakes with Sunday editor Max Frankel. And for the first time in decades, the editorial board would be reshuffled as of January 1, 1977. Eight of the thirteen editorial writers would be returned to the news desk, and others would shift between news reporting and editorial writing. The only two whose jobs would remain unchanged were Wilkins and Ada Louise Huxtable, a turn of events that left Sulzberger vulnerable to charges of tokenism.[45] Disputes over the Moynihan endorsement and other editorial stances and the resulting reshuffling of the editorial page were only one small part of the complicated internal politics at the *Times.* In 1976, Sulzberger was getting ready to name Rosenthal executive editor of the newspaper, and the Sunday *Times*—always autonomous from the daily newspaper—was to be merged with the daily. Sunday editor

Frankel, a powerful force at the newspaper who was considered a top contender for executive editor, would be out of a job with the merger. To placate him and to keep him from leaving the paper, Sulzberger offered him the post of editorial page editor, while at the same time allowing the *Times* to take a fresh approach on its editorial page.

Meanwhile, the issue was where to put Oakes. It was decided that he would be a periodic contributor to the op-ed page, allowing him to continue to voice his strong support of social causes. By offering that position to him, Sulzberger conveyed a sense of loyalty to Oakes for his years of service to the paper. With the mandatory retirement program and continual editorial reshuffling, questions periodically arose as to what positions on the paper former top editors should hold. This was a decision *Times* news managers eventually would have to make regarding their op-ed editor, Charlotte Curtis. Whether executives on the paper felt this loyalty to Charlotte is debatable in light of her final years on the *Times*. Ultimately, their feelings toward her may have surprised and dismayed Charlotte, whose fealty to the paper endured above all else.

12

A Dresden Doll

CHARLOTTE'S JOB REMAINED intact after the startling announcement of the editorial board reshuffling in May 1976, although she
now reported to a different supervisor. With the retirement of John
Oakes and the merging of the Sunday and daily papers, her immediate superior was Max Frankel, or "Max the Ax," as he was referred to
derisively by some staff members after the editorial board shakeup.

Actually, it was publisher Sulzberger and not Frankel who was responsible for one of the most sudden and notorious staff shakeups in
Times history. The unification of the Sunday and daily papers and the
complete revamping of the editorial board received extensive news
coverage in and outside of Manhattan. The *Washington Post*, in an
understatement, noted that the changes "are causing considerable
turmoil, confusion and dismay" among editorial board members. The
Post story noted that shocked editorial writers erroneously believed
they had lifetime appointments.[1]

The affable Sulzberger was again showing his sly side. Besides altering the complexion of the paper's opinion pages, the changes pre-
viewed who would hold the power at the *Times* in the future. The

jurisdiction of Rosenthal, as managing editor, was expanded to include oversight of the daily and Sunday papers (and he would soon be named executive editor). Frankel, the Sunday editor, was not pushed aside when the Sunday and daily papers were merged but instead was given the prestigious post of editorial page editor.

When Frankel took over the editorial pages in early 1977, he assumed tighter control of them than Oakes had, but he was sensitive to the personalities of his employees. He remembered Charlotte as a talented, hard worker but one who did not take orders easily: "She was not somebody to whom you barked orders. She was somebody with whom you tried to dissuade. You didn't say, 'do this tomorrow.' She wouldn't have done it." Frankel said many years later that he respected the changes Charlotte initiated on the op-ed page and that she proved to be a pioneer in the commentary she offered: "She was ahead of her time in shifting interest from everything going on in the far-flung regions of the world to the lives of people here at home. That was certainly the trend of recent decades of journalism [in the 1980s and 1990s] and she was moving in that direction."[2]

Frankel believed, however, that Charlotte occasionally went too far. In early 1979, for instance, the op-ed page was transformed into an "Old Codger's Almanac," a parody of *The Farmer's Almanac*, written by a former *Harvard Lampoon* editor. It was a major departure in appearance and style from the usual op-ed page, and it did not please Frankel. He wrote a memo to her indicating that the two had had previous conversations about such departures from accepted style:

> I thought we agreed that you were going to seek my judgment whenever you plan some major variation in the tone and style or appearance of the Op-Ed page. I not only want to be asked, but asked early enough so that my judgment will count.
>
> Whatever the merits or amusement value of today's Almanac — and I failed to recognize them — I firmly believe that such a thing does not belong on Op-Ed. There is plenty of space in the *Times* for magazine features. But Op-ed is where a large body of readers expects ideas and issues discussed in a serious (which, of course, in-

cludes bright and even humorous) way. Most radical departures of format will detract from that mission, no matter what their inherent interest.[3]

This memo illustrates Charlotte's balancing act as op-ed editor. She was hired for the job because of her creativity and unorthodox news judgment, yet those were the very qualities that sometimes drew criticism from top editors. And then there were those people—like Salisbury—who believed she was not daring enough on her page.

~

By January 1977, the year the staff changes took place, Charlotte had few complaints. She and Hunt traveled extensively, and she went to Columbus every other weekend. Hunt visited her in her tiny Greenwich Village apartment on East Tenth Street, and the couple would socialize with the Sulzbergers or a few others on the *Times* or simply stay at home. Charlotte's New York apartment was barely large enough for two people, and Hunt enjoyed recounting that it was formerly a servants' quarters. Its outstanding feature was its porch, which ran the length of the apartment, allowing Charlotte to establish a lush garden, overflowing with flowers, bushes, and small trees. Charlotte dubbed it her "Ohio garden," and she was very protective about who touched or tended it. She did not even trust her neurosurgeon husband in this regard: "She told me I was a good brain surgeon but I was too heavy handed for her petunias. She wouldn't let me touch her flowers." Charlotte's lifelong interest in gardening was even more intense now that she had more free time. The flowers and shrubs, she told Hunt, reminded her of Ohio and always did wonders for her "Midwestern soul." She often said that if she were not in the newspaper business, she would own a flower shop.[4]

Charlotte's circle of close friends in Manhattan remained small: Clifton and Margaret Daniel now lived in Washington, D.C., as did her college friend Lucky Roosevelt. In New York, Charlotte socialized with journalist Richard Clurman and his wife, Shirley; Joan Whitman, her assistant on the women's pages; David Schneiderman, her assistant on the op-ed page, and a handful of others, primarily journalists. Charlotte could never use her tiny Manhattan apartment for entertaining, but her reluctance to move to a bigger apartment was her one tacit acknowledgment of her illness earlier that decade. Doctors had warned her in 1972 that her cancer would likely recur within five years so she felt it would have made little sense for her to move.

Her cancer had not returned by 1980, though, and she felt healthy. Through the years, Charlotte had suffered skin rashes that came and went, and frequently she experienced fatigue and lack of energy. But she lived with these ailments and compensated for them. Hunt said Charlotte was economical in her actions and movement, never wasting motion and energy. While many hard workers and perfectionists establish an efficiency in movement, Charlotte's came in part as a result of her physical shortcomings.[5]

Charlotte did not question her good health and was pleased to prove her doctors wrong. But Hunt acknowledged that the couple knew she was living on borrowed time. Both were too knowledgeable about medicine to expect a miracle. Hunt maintains that Charlotte was too disciplined mentally to let the specter of an impending illness dampen her enthusiasm for her job or for their lives together. Besides, by the early 1980s, Charlotte was witnessing something that no doubt thrilled her: the coming of age of her hometown, Columbus, and its maturation from a small town to a major city.

~

Leslie Wexner remembers clearly the first few times he saw Charlotte Curtis. In an unobtrusive way, she was oddly distinctive as she sat smoking and reading in the TWA waiting area at LaGuardia Airport.

In the early 1980s, Wexner, like Curtis, lived a double life, residing in both Columbus and New York City. The chairman and chief executive officer of the Limited Corporation apparel chain, he frequently conducted business in Manhattan during the week and returned to his Columbus home on weekends. It was inevitable that the *New York Times* op-ed editor and the CEO of one of the fastest-growing companies in the country would meet, especially since they both treasured their hometown of Columbus, Ohio, and valued their midwestern roots.

Wexner's introduction to Charlotte in the early 1980s, with its co-incidences and twists, sounds like the plot of a screwball comedy, but it was an introduction that he believes dramatically influenced his life and thoughts. After working the week in Manhattan, Wexner routinely flew back on Friday nights to his home and family in sub-urban Bexley on TWA Flight 17. Each week, he would see many of the same people as he sat in the TWA waiting area. One woman in particular remained distinctive for her silence and severity. She re-minded him of Bette Davis: "Certain people would be commuting [each week] and I'd see them frequently. I always saw this really stern woman who never talked. She was tiny, like a schoolmarm. Very tight."[6]

Months later, Wexner's friend and business partner, Columbus developer Jack Kessler, believed Wexner should meet Charlotte. Wexner by this time was an internationally known businessman, and Kessler thought Charlotte, with her ties to the *Times*, could help Wexner professionally. Kessler arranged a small gathering at his home, and when Wexner arrived, there stood the severe-looking woman he had seen at LaGuardia: "When I met her, she had gone from Bette Davis to Marilyn Monroe—I saw the softer side," he said.

The friendship between Charlotte and Wexner grew over the years, and he laughs at how this stern schoolmarm became the sharp, cyni-cal, and funny woman he later came to know. Although they met so-cially only occasionally, Wexner said her influence on him was such that it took him years to accept her death. After her death, he said, he for years carried her newspaper obituary in his pocket because "I couldn't let her go."

Wexner was intrigued that Charlotte enjoyed his company and found him interesting, although he apparently did not see the paral-lels in their personalities. Both appeared conservative and discreet, but their looks were deceiving. Both were radicals who were not afraid to challenge a deeply ingrained status quo, and neither was overly concerned about what people thought of them. Wexner is a self-made man and entrepreneur who built his empire from the ground up. A workaholic, he, like Charlotte, married late in life and maintains close ties to his mother and to his hometown. His professional life is in Manhattan, but he still lives in Columbus. He has become a recognizable celebrity in New York, but he scorns the cocktail parties and much of the social life in favor of evenings with his family.

Wexner admired Charlotte's sincerity, loyalty, and wit: "She was insightful about people. You couldn't have a small-talk conversation with Charlotte, but I never felt I was being interrogated [by her]. There was that inquisitiveness, the intellect, the ability to get people to talk."

What forged the bond between them, he believes, was their love of their hometown. When they grew up in Columbus in the mid-1940s, the town was home to one of the biggest universities in the country and had a population of about a quarter of a million. But it was provincial and unsophisticated, largely influenced by its neighbors to the south, West Virginia and Kentucky, rather than by the more cosmopolitan Cleveland to the northeast. From the 1940s until the 1960s, economic and political clout in the city was consolidated in the hands of two families: the Wolfes, who owned the city's biggest newspaper, the *Dispatch*, as well as one of the three television stations, a radio station, and one of the city's most powerful and biggest banks; and the Lazaruses, who owned the city's only department store. Later, the Jeffrey family, which owned the world's largest mechanical mining manufacturing company, joined them. These families contributed immeasurably to the economic base of the city, but some people believe the city stagnated under their benevolent rule.

Then came Wexner, whose tremendous success as an entrepreneur in the mid-1970s made him an active participant in the Columbus social and cultural scene. As a lifelong Columbus resident, Wexner wanted to help change Columbus, and he felt the time was right. By this time, the city had grown to nearly one million people. With the failure of the steel and other manufacturing industries to the north, Columbus, whose economy was based on government and education, was thriving. Wexner envisioned Columbus as a cultural leader, on par with cities like Baltimore and Atlanta.

Although he was subdued and low-key personally, the maverick Wexner, with his liberal politics, became a controversial figure in Columbus when he donated large amounts of money for buildings and arts centers and challenged wealthy residents to match his contributions. Charlotte loved that Wexner stirred things up—and she believed he was trying to improve the city she adored.

When she became a *Times* columnist, Charlotte wrote two columns about Wexner. Both focused on the tremendous growth of his company over a short time, his vision for Columbus, and his status as a reluctant celebrity who had little interest in the Manhattan social scene: "More than anything, he wants an open, exuberant *esprit de corps* in an uptight town [Columbus] that has always allowed a few rich people to dominate its thinking and set its standards. He and the new leaders are going to get that too. 'It isn't as if we didn't have bright, creative people or leaders,' he said. 'We do. But nobody ever told them it's O.K. to disagree, to lead, to try new ideas, to achieve.'"[7] In the column, Charlotte referred to Wexner as a "2,000-pound gorilla" whose presence and enthusiasm took Columbus by storm. The analogy still amused him a decade later.

~

Charlotte and Hunt suspected they could not live a charmed life forever, and they were right. Charlotte, who for decades had dodged the bullets of change at the paper, was not immune to it. After eight years as op-ed editor, she was given a new assignment in 1982: she would become a weekly columnist in the paper's news section and would once again report to Rosenthal.

Charlotte could be secretive and discreet, even to her closest friends, so her true feelings about her new job are difficult to gauge. Some of her friends, like former colleague Marylin Bender and

Richard Clurman, saw the new assignment as a demotion. Others, like Hunt and such former top executives as Sulzberger, Salisbury, and Frankel, believed the assignment allowed her to indulge in her favorite pastime of writing and was a lateral move. To still others, like Schneiderman, the move was a combination of the two: news executives did not intentionally "demote" her, but instead, her job assignment changed as the result of a string of other reassignments.

On April 15, 1982, the *Times* ran a news story describing changes on its foreign desk and op-ed page. Robert Semple Jr., foreign editor, would become op-ed editor, and his assistant on the foreign desk, Craig Whitney, would become foreign editor. Charlotte Curtis, the article said, would in June become a columnist on the news pages. The publisher praised her work on the op-ed page, noting that its function "is to give readers a broad range of opinion and analysis of current issues . . . [and] Charlotte Curtis has fulfilled that mission with great distinction. I welcome her decision to return to writing," Sulzberger is quoted as saying.[8]

What the article did not say was that Charlotte would no longer carry the title of *Times* associate editor. The same restructuring stripped former Washington bureau chief and op-ed columnist Tom Wicker of his associate editor title. The associate editorship title and its placement on the *Times* masthead is a statement of who holds the power at the paper; as former *Times* columnist Anna Quindlen once said, four words describe the power structure at the *Times*: "Look at the masthead."[9] Thus the removal of Curtis's and Wicker's names told much about their new status on the paper.

Publicly, Charlotte maintained that she was pleased to return to writing regularly, and Hunt says she was happy with her new assignment. But Charlotte, characteristically, would not reveal—perhaps even to her husband—that she was hurt or insulted, nor would she waste her time with negative emotions. Some of her friends, like Schneiderman, believe that pride would have prevented her from acknowledging a demotion.[10] In her own mind, though, she may have concentrated on the positive aspect of the change—the prospect of writing regularly again for the paper and the chance to write in the news section, where she had longed to be decades earlier. But the new job was not as easy as it may have seemed. Charlotte's new assignment as a columnist was fraught with problems, and her opportunity to write for the news pages, her goal for decades, proved bitterly ironic.

~

One of the first actions Charlotte took in her new job was to write a friendly memo to Punch Sulzberger. The courteous and self-deprecating memo was typical Charlotte: it was the polite way of making the best of an awkward situation. She thanked him for her new office, which housed a photo of the *Times* building:

> That's just the prettiest office in the whole New York Times, and I love it. And I'm especially grateful for the wonderful picture of the old, old New York Times.
> More important, many thanks for your support over the years, including the opportunity to do the column (in which I just may fall on my face). The column is one of the great chances (as well as terrors) of a lifetime, and I'll try very hard not to disgrace you or The Times—on general principles—you'd better brace yourself.
>
> Big smooch,
Charlotte[11]

Charlotte's appointment as a *New York Times* columnist might seem prestigious—indeed, the opportunity to write a free-style column in one of the nation's most elite newspapers seems enviable. But one must know the editorial pecking order at that newspaper to understand that Charlotte no longer occupied a top perch in the hierarchy. Her position as news columnist rather than op-ed columnist meant, first, that her work would be printed in the back part of the news section rather than on the more prominent op-ed page, and, more important, the news columnist job did not carry with it the cachet that an op-ed column did. The opportunity to write an op-ed column was the highest praise the *Times* could bestow on an employee, and even a sporadic position on the page—such as the one John Oakes was given—was acknowledgment of talent and intelligence.

The worst part of her new job, however, had nothing to do with the column's placement or prestige: it was that she would now report to her old nemesis, Abe Rosenthal. And Rosenthal had very distinct and specific ideas about the content of her column. He believed that because it was in the news section, it could not be "political" or take a controversial point of view. In a memo to Sulzberger, he spelled out his vision of a Curtis column. He noted, graciously, that he and readers would be happy to read Charlotte's writing again regularly and that she should write about "society, social structure and the mores of living in the United States." Further, he noted, the column could be flexible and appear in other sections throughout the paper.[12] Although the memo at first seems to indicate that she would receive plenty of leeway, the column as outlined by Rosenthal was limiting, as he acknowledged much later, because she could not write about anything he deemed political in nature. "It was a difficult thing to do because it had to reflect her personality and it could not be a political expression [because] we felt that would cross a line between what should be on the news pages and what should be on the editorial pages," he said fifteen years later. "I could say it was caught in the middle. It was difficult to do and she probably did not enjoy walking in the middle."[13]

Frankel also believes Charlotte was in an awkward position as a news page columnist. While she wanted to write, she did not want to repeat what she had done a decade before and had to be careful in how her opinion appeared in her columns: "She didn't want to do just the high society stuff. It's very hard to write a column that sounds opinionated but is essentially analytical and reportorial."[14] Most of Charlotte's columns at the time were lackluster accounts of dinner parties or interviews with cultural or political celebrities of the era, including Alexander Haig, Ted Turner, and John DeLorean.

Even Charlotte's friends acknowledge that her four years as a columnist were disappointing. They thought her writing lost the edge it once had and the subject matter was frequently uninteresting.[15] They speculated on the reasons: it was possible that Charlotte, who for the last eight years did little writing regularly and concentrated on meeting people and "networking" for the op-ed page, simply was out of practice. Or perhaps she had become too close to the people she had met while op-ed editor and could not write about them with the same edge. Or Rosenthal's constraints on subject matter may have put her in a literary no-man's land: it was impossible for her to write anything but fluff if she were to conform to those guidelines.

Her old mentor Salisbury thought she "lost her way on that column," although she could have easily defied Rosenthal's restrictions. Others acknowledge that while such defiance might have been possible for someone of the stature of Salisbury, it was not possible for Charlotte. Salisbury believed it was a mistake for Charlotte to take on the column; she should have left the *Times* for one of the national women's magazines, which would have given her the space and encouragement to regain her edge.

But leaving the paper was out of the question for Charlotte, who had been called "the bride of the *New York Times*."[16] As Marylin Bender noted shortly after Charlotte's death, she never would have been "unfaithful" to the paper: "For more than twenty-five years Charlotte and I had a running conversation really about one topic, our love for the newspaper business, and in particular one newspaper, to which we both came as outsiders with the passion of second marriages. We only disagreed about one thing. What do you do when your lover lets you down? I was for walking out. She was for hanging in. But that takes courage."[17]

To Richard Clurman, another of her longtime friends, changes in her outlook and her associations made the column mediocre: "She didn't know what she'd be writing about and she never defined it. The cutting edge and standoffishness of her original writing was invisible." Clurman, however, thought Charlotte might have forged dangerous personal friendships with her story sources: "It began to get harder to write about people she began to know well," he said. "That wasn't the case in her early writing."[18]

The strict news values she held as a young society page reporter may have faded as she grew older. "In the end, when she tried to go back to reporting, it was like reinflating a soufflé," said Charlotte's former co-worker Joan Whitman. "Times had changed. The people she went back to cover really didn't matter. She had become one of them and she knew it."[19]

Salisbury and Clurman believe that a growing interest in business and entrepreneurs and a growing personal and political conservatism also began to shape her writing, although Hunt and some of her friends disagree. Clurman and Salisbury both think that Charlotte developed a strong and unnatural interest in the activities of CEOs and business titans and that dominated her writing.

Files found after her death in her *Times* office were filled with information about business owners and corporation leaders. Of course, an interest in entrepreneurs does not necessarily mean she became conservative politically, and her concentration on this topic may have stemmed from her early interest in the lives of powerful and wealthy people. Also among her files, however, was a thick folder titled "Homelessness and Hunger," which contained notes in Charlotte's handwriting. Her observations may seem unusual for someone who had always championed the underclass and the underdog: "It's a mistake to characterize them as nice. Perhaps they once were. Now, they are frightened. They hurt. They're hungry. They're frightened and even cynical. So many do-gooders of one sort or another have failed them and failed them so many times. Mostly, they do not like reporters. In the old days, a newspaper story was a way out. People read and responded. Not today. Now they want money for their stories. 'No money, no story,' a woman said."[20] Charlotte believed that society's ills could not be cured simply by throwing money at them. But here, her views are cynical and uncharacteristically pessimistic.

It was unlike Charlotte to become bitter or disillusioned; in fact, her refusal to surrender to such emotions contributed greatly to her professional success. But she must have been hurt by this assignment and the restrictions on the column, even though the cordial note to Sulzberger indicated otherwise. On one hand, Charlotte was smart enough to know her transfer was a business decision, and such decisions were made every day to improve the paper. On the other hand, she could not have helped but feel betrayed by her friend Punch Sulzberger. But many of Charlotte's mentors and supporters, including Daniel and Sulzberger, were long retired, and Sulzberger naturally relied heavily on Rosenthal's opinion when making editorial decisions on the *Times*. Rosenthal was, after all, executive editor of the paper.

~

After she had been writing her column for a year or two, Charlotte's friends and co-workers began to speculate about why her writing had lost its verve and energy. To some people, however, the reason was no mystery. Nearly thirty years of writing and editing at an intense pace may have taken its toll on her. "I think she reached the point in her career where she was just tired," Schneiderman said. "But I knew if she sunk her teeth into a good subject, she could do it well."[21]

As her friends learned later, Charlotte's weariness was not just mental. By the mid-1980s, she began sending regrets to the many people who invited her to dinners, parties, and other events. In 1984, she had plans to attend national political conventions in Dallas and San Francisco but later decided against participating in the frenzied activities related to those conventions. In a short note, Charlotte thanked *Washington Post* publisher Katharine Graham for an invitation: "It was nice getting invited to your always marvelous parties," she wrote, adding that she had been invited to many parties during the convention but had declined most of them. "I'm playing hookey,"[22] she said.

Few people knew that Charlotte was "playing hookey" for health reasons. Although her cancer had not returned, she was suffering from a grinding fatigue that made it a fight to prepare herself for work each morning. It was a weariness that had been creeping up on her over the last two or three years, but now it lasted all day, robbing her of energy. But that did not stop her from moving out of her penthouse apartment on East Tenth Avenue into a bigger apartment on West End Avenue and Eighty-second Street. She bought the apartment so Hunt would be more comfortable during his visits there and so she could have more overnight guests. A frequent guest was Dr. Carole Miller, a neurological surgeon and Dr. Hunt's medical partner at OSU who had become a close friend of Charlotte and Hunt. The move to West End Avenue was not just a practical one: it was an act of faith, initiated long after doctors said her cancer would recur.

By this time, Charlotte was thinking about making a will, although it is unknown what steps she took. A handwritten draft among her papers suggests that by the early 1980s, her sympathies still lay with minority and arts causes. In it she left much of her estate to her mother and to Hunt. Some of the remainder of her personal assets were to go to her sister and her sister's three children; to Hunt's three children; and to Carole Miller and David Schneiderman. Much of her jewelry, art, and other valuables were left to Hunt, Miller, her sister, Mary Davey, and her stepdaughter-in-law, Carol Santangelo Hunt. Charlotte's relationship with Hunt's three children was cordial but distant, a function of time and geography. His two sons, Will and David, were in their twenties when she and Hunt married, and his youngest child, Ginny, was in her early teens. His children did not live in Columbus for most of the years of their relationship.

The bulk of cash assets in the estate were left to causes that were dear to her heart: the Columbus Museum of Art, which would receive $150,000; and the NAACP Legal Defense Fund and "the homeless" in New York City, which would each receive $50,000. According to these notes, she also wanted to leave $10,000 to the Whitney Museum of American Art and $5,000 to Trinity Church in Columbus.[23] Charlotte had earmarked her personal papers for the University of Texas at Austin but later changed her mind and wanted them to go to the Schlesinger Women's Studies Library at Radcliffe College, where they were sent after her death. The Schlesinger Library had expressed an interest in Lucile Curtis's papers after she had been honored by the U.S. State Department as the first woman in the U.S Foreign Service, and Charlotte probably became acquainted with the library at that time and changed her mind about where she wanted her own papers to be deposited.

Charlotte's energy level had declined even further by mid-1985, and she had dramatically reduced her activities. By this time, Lucile Curtis, too, was ill. The ninety-year-old Lucile was forced to curtail her travel and was bedridden. It was a depressing time for Charlotte, who kept in constant communication with her mother throughout her life and even as a middle-aged woman tried to live up to Lucile's high standards. Charlotte and her sister, Mary, visited her on alternate weekends, Charlotte flying in from New York and Mary from northern California. Because of this rotating caretaking schedule, Mary and Charlotte usually missed each other by a day or so.

Her mother's illness and her own poor health were not the only depressing aspects of Charlotte's life in 1985. A friend and co-worker, *Times* reporter Judy Klemesrud, died of breast cancer at the age of forty-six. Charlotte got herself together one cold December day to speak at Klemesrud's memorial service. Nearly twenty years earlier, Charlotte had hired the small-town Iowa woman who became well-known among *Times* readers for her articles about such topics as lesbian mothers, teenage pregnancy, and drug addiction. Charlotte spoke at the service about Klemesrud's innovative and unsentimental writing style. She might have been describing herself:

> Her prose was crisp, deft and irreverent. She had an ear for dialogue. She quoted her subjects wryly. . . . It was Judy Klemesrud's hard work, her drive and talent that got her to the *Times*. Her clips told you she could report as well as write, that she was neither gushy nor superficial, that she believed every story had to have substance as well as style. . . .
>
> She did her stories in what seemed like ten minutes. She cared what happened to her copy. She battled with editors. . . . Uptown pretensions and la-de-dah left her cold. She had little use for fash-

ion, home furnishings, food, social events or any of the other "junk" she found on the style pages. But she wrote the "junk" dutifully, effectively, occasionally hilariously and sometimes brilliantly.

Charlotte noted that in Klemesrud's high school year book in Thompson, Iowa, someone had predicted she would become editor of the *Times*. "I asked her about the prediction shortly after she arrived [at the *Times*]," Charlotte said. "'Is that true?' I said. 'Of course,' she answered. 'But don't tell Punch Sulzberger.'"[24]

Klemesrud's father wrote Charlotte thanking her for the eulogy and noting that he had been told Charlotte was ill and might not attend: "I had been warned that you might not be present because you had been under the weather. Imagine how pleased I was when you arrived—energetic and spunky."[25] Charlotte had everyone fooled.

Charlotte had to deal with another death in late 1985, and this one became the subject of a column. The *Columbus Citizen-Journal* folded. During the first week of 1986, she wrote a column about the paper's demise, proving Schneiderman correct in his assessment that despite of a lack of energy, "if she sunk her teeth into a good subject, she could do it." Her friends considered it one of her best columns.

The paper that first allowed Charlotte to exercise her unusual and irreverent writing style ceased publication on December 31, 1985, leaving Columbus a one-newspaper town. Charlotte's column about the paper's demise was unsentimental but touching. She wrote about the paper's early history, its daring, and its longtime contributions to the community. But she could not resist mentioning how it was the ne'er-do-wells of the 1950s who shaped it. She did not mention that she was a proud member of those ranks:

> In the Middle America of the 50's, newspapering was still often the work of itinerants and ne'er-do-wells. If you could report and write, you could report and write. No questions were asked. And while The Citizen was respectable enough, its staff by today's standards was oddly exotic.
>
> The senior reporter was a former railroad engineer. The society

editor bore the scar of a stray bullet she received in an encounter with one of Al Capone's hoods. The obituary writer sobbed when anyone phoned in a death notice.

The city editor loathed college graduates unless they could drink him under the table. The news editor was a failed Olympic hurdler. And the managing editor, having coined "flash flood," dreamed of leaving to work for Life magazine.[26]

Charlotte accepted the demise of the *Citizen-Journal* as she accepted her own illness and, ultimately, her own death. Her illness was an unexplainable quirk of nature; the paper's demise was an unavoidable result of economics and a changing society. In the last paragraph, she recalled the day the old *Citizen* merged with the *Journal*, noting the sometimes cruel inevitability of change and progress: "The staff, the special few and the dispersed alumni, sense the loss. But there was no wringing of hands when The Citizen went down, no concern for what monopoly newspapering means to a city. The paper was a buggy whip in a jet age, and a frayed buggy whip at that. The economics, to paraphrase Thomas Mann, were in dead earnest." The column drew positive responses, including letters of praise from writers Leo Rosten and Ellen Goodman. Rosenthal wrote her that the column was "lovely. . . . It was warm and not mawkish—very difficult [to write]."[27]

∿

Lucile Curtis died peacefully in her sleep at age ninety-one on May 8, 1986. She had been ill for about six months and until that time maintained a hectic schedule. At her memorial service in Columbus, Mary Davey saw her sister for the first time in a year, and she was shocked. Charlotte, who had always been thin, had lost weight and looked gaunt and pale: "I couldn't believe how awful she looked. I knew something was wrong, but she wouldn't say anything." She mentioned her fears to Hunt, who agreed that Charlotte's appearance and extreme fatigue worried him.[28] Further, he said, he and

Carole Miller noticed she always seemed chilled and wore heavy coats even in warm weather.

Charlotte entered the hospital for a series of tests, and she received some unexpected good news: she had a severely underactive thyroid, which doctors believed caused the fatigue and sensitivity to cold. Hypothyroidism is easily treatable through medication so Charlotte was pleased with the diagnosis. She and Mary were also amused by the irony that their father had been a thyroid specialist. "We went into gales of laughter because that was our father's area," Davey said. "She was so full of the fact that the docs didn't figure this out, and they finally got the hang of it."[29] Their relief was short-lived, although at first treatment for the thyroid condition appeared to be successful; Charlotte gained weight and her energy level improved. In the early summer of 1986, however, she and Hunt learned that the doctors' grim prediction of 1972 had finally come true. The cancer had returned, and this time it was in her liver.

The treatment for Charlotte's hypothyroidism reactivated the cancer, hastening its return and spread. Remarkably, she trudged to work at the *Times* each day until June, when she could no longer do so. Davey and Hunt believed it was sheer will that kept her going that long. "She loved what she did and that was the great motivator," Davey said. "When literally her body was dying on her she wouldn't let it get the better of her."

Charlotte could not go on working, but she still hid the truth from her friends, most of whom were seasoned reporters whose job was ferreting out information. She told them that she was returning to Columbus temporarily for health reasons, and they did not guess the gravity of the situation. "She said, 'I'm going in the hospital, but I'll be back, Davie,'" Schneiderman said. "She didn't mention cancer."[30] Ever the realist, Charlotte probably knew she would never return to the *Times* building. Still, she had outwitted the "docs," as she called them, before.

Near Thanksgiving 1986, Carole Miller called Mary Davey to tell her that Charlotte's condition was deteriorating rapidly. "I got the call, and she said, 'You'd better get out here,'" Davey said. "I got on the first plane. We really did think she was going to die." It was not quite a month until Charlotte's fifty-eighth birthday. Her sister, however, "fooled everyone," Davey said. "She took the treatments, she pulled it out."[31]

~

After Charlotte's name was removed from the *Times* masthead in 1982, no woman was listed, formally, as a top editor of that paper. This would soon change, and the decade of the 1980s was the best of times for women at the paper—although that was not saying much.

The settlement of *Boylan* vs. *Times* in 1978 gave much publicity to the plight of women at that newspaper and other media outlets; though the *Times* publicly acknowledged no wrongdoing, the implication was that the paper settled because mistakes had been made in hiring and promoting women. By this time, however, strides were being made in hiring that would eventually allow women to build up momentum in their efforts for equality at the paper.

One of the most noteworthy of these was the hiring and gradual promotion of Anna Quindlen, who became the first female deputy metro editor at the paper and later a prize-winning op-ed columnist. Quindlen was hired as a news reporter in 1977 at the age of twenty-four, was the first woman to write the long-standing column, "About New York," and in 1990 became the third woman on the paper to have a regular op-ed column. But Quindlen's claim to fame was that her writing focused not on foreign policy or current news but on her life as a mother and wife and on the problems of underprivileged families; she chronicled everyday happenings and opinions of an "average" parent as well as subjects such as drug-addicted babies and domestic violence—certainly new subjects for a regular op-ed columnist. Her style of writing paralleled Charlotte's efforts on the op-ed page through guest comments, and warm and encouraging memos among Charlotte's papers show that Charlotte frequently complimented Quindlen on her writing.[32] Indeed, Quindlen believes that women in a media organization must help each other if they want to achieve equality. She said women must practice "reverse discrimination" and seek out and promote the hiring of talented women. Quindlen, for instance, said she strongly pushed for the hiring of Maureen Dowd, who would later become a widely known *Times* White House reporter and op-ed columnist. Women, she said, "have a moral obligation to not only help other women, but to foster some of the special qualities which make us do an exemplary job as executives."[33]

Still, women had a long way to go both on and off the *Times*. The Associated Press had no women bureau chiefs until 1975 and by 1987 had only six out of seventy-six. In 1975, only 5.2 percent of the top editors at major newspapers were women; that percentage number doubled by 1986 to 12 percent.[34] And salaries were equally bad, according to a 1985 study done of 648 newspaper publishers which showed that, overall, top women editors earned three-fourths the salaries of their male counterparts.[35]

The *Times*, however, was making small strides. In addition to the hiring and promoting of Quindlen, Soma Golden, a former *Times* Sunday business editor and editorial writer, became national editor, earning a spot on the masthead. By the late 1980s, Nancy Newhouse became editor of the *Times*'s revamped lifestyle sections, and Carolyn Lee was photo editor.

～

Charlotte, meanwhile, was consigned to the sidelines, living at the Hunts' high-rise condominium in Columbus. Although her condition worsened gradually over her last ten months, she was not to go idly into that good night. She kept as active as possible, reading voraciously and keeping journals about her thoughts and her illness.[36] She filled nearly ten reporters' notebooks with facts and ideas about her treatment and observations from her sickbed. "The notes are filled with graphs and laboratory tests in detail, with times and hours and symptoms in exquisite detail," Hunt said. "Medical opinions are freely expressed and critiques of the 'big docs,' as she called them, are also there. There are also lengthy comments on local and national politics, Ohio State, the *New York Times*, the stock market and society in general."[37]

Their lifelong proximity to the world of medicine helped Hunt and Charlotte remain stoic during the last few months of Charlotte's life, although it could not have been easy for them. In addition, they both had had many years to prepare for the return of the cancer, and they both knew it would return. Charlotte coped by doing what she had always done—keeping her mind active and occupied. She frequently suggested story ideas to her colleagues at work and kept up on the office gossip about the latest power struggle at the paper: this time the office buzz was about who would replace Rosenthal as executive editor.[38]

By 1987, her co-workers at the paper learned about her condition. Schneiderman visited Charlotte in Columbus that March—nine months after her departure from New York and two weeks before her death. In typical Charlotte fashion, she was impeccably groomed, wearing jewelry, her makeup perfect, and he knew she took pains to pull herself together before he arrived. During his visit, the two discussed current events, *Times* gossip, and mutual friends. They barely discussed her condition.[39]

Charlotte also engaged in another vital activity during her final months: the planning of her own memorial service, a task she tackled "as though she was planning a Christmas party," Hunt said. She spent much time arranging for the location, the music, and the speakers. Even Charlotte acknowledged that someone besides herself would need to carry out her plans, and she enlisted her friend Richard Clurman, whom she thought had done a good job of carrying out the requests of others who planned memorial services. The service would be held in front of the fountains at Lincoln Center, and speakers would include her close friends Clifton Daniel, Punch Sulzberger, Harrison Salisbury, former *Times* executive Sydney Gruson, Schneiderman, Bender, syndicated columnist Liz Smith, her friend and former colleague Roger Wilkins, and Hunt. The list was the result of much thought.

Charlotte's detached attitude about her condition exemplified her mental toughness. Her careful preparation for Schneiderman's visit was classic Curtis—it showed how deceiving her dainty and meticulous physical demeanor could be. At her memorial service, Clifton Daniel, the last one to speak, noted that because of her appearance, Charlotte frequently was compared to a Dresden doll—a somewhat off-target analogy: "She was pretty. But she was not made of porcelain. Intellectually, she was made of cast iron. She had an iron will, an iron determination, an iron integrity."[40]

Her interest in current events never waned, even when she was gravely ill during the last few weeks of her life. In a letter to Bender dated March 1, about six weeks before her death, she suggested a story idea about tycoons for the *Business World*, the *Times* business magazine that Bender edited. "I wrote her back, 'It's a great story, Charlotte. The only problem is I know of one reporter, and only one reporter, who would get the story right.'"[41]

Charlotte's death on April 16, 1987, came in the spring, her favorite time of year because her beloved flowers had just started to bloom. Hunt said that four days before she died she told him it was one of the happiest days of her life "because the Ohio spring came in through open windows."[42]

Before she went, however, Charlotte, ever the writer, made one last request. She left Clurman a note asking that her memorial service be a festive occasion. The note was short and to the point, complete with two exclamation points for emphasis.[43] It read: "With any luck, she will die with her eyebrows and eyelashes properly painted, her hair combed and a smile on her face. She had a glorious life, loved work and was paid to do what she would have done for free. So please celebrate!!"

13

Final Tribute

As Charlotte's friends gathered in front of Avery Fisher Hall for her memorial service on May 20, 1987, Richard Clurman had carried out to the letter her requests for the event: a group of Manhattan musicians provided the music before the service, and her friend from Columbus Beverly Carroll sang at the end. Another friend from New York selected and arranged the flowers for the event.

One by one, the nine people who spoke offered their thoughts and recalled their favorite anecdotes, many of these stories entertaining and some of them poignant. David Schneiderman recalled, for instance, that after meeting an obscure Georgia governor named Jimmy Carter at a *Times* publisher's lunch in the mid-1970s, Charlotte was alone in predicting that he would one day be president. Roger Wilkins recalled the afternoon in 1970 that he sat in the plush apartment of Leonard Bernstein at a Black Panther fund-raiser. Sitting and observing quietly in the corner was a tiny woman with a notebook who suddenly perked up when a guest made a silly and self-serving remark. "Uh, oh, he's in trouble," said the person standing next to Wilkins. "There's Charlotte Curtis." It was his first contact with the woman he would befriend a decade later.

Most telling, however, were the comments of Sydney Gruson, who reminded the group of Charlotte's single-minded devotion to the *Times*. "It was the paper on which she lavished her love, her hope, her attention," he said. "She cared about the paper, almost desperately. And I think her first desire, above everything else in her working life, was try to make it better."[1]

Did Charlotte succeed in making the paper better? Her friends, of course, would argue that she did. But so would those who were not her friends, including A. M. Rosenthal, who said that she contributed to the high quality and fine reputation of the New York Times during her tenure there.[2] More pressing questions remain about her long-term legacy, whether her efforts led to the continued betterment of the paper, whether her innovations stood the test of time, and whether her tenure there as the first women news executive eventually helped make life easier for the women who followed her.

Those are tough questions, and answering them requires a brief examination of what the *Times* left Charlotte. Several former *Times* employees have compared Charlotte's career at the paper to a marriage; Nan Robertson called her the "bride of the New York Times."[3] Gruson noted how she lavished love and tireless effort on it. And Charlotte's colleague and good friend Marylin Bender said Charlotte's relationship to the paper was like a romantic one: "What do you do when your lover lets you down? I was for walking out. She was always for hanging in."[4]

Robertson and some others believe the *Times* ultimately let Charlotte down and that a stellar career ended with a whimper. And Robertson believes that she never regained the respect of many of the women who took part in the lawsuit against the *Times*. Some of these women were still angry and disillusioned with Charlotte two decades later.

As a result of this nonparticipation, Charlotte may have learned the hard way that her subtle lobbying on the behalf of the women — instead of joining the lawsuit — simply did not work. They felt that they needed her open support, and her method of quietly exercising her influence with key executives was not the same thing. As the lawsuit dragged on, however, Charlotte confided to her friend Bender that she may have underestimated the conservatism of her friends in the executive suite. She believed that *Times* officials were unaware of their discriminatory treatment of women, and she felt she could inform them of this and suggest ways to make improvements. She was shocked to learn that perhaps *Times* management was not, consciously, doing all it could to hire and promote women and that she had been misguided in her views about some of her friends.[5] Further, Robertson said, a sadder but wiser Charlotte late in 1983 gave a warning to Anna Quindlen after Quindlen had been named deputy metropolitan editor: "You will only have as much power as they wish you to have," Charlotte said. "Don't fool yourself as to what this promotion means. Do the best you can for yourself and for other women and don't blame yourself if that's not enough."[6] Charlotte learned that she may have been naïve in thinking her behind-the-scenes lobbying could be effective and in her belief that the paper's news executives could always be trusted to do the right thing.

The *Times* may have let her down in other ways. Like any organization, the paper has subtle and "unofficial" ways of rewarding and recognizing longtime employees for jobs well done. After Charlotte was removed from her op-ed job, the assignment to write even an occasional op-ed column would have been considered a reward for her previous work. Longtime editorial page editor John Oakes wrote op-ed columns after he was removed from the editorial page, and Robert Semple, who succeeded Charlotte as op-ed editor, became a member of the *Times* editorial board after he was taken off the op-ed page. And the top editors of the paper—former executive editors Rosenthal and Max Frankel—were given key columns after their retirement, on the op-ed page and in the Sunday magazine, respectively.

Charlotte, however, was given a nebulous assignment as news columnist, her column was consigned to the back pages, and editors imposed great restrictions on its subject matter. Even with the column, as Harrison Salisbury noted, Charlotte could have been "plucked" from her job as columnist to cover breaking news or trends that would have led to prominent play for her stories.[7]

Wilkins, formerly an editorial writer, found, too, that the *Times* could snub someone subtly. Wilkins survived the editorial page purge of 1976 but soon requested and received permission to write a regular urban affairs column covering issues of interest to minority readers. Although the assignment seemed like a plum to him, publication of his columns frequently was delayed or canceled; his columns were not edited by the same person each week and were given such low priority and poor treatment that he soon left the paper.[8]

Longtime assistant women's page editor Joan Whitman, who succeeded Charlotte as editor on the family/style pages, was also treated poorly by the *Times*, some people believe. Whitman was not named an editor when the paper initiated its revolutionary "Home" and "Living" section fronts, and she left the paper.[9] The *Times* is not alone in its unpredictable attitude toward rewarding long-term service. Schneiderman noted that frequently young and middle-aged employees of newspapers are left hanging after they have been removed from key positions: "Unless you're a chief editor, you eventually bump up against a ceiling. There are people there, they're young, and you ask, 'what do you do with them?'" Schneiderman acknowledges, however, that Charlotte "could have had a more graceful last few years."[10]

To some, however, the issue is one of racism and sexism. Wilkins believes his assignment as columnist was poorly handled because of racism at the top levels of the paper.[11] And Betsy Wade Boylan, one of the lead plaintiffs in the sex discrimination lawsuit against the *Times*, was blunt when she said the paper insulted Charlotte at the end of her career: "Lord knows the paper gave her a lot of good jobs and a lot of good opportunities, although I think it should be noted in all fairness . . . that they never gave her the Golden Parachute that they have given all the rest of these turkeys when they were tired of them." Boylan used as an example former foreign and managing editor Seymour Topping, who, after he stepped down from these jobs, was given the assignment of overseeing smaller papers in the *Times* organization, a job she considers a perk: "Now they wouldn't have done that for Charlotte," she said. "They wouldn't have done that for [former architecture and editorial writer] Ada Louise [Huxtable]. They did not do that for [foreign correspondent] Anne O'Hare McCormick. They didn't do it for [foreign correspondent] Flora Lewis. They just don't do it for women. But they take care of men."[12]

It is, of course, impossible to say how Charlotte, Whitman, Lewis, and the others would have been treated at the *Times* today. In the last decade, women have risen to the highest ranks of the newspaper's management and their numbers on newspapers overall have increased considerably, although employment figures indicate they are still not paid as much as their male counterparts.[13] But the numbers do not tell the whole story, and, as Anna Quindlen noted, women may have a moral obligation to help each other in the workforce to ensure their equality there.[14] Charlotte thought that her role as an "insider" at the *Times* gave her access to its top managers, allowing her subtly to influence the treatment of women. This, combined with her willingness to take chances with her own writing and news judgment, could serve as a model for others on the paper, she thought. As she grew older, she realized the importance of more obvious nurturing of talented new writers like Quindlen. She encouraged Quindlen, just as Quindlen, years later, actively promoted the hiring of Maureen Dowd, who would become the first woman at the paper to serve as chief White House reporter.

Charlotte's role as a journalistic pioneer is more evident than her role as a feminist pioneer, although her personality and the era in which she lived camouflage her success in this role. Charlotte shunned the limelight, and she was not prone to self-promotion, which meant that her accomplishments and their legacy inside and outside of the *Times* are obscured. While many magazines and newspapers in the 1960s hailed her as an innovator with her new brand of society writing, little was said later about its influence on other journalists. By virtue of the *Times*'s reputation and wide journalistic influence, this bold type of society reporting was copied by other newspapers. More important is that once the staid and unchanging *Times* starts to vary from long-accepted style and format, it opens a door within the paper, and the innovation becomes accepted. In Charlotte's case, her society and women's page reporting have withstood the test of time and paved the way for current trends in reporting.

Punch Sulzberger, publisher of the *Times* for nearly three decades, liked to say in magazine profiles that the paper was slow to change, and when it did, it did so gradually. He acknowledged that Charlotte's influence stems from a series of small steps and that her legacy lives on more than a decade after her death: "She started a trail and I think a number of people picked it up and carried it along. She was a pioneer. She was to some extent the Maureen Dowd of her day."[15]

It is interesting that Sulzberger compared Charlotte to Dowd, who was promoted to op-ed columnist after her stint as White House reporter. She was viewed in the mid-1990s as an innovator. Dowd's style —a frank, take-no-prisoners style of news reporting that often skewered Washington's most powerful men and women—is eerily similar to Charlotte's brand of society writing. Indeed, many of the profiles written about Dowd describe her writing and razor-sharp observations in the same terms that were used to describe Charlotte's writing in the 1960s and early 1970s. One profile of her noted that "she relies on her uncanny ability to stand in the pack and see what other do not" and "she takes devilish delight in finding the most image-conscious of men in undignified situations."[16]

Another article noted that Dowd "said what others were thinking or muttering but kept hidden under the lid of objectivity," and as White House reporter, "she saw through the absurdity of much of the playacting that comes with being President."[17] That Dowd wrote in a daring style does not mean she was imitating Charlotte or that she was directly influenced by her. But the *Times* published Dowd and rewarded her for her unorthodox writing, which means it was accepted within the paper—and one of the reasons it *was* legitimate was that the paper had already published similar writing much earlier.

Charlotte indirectly influenced the paper's content in another way.

When she took over the op-ed page, she watered down the "official" quality of the page and published commentary from ordinary people with ordinary problems. This, too, led indirectly to the selection a decade later of op-ed columnist Anna Quindlen, who wrote about everyday life rather than solely about government. "She [Charlotte] was ahead of her time in shifting interest from the most-far-flung regions of the world to the lives of people here at home," former *Times* editorial page editor and executive editor Max Frankel said. "That was certainly the trend of recent decades of journalism."[18] As the *Times*'s revolutionary op-ed page was mimicked by other papers, so was its shift in content. Charlotte's news judgment in that area had a definite influence on what is published today.

So why wasn't Charlotte widely hailed as a journalistic innovator? Part of the answer is that she was not a self-promoter and she did not live in the television age of celebrity journalism when print journalists appear regularly on television to offer commentary on everything in and outside of their area of expertise. Charlotte's face and writing became well-known in Manhattan society circles, and for a short period she provided commentary on the *Times*'s radio station. But outside of this world, she was not so well-known. Cable television, the Internet, and other high-tech communication forms today are turning many innovative journalists into celebrities. That was not the case in Charlotte's era.

Like many women, Charlotte's manner was self-effacing, and she was reluctant to take credit for her accomplishments. And her aversion to confrontation often meant that her views on issues were not always known publicly. Even her decades-long disputes with Rosenthal —and her defiance of him—were conducted primarily through memos. She was always cordial to him personally, and they never had openly hostile one-on-one confrontations. The nature and scope of their deep disagreements appeared only on paper.

Of course, it is difficult to gauge the impact of Charlotte's long-term contributions and her legacy. Her contributions, however, should be seen as one link of a chain that led to change; her influence was subtle but important, and she made her contributions not for reasons of power or fame but out of a joy for life and for working and a devilish compulsion to question authority and rattle the status quo. Charlotte might have said about her quarter-century at the nation's most solemn and respected newspaper of record that "it was a hoot."

Notes

Chapter 1

1. See "American Diplomatic Service Has First Woman Appointee," *Christian Science Monitor*, April 16, 1925, p. 1; Constance Drexel, "Woman Diplomat Is Retained Here," *Philadelphia Daily Ledger*, February 12, 1923 (page unknown); and Constance Drexel, "Ohio Woman Seeks Diplomatic Post," *Philadelphia Daily Ledger*, February 17, 1922 (page unknown). Other newspapers, including the *Columbus Dispatch*, had stories about Lucile Atcherson's efforts to enter the Foreign Service.

2. Charlotte Curtis, *New York Times* oral history interview, conducted by Susan Dryfoos, New York, June 21, 1983.

3. Mary Curtis Davey, telephone interview by the author, December 5, 1995.

4. Atcherson's life is reviewed in a newspaper article shortly after his death, "All in a Lifetime," *Ohio State Journal*, March 18, 1950, p. 1.

5. "Columbus Women Prominent in Suffrage Struggle," *[Franklin County] Historian*, vol. 4, no. 165, pp. 8–9. This brief review of Lucile Curtis's early life is included in a résumé in her papers at the Schlesinger Women's Studies Library, Radcliffe College, Cambridge, Mass.

6. "Columbus Women Prominent in Suffrage Struggle," p. 9.

7. Ibid.

8. See "Ohio Woman Seeks Diplomatic Post."

9. Mayme Ober Peak, "Beauty or Brains—Which?" *Philadelphia Public Ledger*, date unknown but believed to be in 1923.

10. Ibid.

11. "Woman Diplomat Is Retained Here."

12. "American Diplomatic Service Has First Woman Appointee."

13. William Hunt, interview by the author, Columbus, Ohio, October 30, 1995.

14. Davey interview.

15. Ibid.

16. Letter, George Morris Curtis to Lucile Atcherson, August 16, 1926.

17. Letter, George Morris Curtis to Lucile Atcherson, June 12, 1927.

18. Letter, Lucile Atcherson to Edward J. Norton, July 13, 1927.

23. Cantwell, *Manhattan*, p. 33.

24. William Hunt, interview by the author, Columbus, Ohio, October 30, 1995.

25. Larry Leeds, telephone interview by the author, January 13, 1996.

26. This letter from Charlotte Curtis to Lucile Curtis is undated, but it is believed to have been written in 1950.

27. Hunt interview.

28. Leeds interview.

29. Hunt interview.

30. Interview with Charlotte Curtis by Susan Dryfoos, June 21, 1983, *New York Times* oral history project, New York City.

31. Ibid.

32. Robert Shamansky, interview by the author, Columbus, Ohio, June 29, 1996.

33. *New York Times* oral history project.

34. Ibid.

35. Charlotte Curtis, "Enthusiastic Group Plans Autumn Prelude," *Columbus Citizen*, August 10, 1947, p. 1D.

36. Charlotte Curtis, "College Girl Makes Own Style Rules," *Columbus Citizen*, August 17, 1948, p. 4.

37. Letter, Charlotte Curtis to George and Lucile Curtis, March 16, 1950.

38. Davey interview.

39. Ibid.

40. Ibid.

41. "Reception in Curtis Home Will Follow Marriage Service," *Columbus Citizen*, July 7, 1950, p. 9.

42. Cantwell, *Manhattan*, p. 37.

43. This letter from Charlotte Curtis to Dwight "Butch" Fullerton is undated, but it is believed to have been written in 1949 or 1950.

44. Davey interview.

Chapter 4

1. Mary Curtis Davey, telephone interview by the author, December 5, 1995.

2. Columbus Newspaper Guild, Program, "Third Annual Page One Ball," April 29, 1954, p. 1.

3. Jane Kehrer Horrocks, interview by the author, Columbus, Ohio, June 18, 1990.

4. Davey interview.

5. Robert Shamansky, interview by the author, Columbus, Ohio, June 14, 1996.

6. Horrocks interview and Mary McGarey, interview by the author, Columbus, Ohio, October 20, 1995.

7. Shamansky interview.

8. Jane Howard, "Charlotte Curtis: First Lady of the *New York Times*," *Cosmopolitan*, January 1975, p. 60.

9. McGarey described this habit of Grove's in her interview by the author.

10. Ibid.

11. Charlotte Curtis, "Stylist Sniffs at Short Hair and Bare Heads," *Columbus Citizen*, June 6, 1951, p. 7.

12. Charlotte Curtis, "Flower Show Puts Pressure on the Posies," *Columbus Citizen*, April 12, 1956, p. 12.

13. Horrocks interview.

14. Ibid.

15. Pauline Wessa, "Charlotte Shares Some Social Insights," *Columbus Citizen-Journal*, November 26, 1976, p. 6.

16. Marylin Bender, memorial service for Charlotte Curtis, New York City, May 20, 1987.

17. Horrocks interview.

18. Davey interview.

19. Interview with Charlotte Curtis by Susan Dryfoos, June 21, 1983, *New York Times* oral history project, New York City.

20. Charlotte Curtis, "Citizen Reporter Sends Notes on Paris Meeting," *Columbus Citizen*, November 12, 1951, p. 4.

21. Charlotte Curtis, "Malik Tries to Grab Spotlight, Photographers Try to Grab Malik," *Columbus Citizen*, November 16, 1951, p. 4.

22. See Harrison Salisbury, *The Soviet Union: The Fifty Years* (New York: Harcourt, Brace and World, 1967).

23. Charlotte Curtis, "Leningrad Streets Are Alive with Walking, Lifeless People," *Columbus Citizen*, September 7, 1956, p. 11.

24. McGarey interview.

25. Ibid.

26. *New York Times* oral history project.

27. Subjects of the stories on her pages varied from the historical, such as a history of how wedding customs evolved over the centuries, to the practical, such as the role and function of the Better Business Bureau.

28. Charlotte Curtis, "Sandburg: A Bird's Eye View of the 'Ulcer Gulch,'" *Columbus Citizen-Journal*, March 8, 1960, p. 12.

29. Charlotte Curtis, "Mrs. Kennedy: Mother Comes to Town," *Columbus Citizen-Journal*, October 19, 1960, p. 15.

30. Charlotte Curtis, "Pat Nixon: The No. 2 Spot," *Columbus Citizen-Journal*, October 10, 1960, p. 15.

31. Letter, Charlotte Curtis to Elizabeth Penrose Howkins, January 28, 1961.

32. *New York Times* oral history project.

33. Letters from Gene Grove to Charlotte Curtis, August 18, September 12, February 11, 1960.

34. Clifton Daniel, interview by author, New York City, June 21, 1995.

35. *New York Times* oral history project.

36. Letter, Elizabeth Penrose Howkins to Charlotte Curtis, January 31, 1961.

37. Letter, Charlotte Curtis to Elizabeth Penrose Howkins, February 9, 1961.

38. *New York Times* oral history project.

Chapter 5

1. Robert Shamansky, interview by the author, Columbus, Ohio, June 29, 1996; Tibi Sterner Johnson, telephone interview by the author, July 18, 1996; and Jane Kehrer Horrocks, interview by the author, Columbus, Ohio, June 18, 1990.

2. Shamansky interview.

3. William Hunt, interview by the author, Columbus, Ohio, November 30, 1995.

4. See letters, Gene Grove to Charlotte Curtis, February 15, March 15, 1961.

5. See Marylin Bender's comments in Kay Mills, *A Place in the News* (New York: Columbia University Press, 1988), p. 120.

6. Nan Robertson, telephone interview by the author, June 15, 1995.

7. Marylin Bender, interview by the author, New York City, October 9, 1989.

8. Memorial service for Charlotte Curtis, New York City, May 20, 1987.

9. Nan Robertson, *The Girls in the Balcony: Women, Men and the New York Times* (New York: Random House, 1992), p. 79.

10. Bender interview.

11. Robertson, *Girls in the Balcony*, pp. 79–83.

12. Robertson interview.

13. Interview with Charlotte Curtis by Susan Dryfoos, June 21, 1983, *New York Times* oral history project, New York City.

14. Ibid.

15. Ibid.

16. Bender interview.

17. Horrocks interview.

18. Charlotte Curtis, "Mr. John and Experts Say His Talent Is Tops," *New York Times*, July 12, 1961, p. 30.

19. Charlotte Curtis, "Italian Designer Enjoys His Life of Adventure," *New York Times*, June 9, 1961, p. 30.

20. The history of the New Journalism is reviewed in Michael and Edwin

Emery, *The Press in America* (Englewood Cliffs, N.J.: Prentice-Hall, 1988), p. 488.

21. Harrison Salisbury, interview by the author, New York City, December 12, 1989.

22. See transcript of interviews with Betsy Wade conducted by Mary Marshall Clark, Washington Press Club Foundation oral history project about women in the media. Interviews with Wade were conducted in October 1994. Transcripts are available at the Washington Press Club, Washington, D.C., and at some university libraries.

23. Lindsy Van Gelder, "You Can't Make News Out of a Silk Purse," *Ms.*, November 1984, p. 112.

24. Maurine Beasley and Sheila Gibbons, *Taking Their Place: A Documentary History of Women and Journalism* (Washington, D.C.: American University Press, 1993), p. 175.

25. Ibid., p. 24.

26. Charlotte Curtis, *First Lady* (New York: Pyramid Books, 1962).

27. Ibid., p. 22.

28. Ibid., p. 24.

29. Ibid., p. 26.

30. Memo, Janet Rosenberg to Don Benson, April 17, 1962.

31. Curtis, *First Lady*, p. 63.

32. Hunt interview.

33. Letter, Gene Grove to Charlotte Curtis, December 13, 1960.

34. Betsy Wade discusses the *Standard* in the Washington Press Club Foundation oral history project.

35. *New York Standard*, January 6, 1963, p. 1.

36. Wade, Washington Press Club Foundation oral history.

37. *New York Standard*, January 8, 1963, p. 1.

38. Wade, Washington Press Club Foundation oral history.

39. Richard Kluger discusses the strike in his *New York Herald Tribune: The Paper* (New York: Knopf, 1986), p. 647; Gay Talese reviews its causes in *The Kingdom and the Power* (Cleveland: World, 1965) pp. 302–6.

40. See Harrison Salisbury's discussion of this in his book *A Time of Change* (New York: Harper & Row, 1988), p. 101.

41. Clifton Daniel, interview by the author, New York City, June 21, 1995.

42. Ibid.

43. Ibid.

44. *New York Times* oral history project.

45. Ibid.

46. Charlotte Curtis, "Notes on England's Social Scene: When a Castle No Longer Feels Like a Home," *New York Times*, April 17, 1964, p. 17.

47. Charlotte Curtis, "Society Glitters in San Francisco," *New York Times*, September 12, 1964, p. 39.

48. Memo, Clifton Daniel to Russell Edwards, November 5, 1963.

49. Daniel interview.

50. See "Sociologist on the Society Beat," *Time*, February 19, 1965, p. 51; and "Upper Crust," *Newsweek*, September 28, 1964, pp. 62–63.

51. "Sociologist on the Society Beat."

52. Daniel interview.

53. Geoffrey Hellman, "View from the 14th Floor," *New Yorker*, January 18, 1969, p. 44.

54. Daniel interview; and A. O. Sulzberger, interview by the author, November 9, 1995, New York City.

55. Salisbury interview.

56. Barbara Tuchman, "History by the Ounce," *Harper's*, July 1965, p. 65.

57. "Sociologist on the Society Beat."

58. Hunt interview.

59. See Jane Howard, "Charlotte Curtis: First Lady of the *New York Times*," *Cosmopolitan*, January 1975, p. 60.

60. This information was included in a resolution in memoriam adopted by the Ohio State University trustees. The document is undated, but it is believed to have been written in early 1966.

61. Horrocks interview.

Chapter 6

1. A. O. Sulzberger, comments made at memorial service for Charlotte Curtis, May 20, 1987, New York City.

2. "I Got My Job Through the *New York Times*," *Women's Wear Daily*, May 18, 1965, pp. 4–5.

3. Ibid., p 4.

4. Sulzberger, memorial service for Charlotte Curtis.

5. *Vanity Fair* ran a long piece on the Capote ball on its thirty-year anniversary. See Amy Fine Collins, "A Night to Remember," July 1996, pp. 122–39. The original article by Curtis, "Capote's Black and White Ball: The Most Exquisite of Spectator Sports," November 29, 1965, appeared in the *Times* on page 53. Enid Nemy, " . . . And Before It Started," appeared on the same day on the same page.

6. See Collins, "A Night to Remember," p. 137.

7. Ibid., p. 129.

8. Ibid., p. 138.

9. Ibid.

10. Curtis, "Capote's Black and White Ball."

11. Pauline Wessa, "Charlotte Shares Some Social Insights," *Columbus Citizen-Journal*, November 26, 1976, p. 6.

12. Leslie Wexner, interview by the author, Columbus, Ohio, January 5,

1996. See Frankel's comments in Robert Sam Anson, "The Best of *Times*, the Worst of Times," *Esquire*, March 1993, p. 198.

13. Gay Talese, *The Kingdom and the Power* (Cleveland: World, 1969), p. 111.

14. Letter to author from Gay Talese, May 16, 1995.

15. Roger Wilkins, memorial service for Charlotte Curtis.

16. "Baroness Von Thyssen Linked Romantically to Onassis's Son," *New York Times*, May 29, 1969, p. 51.

17. Memo, Clifton Daniel to Charlotte Curtis, May 29, 1969.

18. "Princess Auersperg Is Wed," *New York Times*, February 15, 1969, p. 39.

19. Memo, A. M. Rosenthal to Charlotte Curtis, February 17, 1969.

20. Charlotte Curtis, "Plimpton Drops Singles for Doubles," *New York Times*, March 29, 1968, p. 46.

21. "Anita Colby Is Engaged to Wed Phalen Flagler," *New York Times*, June 13, 1969, p. 54.

22. Julie Baumgold, "Charlotte, Star Reporter," *New York*, October 6, 1969, p. 44.

23. Ibid., p. 39.

24. Ibid., pp. 40–41.

25. Ibid., p. 41.

26. This is noted ibid., p. 43, but Curtis also said it publicly in interviews.

27. Ibid., p. 42.

28. Nan Robertson, telephone interview by the author, June 15, 1995.

29. Harrison Salisbury, *The Soviet Union: The Fifty Years* (New York: Harcourt, Brace and World, 1967).

30. Harrison Salisbury, interview by the author, New York City, December 12, 1989.

31. Salisbury, *The Soviet Union*, pp. 33–58.

32. Ibid., p. 35.

33. Ibid., p. 34.

34. Lindsy Van Gelder, "Women's Pages: You Can't Make News Out of a Silk Purse," *Ms.*, November 1974, p. 12.

35. Interview with Charlotte Curtis by Susan Dryfoos, June 21, 1983, *New York Times* oral history project, New York City.

36. Kay Mills quoted Bender in *A Place in the News* (New York: Columbia University Press, 1988), p. 121.

37. See Nan Robertson, *The Girls in the Balcony: Women, Men and the New York Times* (New York: Random House, 1992), p. 115.

38. Carol Felsenthal, *Power, Privilege and the Post: The Katharine Graham Story* (New York: G. P. Putnam's Sons, 1993), p. 266.

39. The history of the "Style" section is outlined in the introduction of *Writing in Style*, ed. Laura Longly Babb and the *Washington Post* Writers Group (Boston: Houghton Mifflin, 1975), pp. iii–vii.

40. Sally Quinn, telephone interview by the author, April 5, 1996.
41. Felsenthal, *Power, Privilege and the Post*, p. 267.
42. *Writing in Style*, p. vii.
43. Quinn interview.
44. Ibid.
45. Liz Smith, interview by the author, New York City, December 13, 1989.
46. Richard Shepard, *The Paper's Papers* (New York: *Times* Books, 1996), p. 277.

Chapter 7

1. Roger Wilkins, comments made at memorial service for Charlotte Curtis, May 20, 1987, New York City.
2. A. M. Rosenthal, telephone interview by the author, November 8, 1995.
3. Sydney Gruson, a close friend of the Sulzberger family, discussed this in an interview by the author in New York City on August 8, 1995.
4. Gloria Steinem, telephone interview by the author, July 18, 1995.
5. Molly Ivins, interview by the author, Athens, Ohio, October 4, 1995.
6. Ibid.
7. William Hunt, interview by the author, Columbus, Ohio, October 30, 1995.
8. The text of this speech, which was among Charlotte's papers, was undated, although it is believed to have been written in 1972 or 1973.
9. See Betty Friedan, *The Feminine Mystique* (New York: Dell, 1963).
10. She made these comments during the speech to the American Association of Advertising Agencies.
11. Mary Curtis Davey, telephone interview by the author, December 5, 1995.
12. Charlotte Curtis, "On Train, Kennedy Elan," *New York Times*, June 9, 1968, p. 1.
13. Letter, Charlotte Curtis to Lucile Atcherson Curtis, June 18, 1968.
14. Ibid.
15. Charlotte Curtis, "California Primary: A Political Test of 'Newness,'" *New York Times*, June 2, 1968, pp. 1, 63.
16. This description was taken from notes in Curtis's papers. They are undated but believed to have been written in August 1968.
17. Ibid.
18. Charlotte Curtis, "Thousands of Jubilant Republicans Celebrate at Six Inaugural Balls in the Capital," *New York Times*, January 21, 1969, p. 26.
19. Marylin Bender, interview by the author, New York City, October 9, 1989. David Schneiderman and Sally Quinn also discussed this aspect of her personality, as did Selwa Roosevelt in a telephone interview with the author

on March 21, 1996, and Leslie Wexner in an interview in Columbus, Ohio, on January 5, 1996.

20. Hunt interview.

21. Lois Melina, "*Times* Editor Doubts Social Responsibility by the Nation's Rich," *Muncie Star*, October 8, 1977, page number unknown.

22. Charlotte Curtis, "Edsel Finally Succeeds: Fords Celebrate First Male to Graduate from College," *New York Times*, September 2, 1973, p. 41.

23. Charlotte Curtis, "The Jules Stein Party: A 3-Day Extravaganza for 600 Fashionable Guests," *New York Times*, March 30, 1969, p. 72.

24. See Julie Baumgold, "Charlotte: Star Reporter," *New York*, October 6, 1969, p. 46.

25. Charlotte Curtis, "The Rich Prepare to Get Through the Energy Crisis, Somehow." This story was written in December 1973 and reprinted in Charlotte's book, *The Rich and Other Atrocities* (New York: Random House, 1976), pp. 128–31.

26. Charlotte Curtis, "The Last Delicious Days of Joey Gallo," *Harper's Bazaar*, June 1972, pp. 86–87.

27. Oliver Skinner, "Covers Diamond and Champagne Beat," *St. Louis Post-Dispatch*, November 24, 1968, p. 2F.

28. Ibid.

29. Ibid.

30. Ibid.

31. Letter, Charlotte Curtis to Lucile Curtis, April 18, 1968.

32. Ibid.

Chapter 8

1. See Curtis's article "Black Panther Philosophy Is Debated at the Bernstcins'," *New York Times*, January 15, 1970, p. 50.

2. See Tom Wolfe, *Radical Chic and Mau-Mauing the Flak Catchers* (New York: Farrar, Strauss & Giroux, 1970).

3. The Black Panthers were formed as part of the black power movement of the 1960s. Although leaders Bobby Seale and Huey Newton said the group was formed to perform community service for the poor, it later became known for violence and skirmishes with police.

4. "False Note on Black Panthers" (unsigned editorial), *New York Times*, January 16, 1970, p. 46.

5. Wolfe, *Radical Chic*, p. 78.

6. Ibid., pp. 79–80.

7. Ibid., p. 83.

8. Ibid., p. 90.

9. Ibid., p. 91.

10. "Panthers' Aid," Felicia M. Bernstein, Letter to the Editor, *New York Times*, January 21, 1970, p. 46.

11. Wolfe, *Radical Chic*, p. 80.

12. Joan Whitman, telephone interview by the author, June 26, 1995.

13. Letter, Charlotte Curtis to Lucile Curtis, January 20, 1974.

14. Charlotte Curtis, "The Black Panther Party for Panther Legal Defense Fund Stirs Talk and More Parties," *New York Times*, January 24, 1970, p. 21.

15. Harrison Salisbury, interview by the author, New York City, December 12, 1989; William Hunt, interview by the author, Columbus, Ohio, October 30, 1995.

16. For a summary of the feminism of the era, see "The New Feminists: Revolt Against 'Sexism,'" *Time*, November 21, 1969, pp. 53–56; and "Women Power," *Newsweek*, March 30, 1970, p. 61.

17. The *Time* article "The New Feminists: Revolt Against Sexism," p. 56, discusses these parallels.

18. Hunt interview.

19. Whitman interview.

20. These stories appeared in the *Times* on August 27, 1970. The story about prominent women was written by Judy Klemesrud and appeared on page 39.

21. Marylin Bender, "Liberation Yesterday: The Roots of the Feminist Movement," *New York Times*, August 21, 1970, p. 29.

22. Memo, Charlotte Curtis to A. M. Rosenthal, January 14, 1971.

23. Letter, Charlotte Curtis to William Hunt, November 24, 1969.

24. See "Charlotte Curtis," *Vogue*, June 1975, p. 116.

25. Charlotte Curtis, "Women's Liberation Gets into the Long Island Swim," *New York Times*, August 10, 1970, p. 32.

26. Charlotte Curtis, WQXR radio broadcast, August 17, 1970. A transcript of the broadcast is among Curtis's papers.

27. "Charlotte Curtis Speaks at Agassiz," *Harvard Crimson*, May 17, 1974, p. 1.

28. Memo, Seymour Topping to A. M. Rosenthal and Charlotte Curtis, January 27, 1971.

29. A. O. Sulzberger, interview by the author, New York City, November 9, 1995.

30. Kay Mills discusses this attitude by some men at the *Times* in her book *A Place in the News* (New York: Columbia University Press, 1988), p. 158.

31. Sulzberger interview.

32. Letter, Charlotte Curtis to William Hunt, January 28, 1972.

33. This memo from A. M. Rosenthal to the staff of the *Times* was reprinted in Joseph Goulden's book *Fit to Print* (Secaucus, N.J.: Lyle Stuart, 1988), p. 158.

34. Gloria Steinem, telephone interview by the author, July 18, 1995.

35. Ibid.

36. Ibid.

37. See Nan Robertson, *The Girls in the Balcony: Women, Men and the New York Times* (New York: Random House, 1992), pp. 213–52.

38. Hunt and Salisbury interviews.

39. Mills, *Place in the News*, p. 147.

40. Ibid., p. 147.

41. Robertson, *Girls in the Balcony*, p. 164.

42. Ibid., p. 147.

43. Ibid., pp. 124–26.

44. Several speakers, including David Schneiderman and Roger Wilkins, mentioned this manner of speaking at the memorial service for Curtis on May 20, 1987, in New York City.

45. Nan Robertson, telephone interview by the author, June 15, 1995.

46. Interview of Wade conducted by Mary Marshall Clark, Washington Press Club Foundation oral history project about women in the media, were October 1994. Transcripts are available at the Washington Press Club, Washington, D.C., and at some university libraries.

47. Robertson, *Girls in the Balcony*, p. 187.

48. Ibid., pp. 207–11.

49. Hunt made this comment during an interview with the author on October 30, 1994. Rosenthal and Clifton Daniel also voiced that opinion, Daniel during an interview with the author in New York City on June 21, 1995, and Rosenthal during the telephone interview with the author.

50. Sulzberger interview.

51. Rosenthal interview.

52. See Ellen Bilgore, "Charlotte Curtis: She Did It Her Way," *Harper's Bazaar*, May 1981; and Jean Tarzanian, "We Can Do Anything a Man Can Do," *Editor & Publisher*, December 14, 1963.

53. Steinem interview.

54. See Gloria Steinem, *Moving Beyond Words* (New York: Simon & Schuster, 1994), pp. 179–81.

55. Letter, Iphigene Sulzberger to Charlotte Curtis, October 10, 1969.

56. Letter, Charlotte Curtis to Iphigene Sulzberger, October 25, 1969.

Chapter 9

1. Telegram, A. M. Rosenthal to Charlotte Curtis, July 11, 1972.

2. Letter, A. M. Rosenthal to Charlotte Curtis, September 8, 1982.

3. Nan Robertson, *The Girls in the Balcony: Women, Men and the New York Times* (New York: Random House, 1992), pp. 188–99.

4. A. M. Rosenthal, telephone interview by the author, November 8, 1995.

5. Letter, Charlotte Curtis to Lucile Curtis, July 29, 1969.

6. Lisa Hammel, "The Partners Are Three Nuns and 1,000 Maine Crafts-men," *New York Times*, September 28, 1973, p. 26.

7. Memo, A. M. Rosenthal to Charlotte Curtis, September 28, 1973.

8. Memo, A. M. Rosenthal to Charlotte Curtis, March 29, 1972.

9. Georgia Dullea, "Suburban Parties: Token Integration Is on the De-cline," *New York Times*, February 6, 1973, p. 42.

10. Memo, A. M. Rosenthal to Charlotte Curtis, February 6, 1973.

11. Charlotte Curtis, "Experiment in Fund-Raising: A Greek 'Love Fest' Raises $5,000," *New York Times*, March 12, 1971, p. 46.

12. Memo, John G. Morris to Charlotte Curtis, March 12, 1971.

13. Judith Weinraub, "Princess' Etiquette Book Certainly not Emily Post," *New York Times*, February 23, 1972, p. 36.

14. Memo, Seymour Topping to Charlotte Curtis, February 23, 1972.

15. Memo, A. M. Rosenthal to Charlotte Curtis, November 29, 1971.

16. Memo, A. M. Rosenthal to Charlotte Curtis, June 22, 1970.

17. Memo, A. M. Rosenthal to Charlotte Curtis, May 13, 1969.

18. Letter, Charlotte Curtis to Lucile Curtis, May 22, 1968.

19. See Harrison Salisbury, *A Time of Change* (New York: Harper & Row, 1988), p. 297, and Joseph Goulden's biography of Rosenthal, *Fit to Print* (Secaucus, N.J.: Lyle Stuart, 1988), pp. 156–60.

20. Gloria Steinem, telephone interview by the author, July 18, 1995.

21. John Tebbel, *A Compact History of the American Newspaper* (New York: Hawthorn Books, 1969), pp. 262–63.

22. Gerald Lanson and Mitchell Stephens, "Abe Rosenthal: The Man and His Times," *Washington Journalism Review* (July–August 1983), p. 24.

23. Edwin Diamond, *Behind the* Times (New York: Villard Books, 1993) p. 146.

24. Lanson and Stephens, "Abe Rosenthal," p. 24.

25. Memo, A. M. Rosenthal to Charlotte Curtis, November 2, 1971.

26. William Hunt, interview by the author, Columbus, Ohio, October 30, 1995.

27. Harrison Salisbury, interview by the author, New York City, Decem-ber 12, 1989.

28. A. M. Rosenthal, telephone interview by the author, November 8, 1995.

29. The newspaper's Washington bureau and its relationship to the New York office has been a topic of discussion among those writing about the *Times*. See, for instance, Gay Talese, *The Kingdom and the Power* (Cleveland: World, 1969), pp. 504–11; and Salisbury, *Time of Change*, pp. 422–27, 449.

30. Letter, Clifton Daniel to Charlotte Curtis, February 5, 1973.

31. Harrison Salisbury, interview by the author, New York City, December 12, 1989; and Clifton Daniel, interview by the author, New York City, June 21, 1995.

32. Sydney Gruson, interview by the author, New York City, August 8, 1995.

33. Enid Nemy, "They Came to Look at Designs—and Designers," *New York Times*, April 5, 1972, p. 50.

34. Memo, Marian Heiskell to Charlotte Curtis, undated.

35. Memo, Charlotte Curtis to Marian Heiskell, undated.

36. David Schneiderman, interview by the author, New York City, June 22, 1995.

37. Salisbury interview.

38. Mary Curtis Davey, telephone interview by the author, December 5, 1995.

39. Schneiderman interview.

40. Hunt interview.

41. Davey interview.

42. Ibid.

43. Hunt interview.

44. Davey interview.

45. Transcript of memorial service for Charlotte Curtis, New York City, May 20, 1987.

46. Joe Gillette, "Area Doctors Clash Over Civil Disobedience Roots," *Columbus Citizen-Journal*, November 23, 1967, p. 6.

47. Letter, William Hunt to Charlotte Curtis, November 30, 1967.

48. Letter, William Hunt to Charlotte Curtis, December 21, 1967.

49. Mark Somerson, "Military School 'Runt' Grows Up to Be Man of Year," *Columbus Dispatch*, July 30, 1995, p. 3D.

50. Hunt interview.

51. Letter, Charlotte Curtis to William Hunt, April 22, 1970.

52. Letter, Charlotte Curtis to William Hunt, December 24, 1969.

53. Letter, Charlotte Curtis to William Hunt, January 8, 1969.

54. Letter, William Hunt to Charlotte Curtis, November 8, 1969.

55. Letter, Charlotte Curtis to Lucile Curtis, August 18, 1970.

56. Davey interview.

57. Letter, William Hunt to Lucile Curtis, August 9, 1970.

58. Ibid.

59. Davey interview.

60. Mary McGarey, interview by the author, Columbus, Ohio, October 25, 1995.

61. Letter, Charlotte Curtis to Lucile Curtis, September 15, 1970.

62. Letter, Charlotte Curtis to Lucile Curtis, January 24, 1970.

63. Letter, Charlotte Curtis to Lucile Curtis, September 8, 1970.

64. Davey interview.

65. Letter, Charlotte Curtis to Lucile Curtis, December 9, 1969.

66. Letter, Charlotte Curtis to Lucile Curtis, November 24, 1969.

67. Davey interview.
68. Ibid.

Chapter 10

1. Mary Curtis Davey, telephone interview by the author, December 5, 1995.
2. Sally Quinn, telephone interview by the author, April 5, 1996.
3. Interview by author with William Hunt, Columbus, Ohio, June 13, 1988.
4. For instance, a memo Sulzberger sent Charlotte on September 25, 1972, compliments her on the design of her page. He also sent her a telegram when she was in Tucson, Arizona, on February 22, 1973, complimenting her on a special fashion section in the *Times*.
5. See "Winners & Sinners," 1971, undated by month, although stories discussed in this edition were dated September and October 1971. The story it referred to was Virginia Lee Warren, "Round-the-Clock Care Centers Envisioned by New City Aide," *New York Times*, September 28, 1971, p. 34. The story focuses on "night care" centers for children and adolescents in New York's Harlem and Bedford-Stuyvesant areas and also profiles the efforts of a black woman who was recently named head of the city's newly formed Agency for Child Development.
6. Sydney Gruson, interview by the author, New York City, August 8, 1995. Edwin Diamond discusses the "cabal" in *Behind the* Times (New York: Villard Books, 1993), pp. 189–91.
7. Joseph Goulden, *Fit to Print* (Secaucus, N.J.: Lyle Stuart, 1988), pp. 170–77.
8. Sally Quinn, telephone interview by the author, April 5, 1996.
9. Simmons Traffic Study, 1973 (undated by month and day).
10. Ibid.
11. Memo, A. M. Rosenthal to Charlotte Curtis et al., May 26, 1972.
12. Memo, Charlotte Curtis to A. M. Rosenthal, May 31, 1972.
13. Memo, Peter Millones to *Times* editorial department heads, January 22, 1973.
14. Memo, Peter Millones to *Times* editorial department heads, January 9, 1973.
15. Memo, Harding F. Bancroft to *Times* staff members, November 2, 1972.
16. David Schneiderman, interview by the author, New York City, June 22, 1995.
17. Harrison Salisbury, *A Time of Change* (New York: Harper & Row, 1988), pp. 316–17.
18. Schneiderman interview.
19. Ibid.

20. Harrison Salisbury, interview by the author, New York City, December 12, 1989.

21. Schneiderman interview; and Clifton Daniel, interview by the author, New York City, June 21, 1995.

22. Salisbury interview.

23. A. O. Sulzberger, interview by the author, New York City, November 9, 1995.

24. A. M. Rosenthal, telephone interview by the author, November 8, 1995.

25. Gruson interview.

26. Leslie Kaufman, "Mo Knows," *Washington Journalism Review*, October 1992, p. 16.

27. "Op-Editor in Pink," *Time*, October 1, 1973, p. 58.

28. Ellen Bilgore, "Charlotte Curtis: She Did It Her Way," *Harper's Bazaar*, March 1981, pp. 72, 128.

29. Lee Rosenbaum, "Charlotte Curtis: Opting for Op-Ed," *Quill*, January 1974, p. 24.

30. "You and Your Job: *Harper's Bazaar's* Guide to the Executive Suite," *Harper's Bazaar*, August 1978, pp. 80–81.

31. Trucia D. Kushner, "People You Should Know," *Viva*, March 1974, p. 41.

32. Organizations such as the Newspaper Enterprise Association and *Harper's Bazaar* designed these lists. Usually the wire services distributed them to news organizations around the world.

33. Hunt interview.

34. "Charlotte Curtis," *Vogue*, June 1975, p. 141.

35. Schneiderman interview.

36. Jane Howard, "Charlotte Curtis: First Lady of the *New York Times*," *Cosmopolitan*, January 1975, p. 60.

37. Schneiderman interview.

38. Ibid.

39. Schneiderman told this anecdote at the memorial service for Charlotte Curtis, May 20, 1987, New York City.

40. Hunt interview.

41. Sulzberger interview.

42. This page of notes was dated June 13, 1974 and was among Curtis's personal papers.

43. This page of notes was dated October 4, 1974 and was among Curtis's personal papers.

44. Curtis said this during an interview with Mary Marshall Clark on June 21, 1983 as part of the *New York Times* oral history project. A transcript is available at the *New York Times*.

45. Schneiderman, memorial service for Curtis.

Chapter 11

1. Charlotte Curtis, *The Rich and Other Atrocities* (New York: Random House, 1976).
2. Some of these news outlets include the *Washington Post, Newsday* in New York, and the Associated Press. See Kay Mills, *A Place in the News* (New York: Columbia University Press, 1988), pp. 149–72.
3. See "A Souped-up *New York Times* Gets Going," *Business Week,* July 17, 1978, pp. 72–73.
4. Earl Shorris, "Cutting Velvet at the *New York Times," Harper's,* October 1977, p. 109.
5. See Lester David, *Jacqueline Kennedy Onassis* (New York: St. Martin's Paperbacks, 1994), p. 21.
6. John Fairchild, *Chic Savages* (New York: Simon & Schuster, 1989), p. 102.
7. Leslie Wexner, interview by the author, Columbus, Ohio, January 5, 1996.
8. William Hunt, interview by the author, Columbus, Ohio, October 30, 1994.
9. See Selwa Roosevelt, *Keeper of the Gate* (New York: Simon & Schuster, 1990), p. 24.
10. This poem was among Charlotte's personal papers. It was given to her by Selwa Roosevelt and dated October 14, 1978.
11. Selwa Roosevelt, telephone interview by the author, March 21, 1996.
12. Ibid.
13. Ibid.
14. Amy Schildhouse, draft of article for Vassar College *Quarterly,* undated.
15. "Press," *Time,* January 21, 1974, p. 60.
16. David Shaw, "Newspapers Offer Forum to Outsiders," *Los Angeles Times,* October 13, 1975, p. 16.
17. Harrison Salisbury, interview by the author, New York City, December 12, 1989.
18. Roger Wilkins, telephone interview by the author, June 20, 1995.
19. David Schneiderman, interview by the author, New York City, June 21, 1995.
20. Schneiderman and Salisbury interviews.
21. Memo, A. O. Sulzberger to Charlotte Curtis, March 16, 1972.
22. Memo, Charlotte Curtis to A. O. Sulzberger, March 21, 1972.
23. Memo, A. O. Sulzberger to Charlotte Curtis, April 4, 1972.
24. This April 26, 1972, article "Journalism's New Nation," by Sally Quinn was reprinted in *Writing in Style,* ed., Laura L. Babb and Washington Post Writer's Group (Boston: Houston Mifflin, 1975) p. 75.

25. Memo, Charlotte Curtis to Clifton Daniel, April 25, 1972.
26. "Continuing Sagas," *More*, July 1974, page number unknown.
27. Roger Morris, "The Press as Cloak and Suitor," *New York Times*, May 11, 1974, p. 31.
28. Memo, A.M. Rosenthal to Charlotte Curtis and John Oakes, May 15, 1974.
29. "Continuing Sagas," *More*, July 1974.
30. Schneiderman interview.
31. Memo, A. O. Sulzberger to John Oakes, A. M. Rosenthal, and Max Frankel, May 13, 1974.
32. Memo, A. O. Sulzberger to Charlotte Curtis, May 13, 1974.
33. Wilkins interview.
34. Ibid.
35. Ibid.
36. Ibid.
37. See Edwin Diamond, *Behind the* Times (New York: Villard Books, 1993) pp. 140–41, for a discussion of the history of the *Times's* editorial page.
38. James Brady, "The *Times* They Are A'Changing," *New York*, February 5, 1973, p. 56.
39. Sally Quinn, telephone interview by the author, April 5, 1996.
40. Diamond recounts this story in *Behind the* Times, pp. 128–34.
41. Hunt interview.
42. Diamond, *Behind the* Times, p. 134.
43. Ibid., p. 129.
44. Ibid., p. 133.
45. Ibid., p. 134.

Chapter 12

1. Jack Egan, "Changes at the *New York Times*," *Washington Post*, May 1, 1976, p. D4.
2. Max Frankel, telephone interview by the author, May 28, 1996.
3. Memo, Max Frankel to Charlotte Curtis, January 19, 1979. The "Old Codgers's Almanac" was written by Mark O'Donnell and appeared in the *Times* on January 19, 1979, p. A23.
4. William Hunt, interview by the author, Columbus, Ohio, October 30, 1995.
5. Ibid.
6. Leslie Wexner, interview by the author, Columbus, Ohio, January 5, 1996.
7. Charlotte Curtis, "A Restless Philanthropist," *New York Times*, April 3, 1984, p. C3.

8. "3 Editors at The Times Get New Assignments," *New York Times*, April 15, 1982, p. C28.

9. Quindlen is quoted in Nan Robertson, *The Girls in the Balcony: Women, Men and the* New York Times (New York: Random House, 1992), p. 232.

10. David Schneiderman, interview by the author, New York, June 22, 1995.

11. Memo, Charlotte Curtis to A O. Sulzberger, May 12, 1982.

12. Memo, A. M. Rosenthal to A. O. Sulzberger, February 17, 1982.

13. A. M. Rosenthal, telephone interview by the author, November 8, 1995.

14. Frankel interview.

15. Interviews with Salisbury, Bender, Schneiderman, and others.

16. Robertson, *Girls in the Balcony*, p. 114.

17. Marylin Bender in transcript of memorial service for Charlotte Curtis, New York City, May 20, 1987.

18. Richard Clurman, interview by the author, New York City, December 12, 1989.

19. Joan Whitman, telephone interview by the author, June 20, 1995.

20. This folder was found in a 1990 file in Charlotte's office at the *New York Times*.

21. Schneiderman interview.

22. Letter, Charlotte Curtis to Katharine Graham, August 7, 1984. A copy was in Charlotte's files at the *Times*.

23. This undated draft of a will was among Charlotte's personal papers.

24. This transcript of Charlotte's comments is undated.

25. Letter, Theo Klemesrud to Charlotte Curtis, December 20, 1985.

26. Charlotte Curtis, "A Newspaper Is Elegized," *New York Times*, January 7, 1986, p. C14.

27. Memo, A. M. Rosenthal to Charlotte Curtis, January 8, 1986, among Charlotte's files at the *Times*.

28. Mary Curtis Davey, telephone interview by the author, December 5, 1996.

29. Ibid.

30. Schneiderman interview.

31. Davey interview.

32. These were among Charlotte's files at the *Times*.

33. Quindlen is quoted in Robertson, *Girls in the Balcony*, p. 218.

34. See Kay Mills, *A Place in the News* (New York: Columbia University Press, 1988), p. 276–77.

35. Ibid., pp. 279–80.

36. Hunt interview.

37. Hunt made these comments at Charlotte's memorial service.

38. Schneiderman interview. See also Marylin Bender's comments at Charlotte's memorial service.

39. Schneiderman interview.

40. Daniel, memorial service for Charlotte Curtis.

41. Bender, memorial service.

42. Hunt, memorial service.

43. Clurman, memorial service.

Chapter 13

1. All these comments were made at Charlotte's memorial service, May 20, 1987, New York City.

2. A. M. Rosenthal, telephone interview by the author, November 8, 1995.

3. See Nan Robertson, *The Girls in the Balcony: Women, Men and the New York Times* (New York: Random House, 1992), p. 114.

4. Bender made these comments at Charlotte's memorial service.

5. Robertson, *Girls in the Balcony*, p. 187.

6. Ibid., p. 216.

7. Harrison Salisbury, interview by the author, New York City, December 12, 1989.

8. This incident is described in Joseph Goulden's biography of A. M. Rosenthal, *Fit to Print* (Secaucus, N.J.: Lyle Stuart, 1988), pp. 392–95.

9. Nan Robertson, telephone interview by the author, June 15, 1995.

10. David Schneiderman, interview by the author, New York City, June 22, 1995.

11. Goulden, *Fit to Print*, p. 392.

12. Boylan was interviewed by Mary Marshall Clark in October 1994 as part of an oral history project about women in the media sponsored by the Washington Press Club Association. Transcripts of this interview and others done as part of the project are available at the Washington Press Foundation, Washington, D.C., and at many university libraries.

13. In 1971, 20 percent of newsroom employees on newspapers were women; that proportion grew to 39 percent in 1992, according to journalism historian Marion Tuttle Marzoff. See her article, "Deciding What's Women's News" in the *Media Studies Journal*'s issue, "The Media and Women Without Apology," Winter–Spring 1993, pp. 33–48. The salaries of women newsroom employees also lagged behind those of their male counterparts in 1992, when women on daily newspapers made an average of $30,887 a year compared to the $36,959 for men. These salary figures were quoted in the same issue of *Media Studies Journal* on page 88. They were taken from a salary survey conducted by David Weaver and G. Cleveland Wilhoit, "The American Journalist in the 1990s," Report to the Freedom Forum, 1992.

Through much of the 1990s, two women on the *Times* were listed on the masthead as deputy managing editors of the paper: Soma Golden and Carolyn Lee.

14. Robertson, *Girls in the Balcony*, p. 218.

15. A. O. Sulzberger, interview by the author, New York City, November 9, 1995.

16. Leslie Kaufman, "Mo Knows," *Washington Journalism Review*, October 1992, p. 19.

17. James Wolcott, "Hear Me Purr," *New Yorker*, May 20, 1996, pp. 54–55.

18. Max Frankel, telephone interview by the author, May 28, 1996.

Index

Abzug, Bella: as senatorial candidate, 188
Adler, Renata, 174
Atcherson, Charlotte Ray (Charlotte's maternal grandmother), 2, 15–16
Atcherson, Fred (Charlotte's maternal grandfather), 2, 3, 16, 38
Atcherson, Lucile. *See* Curtis, Lucile Atcherson (Charlotte's mother)

Baumgold, Julie, 89
Bender, Marylin: admiration for A. O. McCormick, 49; as friend at the *Times*, 62, 105, 212, 214; women's issues, 93
Bernstein, Leonard: and Black Panther fund-raiser, 110–15
Bexley, Ohio, 43; move to, 17–18, 38
Black Panthers: Bernstein fund-raiser, 110–15, 213; sympathy for, 149, 154
Bouvier, Jacqueline. *See* Onassis, Jacqueline Bouvier Kennedy
Boylan, Betsy Wade: as copy editor on foreign desk, 68; and newspaper strike, 72, 73; and discrimination lawsuit, 125, 126–27, 128, 216
Boylan vs. the New York Times, 125–29; settlement out of court, 127; and Charlotte's promotion, 161–62; publicity for women, 209

Bradlee, Ben: as editor of "Style" section, 93–94, 95
breast cancer, 131; mastectomy in 1972, 140–41
bridal announcements, 88–89; as sociological events, 96
Brody, Jane, 125
Brookwood (country house), 12, 15
Brown, Edmund G.: as California gubernatorial candidate, 103

"cabal" group, 153
California: as easy target for Charlotte, 103
Cantwell, Mary, 32
Capote, Truman: "New Journalism," 67; frank writing style, 81; masked ball, 81–83
Carter, Jimmy, 168, 213
Catledge, Turner, 73
"Charlotte's Ruse" column, 54–55
Citizen-Journal. See Columbus Citizen Journal
civil rights: interest in, 50, 106, 109, 116, 117
Claiborne, Craig: as food writer, 63, 74, 132
Clark, Evalyn, 28
clothing: discussion at women's liberation fund-raiser, 119–20
Clurman, Richard: Charlotte's memorial service, 211, 212; as friend of Charlotte's, 193; opinion of Charlotte's column, 201–2

243

travel at own expense, 48, 50–52
contradiction as union officer
and civil rights advocate, 50
awards, 58
as *Times* home furnishings reporter, 59
Four F's job, 60–69
freedom to write in unconventional way, 65
First Lady (Curtis), 69–71
New York Standard, 72–73
society writer at the *Times*,
74–79, 80–81
typing-revising method, 78–79
close circle of friends, 84, 97,
193–94
as women's news editor, 84–96
as egalitarian manager, 89–90
fame outside the *Times*, 90
changing role of women in society, 91–92
Ohio twang, 98
criticism by readers, 107–8
conservatism in social sense, 109
rigid loyalties and principles, 111,
115–16
sacrificing personal friendships,
124, 125, 126–29
breast cancer, 131, 140–41
loyalty to the *Times*, 137, 201
relationship with William Hunt,
140–47
medicine: Charlotte's interest
in, 142, 194
marriage to William Hunt, 147
as reporter-editor and wife,
151–52
praise for her work, 152–53
as member of "cabal" group,
153–54
as op-ed editor, 160–69, 179,
192–93
as political animal, 162
view of power, 164, 165
self-deprecating manner, 165, 219

eye for detail, 166–67
The Rich and Other Atrocities
(Curtis), 170
mixing with New York society,
174–75
awards and speeches, 175
Greenwich Village apartment,
178, 193
party planning, 178–79
journalism counterconvention,
181–82
as news section columnist,
197–203
writing lost its verve, 201, 203
growing conservatism, 202
illness, 203–4, 207–9, 210–12
draft will, 204
move to larger apartment, 204
death of, 212
memorial service, 213–14
Curtis, George Morris (Charlotte's
father): as physician, researcher
and educator, 1, 12–13, 21–23;
meeting L. Atcherson, 7–9;
deteriorating health of, 43;
death of, 79
Curtis, Lucile Atcherson (Charlotte's mother), xxii, 1–11; Normandie Hotel, 12; depression,
13, 14, 24, 26; public service
awards, 13–14; and social
causes, 23; death of G. Curtis,
38, 39; suffrage movement,
117–18; cancer survival, 141;
travels, 148; suicide attempt,
150; illness and death, 205, 207

Daniel, Clifton: as friend, xx, 84, 137,
138–39, 193; marriage to Margaret Truman, 74; as assistant
managing editor, 74–75, 76,
77; influence on Charlotte's
writing, 85–86, 87–88; management style, 95; as Washington bureau chief, 98, 138;

National Women's Party, 5
nature: respect for, 16, 21. *See also*
	gardening: love for
Nemy, Enid, 82
"New Journalism," 67, 94
New York City: exposure during
	college, 25, 27
New York Herald Tribune: as top
	choice when job-hunting, 58;
	demise of, 136
New York Post: job opportunity on
	news desk, 61
New York Standard: unofficial sub-
	stitute during strike, 72–73
New York Times: See also *Boylan vs.
	the New York Times*; male-
	dominated management, xx,
	99; betrayal of Charlotte, xxiii,
	215; as family-owned newspa-
	per, 61; merger of society sec-
	tion and women's news
	section, 84; during the 1960s,
	85–87; response to women's
	movement, 118, 121; naming
	women's pages, 121–22; use of
	"Ms.," 122–24; circulation, 135,
	136, 156; internal politics, 138;
	"Winners & Sinners" sheet,
	153; "Simmons Traffic Study"
	(reader survey), 156; cost-cut-
	ting, 157; op-ed page, 158–69,
	178–80; addition of themed
	sections, 171–72; editorial
	reshuffling, 189–90, 191;
	charges of sexism at the *Times*,
	214–17
Newhouse, Nancy: as lifestyle edi-
	tor, 210
Newspaper Guild, 42; Charlotte as
	union officer, 50; payment of
	salaries during strike, 72
newspaper strike (1962–63), 71–74,
	136
Newspaper Women's Club of New
	York award, xvii

newspapering: reputation of, 35–36;
	closed fraternity of 1950s, 42.
	See also women in newspaper
	management
Newsweek: article on Curtis, 77
Nixon, Pat, 56, 57, 103
Nixon, Richard, 109
Normandie Hotel (Columbus), 12,
	15, 16

Oakes, John B.: as editorial page edi-
	tor, 186; opposition to hiring
	W. Safire, 187; opposition to
	endorsement of Patrick Moyni-
	han, 187–89; retirement of,
	189–90; as op-ed columnist, 215
Ochs, Adolph ("Punch" Sulzberger's
	grandfather), 77, 186
Ohio Club (Columbus Athletic
	Club), 3
Ohio Newspaper Women's Associa-
	tion award, 58
Ohio State Journal, 44; merger with
	Columbus Citizen-Journal, 57
Ohio State University School of
	Medicine: W. Hunt at, 141
Ohio Suffrage Association, 5
Onassis, Jacqueline Bouvier
	Kennedy: as college classmate,
	27; *First Lady* (Curtis), 69–71;
	as book editor and friend of
	Charlotte, 173
opinion-sharing: in the Curtis home,
	20; at Vassar, 28–29
Orbach, Jerry and Marta: and
	"Mafia chic," 107

photographer: Charlotte as, 170
Plimpton, George, 88
political wives, 55–57; *First Lady*
	(Curtis), 69–71
politics: discussion at CSG, 20; as
	part of college education,
	28–29; Republican National
	Convention (1968), 103–4;

Charlotte's liberalism, 109;
Charlotte as political animal,
162; of everyday life, 164–65
public service: L. Atcherson and, 4,
14
Pucci, Emilio (profile), 66–67
Pulitzer, Joseph, 67

Quindlen, Anna: writing style,
209–10, 219; advice to, 215, 217
Quinn, Sally, 142; comments over
hiring of William Safire, 187;
"Style" section, 94–95; *New
York Times* job offer, 154–55;
"counterconvention," 182
quotations: letting subjects indict
themselves, 45–46, 66

race relations: Black Panther fund-
raiser, 114
racism at the *Times*, 216
"radical chic," 106, 110
radio commentary, 101, 120–21
reader survey: "Simmons Traffic
Study," 156
Reagan, Ronald: as governor of California, 103; breakfast meeting
with, 175–76
religion: at Columbus School for
Girls, 18
Republican National Convention
(1968), 103–4
Reston, James: as Washington bureau chief, 73; R. Morris criticism of the *Times*, 184;
column praising Patrick
Moynihan, 188
The Rich and Other Atrocities (Curtis), 170
Robertson, Nan, 213–14; women's
news reporter, 62–63; attitude
toward covering Washington
parties, 90; discrimination lawsuit, 126–27; relationship with
Rosenthal, 132

Rolling Stone: freelance writing,
109, 170
"Romanticism": at Vassar, 27–28
Roosevelt, Archibald, 176–77
Roosevelt, Selwa Showker
("Lucky"): as college friend,
26, 27, 28–29; as friend in the
1970s, 176–78
Rosenberg, Janet: editing of *First
Lady*, 70
Rosenthal, A. M.: criticism of Charlotte, xxi, 86–88, 98, 131–38,
219; use of "Ms.," 122; friendship with G. Steinem, 124; discrimination lawsuit, 128;
sentimentalism, 131–32; domi-
nation of Charlotte, 140; reaction to R. Morris column,
183–84; as Charlotte's superior
once again, 200; as executive
editor, 203; as columnist after
retirement, 215
"Rusty" (Charlotte's college nickname), 26

Safire, William: controversy over
hiring, 186–87
Salisbury, Harrison: as friend of
Charlotte, xx, 137, 162; as part
of Sulzberger inner circle, 84;
book on Soviet Union, 90–91;
respect for Charlotte, 140; as
editor of op-ed page, 158–60;
dedication of *The Rich and
Other Atrocities* to, 170–71;
stature and reputation of, 179;
critique of Charlotte's op-ed
page, 180
Sandburg, Carl (interview), 55
Saroyan, William, 168
Schlesinger Women's Studies Library (Radcliffe College), xxiv,
204–5
Schneiderman, David: as assistant
editor of op-ed page, 158–60,